Cyber Society, Big Data, and Evaluation

Comparative Policy Evaluation Series
Ray C. Rist, editor

The Comparative Policy Evaluation Series is an interdisciplinary and international series that evaluates governance issues from the perspectives of sociology, anthropology, economics, policy science, law, and human rights. The books draw from many different nation-states and provide a longitudinal perspective: this series has been in existence for nearly thirty years and includes more than twenty volumes.

Titles in this series include:

Cyber Society, Big Data, and Evaluation
Doing Public Good?
Success in Evaluation
Speaking Justice to Power
Evaluation and Turbulent Times
Evaluation Cultures—Sense-making in Complex Times
Evaluating the Complex
Evaluation
Mind the Gap
The Evidence Book
Making Accountability Work
Open to the Public
From Studies to Streams
Quality Matters
Collaboration in Public Services
International Atlas of Evaluation
Building Effective Evaluation Capacity
Politics and Practices of Intergovernmental Evaluation

Cyber Society, Big Data, and Evaluation

Comparative Policy Evaluation
Volume 24

Gustav Jakob Petersson and
Jonathan D. Breul, editors

With a foreword by Caroline Heider

Routledge
Taylor & Francis Group
LONDON AND NEW YORK

First published 2017 by Transaction Publishers

2 Park Square, Milton Park, Abingdon, Oxfordshire OX14 4RN
711 Third Avenue, New York, NY 10017

Routledge is an imprint of the Taylor & Francis Group, an informa business

First issued in paperback 2018

Copyright © 2017 Taylor & Francis

All rights reserved. No part of this book may be reprinted or reproduced or utilised in any form or by any electronic, mechanical, or other means, now known or hereafter invented, including photocopying and recording, or in any information storage or retrieval system, without permission in writing from the publishers.

Notice:
Product or corporate names may be trademarks or registered trademarks, and are used only for identification and explanation without intent to infringe.

Library of Congress Catalog Number: 2016030729

Library of Congress Cataloging-in-Publication Data

Names: Petersson, Gustav Jakob, editor. | Breul, Jonathan D., editor.

Title: Cyber society, big data, and evaluation / Gustav Jakob Petersson and Jonathan D. Breul, editors.

Description: New Brunswick: Transaction Publishers, [2017] | Series: Comparative policy evaluation; volume 24 | Includes bibliographical references and index.

Identifiers: LCCN 2016030729 (print) | LCCN 2016046182 (ebook) | ISBN 9781412864367 (hardcover) | ISBN 9781412864510

Subjects: LCSH: Big data–Social aspects. | Social sciences–Research. | Quantitative research. | Evaluation research (Social action programs) | Policy sciences–Statistical methods.

Classification: LCC H62 .C89 2017 (print) | LCC H62 (ebook) | DDC 303.48/33–dc23

LC record available at https://lccn.loc.gov/2016030729

ISBN 13: 978-1-4128-6436-7 (hbk)
ISBN 13: 978-1-138-48303-3 (pbk)

Contents

Foreword, by *Caroline Heider*   vii

1. Cyber Society, Big Data, and Evaluation: An Introduction   1
   Gustav Jakob Petersson, Frans Leeuw, Jonathan Breul, and H.B.M. Leeuw

2. What Is Big Data?   19
   Frédéric Lefebvre-Naré, Sebastian Lemire, and Gustav Jakob Petersson

3. The Current Use of Big Data in Evaluation   35
   Steven Højlund, Karol Olejniczak, Gustav Jakob Petersson, and Jakub Rok

4. Getting Started with Big Data: The Promises and Challenges of Evaluating Health-Care Quality   61
   Maria Barrados and Jonathan I. Mitchell

5. Big Data, Real-World Events, and Evaluations   77
   Frank Willemsen and Frans Leeuw

6. Using Big Data to Study Digital Piracy and the Copyright Alert System   97
   H.B.M. Leeuw

7. Protecting America's Biggest Sporting Spectacle   117
   Jonathan D. Breul

8. Keeping Traffic and Transit Passengers Moving—The Use of Big Data   129
   Peter Wilkins

9. Exploring Big (Data) Opportunities: The Case of the Center for Innovation through Data Intelligence (CIDI), New York City   147
Steffen Bohni Nielsen, Nicolaj Ejler, and Maryanne Schretzman

10. Using "Big Data" for Equity-Focused Evaluation—Understanding and Utilizing the Dynamics of Data Ecosystems   171
Kim Forss and Jonas Norén

11. Real-Time Monitoring and Evaluation—Emerging News as Predictive Process Using Big Data-Based Approach   191
Francesco Mazzeo Rinaldi, Giovanni Giuffrida, and Tom Negrete

12. Big Bang or Big Bust? The Role and Implications of Big Data in Evaluation   215
Sebastian Lemire and Gustav Jakob Petersson

13. Cyber Society, Big Data, and Evaluation: A Future Perspective   237
Gustav Jakob Petersson, Frans Leeuw, and Karol Olejniczak

Contributors   255

Index   261

Foreword

Growing complexity and big data are reshaping the evaluation profession in fundamental ways. Increasing complexity is pushing evaluators to move from simple linear models to a more realistic way of evaluating development processes and their outcomes. The emergence of big data has the potential to help us overcome the perpetual search for more and better data, which is necessary to have a better, more robust understanding of change.

Cyber Society, Big Data, and Evaluation offers a visionary and insightful look at how societal and technological changes provide unprecedented opportunities and challenges for evaluators, in particular.

For decades, the evaluation profession has pointed to the need for more and better data. The *cyber society* now produces a constant stream of data, some through self-selected engagement with the Internet and social media, some because of data tracking built into devices we use on a daily basis.

This book shows how technological advances can help fill some of the data gaps that have hamstrung evaluation until now. Big data can usefully complement more traditional sources of evaluation data. It moves us away from the notion that data is generated only for the purpose of understanding a particular intervention, policy, or project—a linear results chain—to recognizing that data on behavior change is much more dispersed and can capture a complex set of factors that trigger such change.

Furthermore, this book illustrates how technological advances in data processing exponentially improve our data processing capacity. This is important in light of the sometimes overwhelming quantities of data. New tools can help evaluators in identifying patterns and making sense of data that otherwise would be difficult to see. Importantly, these tools can also help us become nimbler, faster, and cheaper to address a long-running concern of policy-makers, namely that evaluators take too long to come up with evidence, analyses, and recommendations.

Technological advances allow us—policy-makers, researchers, evaluators—to test hypotheses in real time with very short feedback loops. Experimentation can help us understand how incentives change behaviors. The book provides illustrative examples of how this has and can be done.

The book also challenges evaluators to take up the opportunities that big data provides. The authors found that very few evaluators are tapping into big data or data science in meaningful ways. One example of how evaluators can do this is to provide data scientists with relevant evaluative frameworks—theories of change, hypotheses that can be tested against evidence, including from big data—and more traditional approaches. The authors have not been blind to the limitations of big data, but they validly point out the risks to the evaluation profession, if we don't seize the opportunities.

This book is a great resource that will stimulate debate and practice among evaluators, and hopefully in exchange with data scientists. It has the potential to ground evaluation in more evidence and make it faster than could be done with traditional means, if new technologies are adopted and adapted to complete current evaluation methods.

Caroline Heider

1

Cyber Society, Big Data, and Evaluation: An Introduction

Gustav Jakob Petersson, Frans Leeuw, Jonathan Breul, and H.B.M. Leeuw

We are living in a new world of data. Crime cameras and other sensors generate data as we move. The global usage of mobile devices, social media activity, and Internet behavior leave behind a digital trail of "data exhaust." The economic world has largely moved online, reducing transaction costs and enhancing cross-border money flows. New "peer-to-peer" markets have been developed, including Internet auction "houses" such as eBay (Margetts, 2009: 3). Enormous amounts of data are created also through online media, radio, telecommunications, energy consumption, remote sensing, and program data (e.g. logistics). Machine-generated real-time data thereby constitute an increasing share of the data stored globally. Further expanding the digital world of data, registers as sources of (administrative) data have been increasingly digitalized and made more available.

The resulting dramatic growth in digital data volumes spans nearly every part of our lives from gene sequencing to consumer behavior (King, 2011). The article on the Internet and public policy by Margetts (2009: 3) showed that "for many people across the world, large chunks of their social, economic and political life have moved online." This is sometimes referred to as a "datafication" of our everyday lives.

Datafication is, however, not only about people starting to do things online rather than offline but also about people doing new things, particularly with the growth of the so-called Web 2.0 applications, where users can easily produce as well as consume content by themselves. Examples include social networking sites used by around one-third of Internet users; photo- and video-sharing sites and social media; and peer-produced information goods such as the online user-generated encyclopedia Wikipedia, the English language version of which has over three million articles and eleven million registered users (Margetts, 2009: 3). Such developments regard a large and increasing share of the world's population as Internet penetration has now reached approximately fifty percent globally, almost seventy-five percent in Europe[1] and close to eighty-seven percent in the United States.[2]

Another aspect of the ongoing datafication is that we increasingly monitor *ourselves*. The *Quantified Self-Movement* "involves individuals engaged in the self-tracking of any kind of biological, physical, behavioral, or environmental information as individuals or in groups. Health is an important but not exclusive focus, where objectives may range from general tracking to pathology resolution and to physical and mental performance enhancement."[3]

The *Quantified Self-Movement* works through technology: wearable sensors, mobile apps, software interfaces, and online communities, ranging from simple things like smart watches and electronic T-shirts to electronic tattoos and wearable personal information ecosystems (Swan, 2013).[4]

When such highly diversified sources of data are combined to form massive data sets, they are referred to as *Big Data*. And data sets indeed grow big. In fact, "big" may be translated into "too big." Data sets grow bigger than what can be processed by the memories of individual computers; the development of tools to make the most of Big Data, such as machine learning, data mining, and Big Data analytics, is sometimes depicted as just as transformative as the development of the Internet (for instance, Cukier and Mayer-Schoenberger, 2013).

When Big Data is anonymized, aggregated, and analyzed, it can reveal significant new insights and trends about human behavior. The basic idea is that Big Data makes it possible to learn things that we could not comprehend with smaller amounts of data, creating new insights and value in ways that change markets, organizations, the relationship between citizens and government, and more (Mayer-Schoenberger and Cukier, 2013). We can also learn about phenomena that have been previously difficult to capture, for example, personal connections, such as those within Facebook, and geolocation, such as the place from which a "tweet" was sent via Twitter (Taylor et al., 2014).

Private businesses have found use for Big Data in various fields as the development of new data products has grown to big business. A data product may, for instance, estimate the potential of various business strategies, for instance, by assessing how likely an individual with certain characteristics is to respond to a certain marketing campaign or how likely an investment is to yield the expected return (see for instance Siegel, 2013). And such analyses may be performed almost in real time.

At the same time, it is well known that in our world of evaluations, our work sometimes does not meet the informational needs of decision makers. There is a need for varied and rapidly delivered information to inform decision making. Studies taking years to finish are increasingly believed to be of limited societal or political relevance in a society where every (Internet) year lasts "three months," as the proverb goes. Ex ante evaluations, including regulatory impact assessments, are sometimes even done and reported before the program has been fully implemented, and also real-time evaluations and 'RIPI-evaluations' (evaluating recently implemented program interventions) are more and more seen as answers to these challenges. Another central invention has been to evaluate theories underlying policies and programs (also before they are fully implemented) with the help of knowledge repositories where systematic reviews and synthesis studies have been collected, reviewed, and summarized. The Campbell Collaboration, EPPI, 3ie, and other "secondary knowledge production institutes" (Hansen and Rieper, 2009) provide syntheses that aggregate the samples of different studies, for instance, in the form of meta-analysis or realist synthesis. And yet the calls for more rapidly delivered and broadly generalizable results persist. This is while Big Data provides new opportunities to take the pulse of communities in real time.[5]

Big Data therefore seems to hold the potential to meet needs already noted and experienced by the evaluation community. And yet we will show that Big Data is hardly utilized by evaluators—this in spite of the never-ending call for evidence-based policymaking and in spite of Big Data permitting a dramatically increased range of other agents to analyze social developments (Burrows and Savage, 2014), implying competition from evaluation-like activities. In the adjacent discipline of empirical sociology, the challenge is considered profound and very real (Burrows and Savage, 2014).

In the face of the rapid growth in the global data production, and given the development of analytical techniques to make the most of Big Data, we believe that evaluators should work with and use Big Data. Otherwise, the evaluation community will see tightening competition from more innovative communities representing a rival form of knowledge production that may promise insights quicker, cheaper, and more useful than those of evaluators.

The lack of attention to Big Data also seems surprising since there has been a debate within the evaluation community on the need for integrating evaluation and monitoring. In our view that debate illustrates the need to incorporate also Big Data since Big Data—just like monitoring—refers to a continuous collection of data.

We, therefore, encourage evaluators to engage with Big Data—*and keep turning the pages of this book.*

The Purpose

The purpose of this book is, first, to highlight lessons learned from rare but valuable examples of how Big Data has been rewardingly utilized in evaluation and, second, to discuss how Big Data could be used more widely and systematically in evaluation in various policy fields. We will also discuss how the advent of Big Data may transform the role of evaluators in knowledge production and policy making.

We see at least four reasons why evaluators should engage with Big Data. First, Big Data sources are frequently available in real time, improving the opportunities of evaluators to produce their results while still relevant for decision making. Second, the size of the data makes statistical analysis more powerful and possibly more accurate. Third, Big Data often involves aspects of human behavior that have been previously difficult to observe, for example, personal connections and geolocation. This characteristic makes Big Data important to enhance the relevance of evaluation. Fourth, since the data are already there, it may be comparatively cheap to use as compared to other sources of data, such as surveys.

We will discuss Big Data in relation to various evaluative activities, such as impact analysis, effectiveness assessments, monitoring, and predictive work (ex ante evaluation). Distinctions between such activities are not our primary focus. This book focuses on the *use of Big Data in the production of evidence-based knowledge for decision making.*

Getting started with Big Data is of course associated with a number of challenges. Often discussed in relation to Big Data are ethical concerns associated with having access to data that mirrors numerous aspects of people's lives, that is, privacy concerns, and also challenges of other sorts must be met. The fact that data have been stored does not guarantee that it will be accessible for evaluators or other analysts, as it may be owned, for instance, by business firms. Another pertinent concern is whether the evaluation community is equipped to make valuable contributions also in the Big Data era. Would we best fade out and leave room for Big Data analysts to help produce evidence-based policies? We believe not. Evaluators harness skills which will remain valuable and which make a good starting point for collaboration with Big Data analysts, when needed. And sometimes collaboration will not be needed—if evaluators acquire basic insights and skills needed to work with Big Data. We will discuss both challenges and valuable evaluation skills throughout this volume and summarize in the concluding chapter.

This chapter proceeds by first discussing the meaning of the concept of Big Data. It then gives some first indications of how Big Data may be of value in evaluation. Thereafter, some critique of Big Data is discussed. The chapter concludes by lining out the structure of this volume.

The Concept of Big Data

The term Big Data is today used in a number of different ways. While some observers emphasize characteristics of the data as such, others highlight the implications of the data and their derivatives—processing algorithms and data products—for decision making as well as society as a whole. Chapter 2 of the present volume will provide a discussion of different definitions of Big Data. For now, we will illustrate the breadth by referring to a definition presented by Boyd and Crawford (2012: 663):

> *We define Big Data as a cultural, technological, and scholarly phenomenon that rests on the interplay of:*
>
> *(1) Technology: maximizing computation power and algorithmic accuracy to gather, analyze, link, and compare large data sets.*
> *(2) Analysis: drawing on large data sets to identify patterns in order to make economic, social, technical, and legal claims.*
> *(3) Mythology: the widespread belief that large data sets offer a higher form of intelligence and knowledge that can generate insights that were previously impossible, with the aura of truth, objectivity, and accuracy.*

Other observers, however, use the term Big Data to refer only to data, frequently with an emphasis on automatically generated data. Bail (2014: 469) uses the term Big Data "to refer to the increasingly large volume of text-based data that is often – though not always – produced through digital sources. ... These data are also unique because they are 'naturally occurring,' unlike survey data which result from the intrusion of researchers into everyday life."

Different chapters of the present volume will analyze different aspects of Big Data in relation to evaluation. Some chapters dig into data sources seldom used by evaluators. Other chapters use combinations of data sources which would not have been conceivable only a few years ago, when processing capacity and algorithms were less developed. Yet other chapters discuss the political and cultural framework within which evaluation meets Big Data.

Which of these aspects of Big Data are new? Some observers hold that the data as such are not very revolutionizing and that the revolutionizing power lies rather in (1) the development of a new frame of mind where data are conceived as a commodity with high scientific, economic, political, and social value and (2) in the development of new methods, infrastructures, technologies, skills, and knowledge to handle data (Leonelli, 2014). We will develop our perspective on what is new and what is now so new about Big Data in Chapter 2.

Using Big Data

Big Data has received substantial attention in different spheres. In the scientific community, Big Data journals have been established, and funding for the development of new analytical tools to utilize Big Data is growing. Private businesses utilize Big Data to create various data products, drawing on the development of machine learning, data mining, and Big Data analytics. Such tools make it possible to manage far larger data volumes than previously and to analyze non-structured data, such as free-text documents, images, motion pictures, and sound recordings (Mayer-Schoenberger and Cukier, 2013; O'Reilly Media, 2011). Big Data has also been used in ex ante evaluation, for instance, in Global Development and epidemiological work (Kirkpatrick, 2012). Still there is no doubt that Big Data generally remains under-utilized in policymaking, as highlighted, for instance, in Decker's APPAM Presidential Address (Decker, 2014). The potential of Big Data has probably not yet been fully understood by policy makers and evaluators, as there is no reason to hold that Big Data is less promising for the public sector than for the for-profit sector (Mayer-Schoenberger and Cukier, 2013). For one, Big Data provides as yet unexplored opportunities for manipulating and controlling individuals and communities on a large scale (Leonelli, 2014).

Giving some examples of how Big Data has been utilized for evaluation-like activities may give a first glimpse of the potential of Big Data in evaluation. Let's look into a few developments.

First, Big Data has made it possible to capture aspects of human behavior, which have previously been difficult to observe. Affecting such phenomena—for instance, human interaction—is frequently a focus of public interventions. Interaction and networks may be captured, for instance, over social media, but various difficulties such as validity issues have been obstacles in utilizing the potential of such data. Work is however being done to manage such difficulties. Note, for instance, that Bail (2015) provides an example of how Big Data generated through social media may be effectively combined with conventional survey techniques to enable more comprehensive analysis of collective behavior online. Bail had noted that although social media websites such as Facebook and Twitter provide an unprecedented amount of qualitative data about organizations and collective behavior, these new data sources lack critical information about the broader social context of collective behavior—or protect it behind strict privacy barriers. Therefore, Bail introduced the idea of social media survey apps (SMSAs), which may be used to (1) request permission to access public and non-public data from users of an organization's social media page and (2) distribute a survey among the users in order to capture additional data of interest to a researcher. Finally, social media survey apps may be used to return the results of a scholarly analysis back to the organization as an incentive to share data and participate in social science research. Bail concludes that app technology provides a powerful new platform for social science research. Why should evaluators not use similar technology to map changes in norms or behavior related to interventions?

Another example of a difficult-to-observe phenomenon is deforestation or failure to preserve biodiversity, simply because vast areas would have to be monitored. So how are we to evaluate interventions to tackle such problems? An emerging trend is the development of remote monitoring to map developments over vast geographical areas. Such monitoring has been made possible by the rapid decline in the cost of recording devices, the ability to transmit the information over the Internet, and the availability of free or low-cost tools such as Google Earth make sense of that data by using annotation and sharing features in tools. A recent example is a tool called FORMA (Forestry Monitoring for Action), developed by the Center for Global Development and the Danish government. It uses satellite imagery to produce monthly maps of deforestation down to a very small scale (Hammer et al., 2009). Such technology could also be used, for instance, to monitor the use of green spaces in urban areas, in order to determine which areas are of importance, for instance, for recreation and which would better be used for other purposes.

To further highlight the importance of capturing difficult-to-observe phenomena, think of the role of "culture" and "contexts" when evaluators study the ways in which organizations operate and are realizing their goals. Naturally, the culture of organizations like prisons and psychiatric wards differs from the culture of universities or IT firms. To describe crucial aspects of such different kinds of cultures and sort out the weight of these factors in understanding the efficiency or effectiveness of organizations, often surveys or case studies (including focus groups) are done. This could, however, alternatively be done, for instance, by screen scrapping technologies or automated extraction of text from websites. This is demonstrated by Bail (2012). To classify cultures, Bail (2014: 469) suggests start doing what "cultural sociologists have scarcely explored, i.e. the promise of automated text analysis to classify texts." This new field resulted from collaboration between linguists and computer scientists designed to identify hidden or latent themes within large corpora. Additionally, new techniques have been developed to exploit the relational nature of many sources of Big Data—particularly those from the Internet. For example, Gong (2011) introduced new software that fuses snowball sampling methods with screen-scraping technologies.

Big Data may also be rewardingly used to capture various kinds of phenomena quicker or with greater accuracy than by traditional methods. For one, using online search behavior and data, it can act as a baseline measurement as well as the follow-up measurements. The influenza example is nowadays well known. Although not designed to act as baseline measurement, evaluators could use these data in such a way. It concerns Google Flu Trends, a tool launched in 2008 based on the prevalence of Google queries for flu-like symptoms. Because the relative frequency of certain queries is highly correlated with the percentage of physician visits in which a patient presents with influenza-like symptoms, it was possible to estimate the current level of weekly influenza activity in each region of the United States, with a reporting lag of about one day. When applied to public health, online data have been used as a part of syndromic surveillance efforts also known as infodemiology. According to the US Center for Disease Control and Prevention, mining vast quantities of health-related online data can help detect disease outbreaks before confirmed diagnoses or laboratory confirmation.

Evaluators of (e-health) policies could do regular measurements through the year and over different regions that are capable of functioning as baseline data on the spread of the flu. Then, when new interventions are applied, regular follow-up measurements are possible against hardly any costs and almost in real time.

Evaluators could also use Big Data to contribute to the development of more individualized interventions. Big Data has allowed for the development of precision medicine, that is, the development of individualized care. The Obama administration recently reported about a new initiative: "Launched with a $215 million investment in the President's 2016 Budget, the Precision Medicine Initiative will pioneer a new model of patient-powered research that promises to accelerate biomedical discoveries and provide clinicians with new tools, knowledge, and therapies to select which treatments will work best for which patients."[6]

It is also said that having access to more data on how patients with different characteristics respond to different treatments allows for more individualized treatments. The generation of more data on social interaction, for instance, from the Internet, and combining different data sets, potentially allows for similar developments in social interventions.

This list of evaluation-like activities adopting Big Data could go on and on—including, for instance, regulatory impact assessment—as Big Data has been used in several different disciplines and for different purposes.

Using Big Data for evaluative purposes, however, must not always be quite this advanced. One of the perhaps biggest changes Big Data bring in the evaluation paradigm is in realizing that much relevant data may exist and that there is the option to dive into it quite early in the evaluation process. Quite early means here: after the evaluation has reviewed the key questions of policymakers and stakeholders, and the issues for the future, but before the evaluators develop an investigation scheme and start collecting primary data. A number of log files may exist in different places, about the behaviors of people before and after they received the program outputs.

Imagine an everyday example: an evaluation of resource allocation in a public town library. Entrances as well as book loans are digitally recorded: increasing entrances, and a sharp fall in physical book loans, may easily suggest that users now come to the library for another reason than books—maybe they switched to digital media, and appreciate the library as a cellular-free and Facebook-free working space. That will suggest to modify room allocation and possibly to review the profiles, job descriptions, and training of the staff.

Further and more elaborated examples of what Big Data may bring in evaluation are provided throughout this volume.

Critique of Big Data

There is, however, also skepticism about the beliefs currently held in the potential of Big Data. Gartner, a leading IT research company, annually publishes its "Hype Cycle for Emerging Technologies." Gartner holds that every emerging technology passes through a number of phases in terms of expectations. First, a new innovation triggers new expectations. Then, these expectations reach the peak of inflated expectations. This phase is followed by a period of disillusionment. Only thereafter do expectations slowly rise to a reasonable level. According to a recent Gartner issue, Big Data is about to hit the peak of inflated expectations, where expectations are unreasonably high.[7]

Indeed, the expectations on Big Data are sometimes high. Some authors hold that Big Data will be sufficient and make the use of sampling techniques less important in many contexts (Mayer-Schoenberger and Cukier, 2013). This view has however been shown to create difficulties in cases where quantity has been conceived as a substitute for attention to issues of measurement and construct validity, reliability, and dependencies among data. The belief that Big Data is a substitute for, rather than a supplement to, traditional data collection and analysis is, therefore, sometimes referred to as "Big Data hubris" (Lazer et al., 2014).

Difficulties relating to validity issues must therefore be admitted. For instance, social forums emerge and become associated with certain groups, which evolve over time, for instance, by aging, meaning that data from such forums are not stable indicators over time. Also, as has been highlighted by Lermon (2013), validity concerns may arise due to Big Data exclusions. It concerns "the non-random, systemic omission of people who live on Big Data's margins, whether due to poverty, geography, or lifestyle, and whose lives are less "datafied" than the general population. In key sectors, their marginalization risks distort data sets and, consequently, skew the analysis on which private and public actors increasingly depend."

In our view, evaluators should be aware of such validity dilemmas and treat them by providing appropriate combinations of Big Data and "small data"—that is, the different kinds of primary data traditionally produced by evaluators. This view will be further elaborated throughout this volume and in the concluding chapter.

Worthy of note is also the difficulties of Google Flu Trends to repeat its initial success. In 2008, it was possible to most accurately predict the spread of the flu, but in later years, this has proven difficult. Why? Possible explanations are affluent. Some regard algorithm dynamics, which refers to the fact that search algorithms, for instance, the ones used by Google, are constantly modified so as to improve the commercial service. This means, for instance, providing users more useful search results and making advertising more effective (Lazer et al., 2014). These challenges mean that indicators will have to be continuously and critically assessed.

Another frequently held high expectation is that Big Data will render knowledge about causality obsolete in many contexts since Big Data can provide unsurpassed insights on correlations. Examples are often drawn from automatic modifications of technological systems or from medicine (Cukier and Mayer-Schoenberger, 2013; Mayer-Schoenberger and Cukier, 2013). Others have, however, argued that society is different, for one since past correlations will not always mirror the future. If the environment of a correlation evolves, for instance, through political decision making or through changes in preferences, blind prediction algorithms can fail since they are informed by the world as it was (Hilbert, 2013: 30).

We agree that some contemporary expectations on Big Data are not realistic. However, although too high expectations are likely to throw Big Data into a phase of damnation—as was the case for artificial intelligence a few decades ago—that phase will—if we are to believe Gartner's hype cycle—be followed by a phase of more realistic expectations. Big Data is here to stay.

Moreover, we do not see an immediate risk of inflated expectations in Big Data *in evaluation—simply because evaluators so far have largely been reluctant or ignorant to embrace the promises of Big Data.* Nonetheless, we will avoid adding to the already inflated expectations on Big Data. Instead, we hold that if Big Data is to reach its full potential, it will need to be combined with "small" data—for example, sample data—and with theories of causality, such as the tool kit of evaluators, for example, program theories and the theories borrowed from the social sciences. And as pointed out by many, not the least Ray Pawson, causal explanation is central if we seek to arrive at conclusions usable for the commissioners of evaluations. We will, therefore, need to trace also the mechanisms which give rise to correlations—and this may frequently have to be done using carefully selected primary qualitative data (Pawson, 2013). These points and related points will be further elaborated in the concluding chapter of this book. For now, we state that this book does not advocate Big Data as *thé* alternative but as a most valuable supplement to evaluators' traditional tools.

Structure of the Book

The book proceeds by the following chapters.

Chapter 2, "What Is Big Data" by Frédéric Lefebvre-Naré, Sebastian Lemire, and Gustav Jakob Petersson, provides a summary of the historical development of Big Data, distinguishes between different kinds of Big Data, and discusses which technological shifts have made Big Data possible. The chapter also discusses the emerging data science.

Chapter 3, "The Current Use of Big Data in Evaluation" by Steven Højlund, Karol Olejniczak, Gustav Jakob Petersson, and Jakub Rok, discusses the use of Big Data so far. The chapter draws on a survey aimed at the members of the European Evaluation Society and the American Evaluation Association LinkedIn groups. The findings seem to indicate that Big Data are hardly used by evaluators and that the concept of Big Data is not clear to the majority of evaluators. This chapter also draws on a systematic review of academic journals from the SCOPUS database.

Chapter 4, "Getting Started with Big Data: The Promises and Challenges of Evaluating Health-Care Quality" by Maria Barrados and Jonathan Mitchell, argues that it is a challenge for evaluators to make use of Big Data since they have extensive experience in the collection of data from primary sources but will have to gather more experience on how to make the most of secondary data. The authors illustrate how evaluators may get started with Big Data by discussing a study of the effectiveness of accreditation in promoting the quality of care outcomes in acute care institutions (hospitals).

Chapter 5, "Big Data, Real-World Events, and Evaluations" by Frank Willemsen and Frans Leeuw, presents several real-world case studies showing the relevance of working with Big Data. The authors review a study on consumer confidence, measured, first, through a traditional survey and, second, through Dutch social media messages in public Facebook and Twitter, revealing a strong association between the two measures. The authors also provide examples of how correlations with Google search queries may be used to predict, for instance, influenza and bankruptcies. This example is used to demonstrate the importance of working with social scientific theories about causal mechanisms when building predictive models. The authors conclude that Big Data, when combined with theories, may enhance the opportunities for evaluators to provide results almost in real time and at very low costs.

Chapter 6, "Using Big Data to Study Digital Piracy and the Copyright Alert System" by H.B.M. Leeuw, presents a case study assessing the Copyright Alert System as an anti-piracy intervention. To find out whether an effect of this digital intervention can be expected, Big Data in the form of search queries is used as a screening tool. Benefits of this method are presented, and it is suggested that this method, when combined with more robust tools, can serve as a useful addition to the evaluator's arsenal.

Chapter 7, "Protecting America's Biggest Sporting Spectacle" by Jonathan D. Breul, gives insight into complex logistical and security challenges of Super Bowl XLVIII held in the New York–New Jersey metropolitan area. It takes us through the step-by-step process of advanced planning and implementation of this event and explains how Big Data technology allowed things to work safely. The author explains how evaluative elements integrated into the process played a crucial role in maintaining links between the event and improved planning.

Chapter 8, "Keeping Traffic and Transit Passengers Moving—The Use of Big Data" by Peter Wilkins, provides an overview of opportunities and practices of Big Data applications in the field of transport (both traffic and public transport) by contrasting them with traditional use of data. Based on that overview, the author puts forward four key lessons for evaluators.

Chapter 9, "Exploring Big (Data) Opportunities: The Case of the Center for Innovation Through Data Intelligence (CIDI), New York City" by Steffen Bohni Nielsen, Nicolaj Ejler, and Maryanne Schretzman, presents pioneering experience of New York City in the application of Big Data for coordinating different interventions. The authors use this case study to compare the use of Big Data to a hypothetical, alternative approach based on traditional evaluation insights. They point to differences as well as complementarities and conclude that an exchange of experience between the two fields could provide valuable insights and knowledge for public managers.

Chapter 10, "Using 'Big Data' for Equity-Focused Evaluation—Understanding and Utilizing the Dynamics of Data Ecosystems" by Kim Forss and Jonas Norén, discusses the possibilities for Big Data to revolutionize the way evaluators gather and analyze data and provide policy recommendations. They look at a sample of twenty-five evaluation Terms of Reference from selected international development agencies and find that, at present, Big Data is not much used, partly because Terms of References sometimes close the door for Big Data. They conclude that evaluations need to tap into data that can monitor and gather information regarding digital interaction and that commissioners of evaluations should encourage such innovative approaches.

Chapter 11, "Real-Time Monitoring and Evaluation—Emerging News as Predictive Process Using Big Data-Based Approach" by Francesco Mazzeo Rinaldi, Giovanni Giuffrida, and Tom Negrete, looks at the question of Big Data from the vantage point of journalism, based on user traffic on the online newspaper Sacramento Bee. They argue that "modern" evaluators have to work with a team of experts from various disciplines, such as data mining, data analytics and visualization, computational sociology and social simulation, data journalism, and storytelling. They conclude that co-production may be a key concept for the future.

Chapter 12, "Big Bang or Big Bust? The Role and Implications of Big Data in Evaluation" by Sebastian Lemire and Gustav Jakob Petersson, discusses what we should and should not expect from Big Data in evaluation. The authors start with the promise made by proponents of Big Data that new data analytics will fundamentally transform how we produce—or ought to produce—knowledge about society, such as in evaluation. In the view of the authors, this promise may be formulated in the form of four fundamental shifts, which should all be viewed with a critical eye. The authors conclude that Big Data should be treated as a most valuable new tool in the evaluator's toolbox, rather than a replacement for program theories, theories borrowed from other social science disciplines, causal reasoning, or "small" primary data.

Chapter 13 "Cyber Society, Big Data, and Evaluation: A Future Perspective" by Gustav Jakob Petersson, Frans Leeuw, and Karol Olejniczak, points to different possible future scenarios. We picture that evaluators must either accept to play a small role or embrace Big Data. We discuss four challenges that must be met by evaluators to stay relevant. The first challenge is to redefine the tools used for evaluative purposes. We highlight work done within other communities, which could be used to analyze results of interventions—a task at the very heart of the evaluator profession. The second challenge is to reinvent the role of the evaluator in the policy process. We imagine that evaluators must seek to fill new roles, not the least contribute in new ways to predictive work when new interventions are designed. The third challenge is to obtain various competencies necessary to work with Big Data. These competencies are not only of a technical nature, for evaluators will have to adopt a new mindset to (secondary) data. The fourth and final challenge is to obtain co-creation with communities who already are active in working with Big Data. We believe that evaluators should not only seek to do Big Data work themselves but also seek collaboration with Big Data experts and other innovative communities and add insights coming from theory-driven evaluations, knowledge repositories, expertise in stimulating utilization of findings, and much more.

Notes

1. "Internet World Stats: Usage and Population Statistics" http://www.internetworldstats.com/stats4.htm (accessed August 26, 2016).
2. "Number of Internet Users (2016) – Internet Live Stats" http://www.internetlivestats.com/internet-users/ (accessed August 26, 2016).
3. Swan (2013: 85) refers to the history of self-tracking. "One of the earliest recorded examples of quantified self-tracking is that of Sanctorius of Padua, who studied energy expenditure in living systems by tracking his weight versus food intake and elimination for 30 years in the 16th century."
4. Swan (2013: 86) presented some self-tracking statistics for the USA: 60% US adults track weight, diet, or exercise, 33% US adults monitor blood sugar, blood pressure, headaches, or sleep pattern, and 9% receive text message health alerts.
5. "Big Data for Development: Opportunities & Challenges" http://www.unglobalpulse.org/projects/BigDataforDevelopment (accessed August 26, 2016).
6. "Our Data, Our Health: Thoughts on Using mHealth for the Precision Medicine Cohort" http://quantifiedself.com/?s=M+health+Obama+&x=12&y=7 (accessed August 26, 2016). See also "About the Precision Medicine Initiative Cohort Program" https://www.nih.gov/precision-medicine-initiative-cohort-program (accessed August 26, 2016).
7. "Gartner's 2013 Hype Cycle for Emerging Technologies Maps Out Evolving Relationship Between Humans and Machines" http://www.gartner.com/newsroom/id/2575515 (accessed August 26, 2016).

References

Bail, C. 2012. "The Fringe Effect: Civil Society Organizations and the Evolution of Media Discourse about Islam." *American Sociological Review* 77 (7): 855–79.

———. 2014. "The Cultural Environment: Measuring Culture with Big Data." *Theory and Society* 43 (3): 465–82.
———. 2015. "Taming Big Data: Using App Technology to Study Organizational Behavior on Social Media." *Sociological Methods & Research* 43: 1–29.
Boyd, D., and K. Crawford. 2012. "Critical Questions for Big Data." *Information, Communication & Society* 15 (5): 662–79.
Burrows, R., and M. Savage. 2014. "After the Crisis? Big Data and the Methodological Challenges of Empirical Sociology." *Big Data & Society* 1 (1): 1–6.
Cukier, K., and V. Mayer-Schoenberger. 2013. "The Rise of Big Data: How It's Changing the Way We Think about the World." *Foreign Affairs* 92 (3): 28–40.
Decker, P. 2014. "False Choices, Policy Framing, and the Promise of 'Big Data.'" *Journal of Policy Analysis and Management* 33 (2): 252–62.
Gong, A. 2011. *An Automated Snowball Census of the Political Web.* http://papers.ssrn.com/sol3/papers.cfm?abstract_id=1832024 (accessed August 26, 2016).
Hammer, D., D. Kraft, and D. Wheeler. 2009. *Forma: Forest Monitoring for Action – Rapid Identification of Pan-Tropical Deforestation Using Moderate-Resolution Remotely Sensed Data.* Working Paper. Washington, DC: Center for Global Development.
Hansen, F., and O. Rieper. 2009. "Institutionalization of Second-Order Evidence-Producing Organizations." In *The Evidence Book. Concepts, Generation and Use of Evidence*, edited by O. Rieper, F. Leeuw, and T. Ling, 27–52. New Brunswick: Transaction Publishers.
Hilbert, M. 2013. *Big Data for Development: From Information- to Knowledge Societies.* Accessed August 26, 2016. http://papers.ssrn.com/sol3/papers.cfm?abstract_id=2205145.
King, G. 2011. "Ensuring the Data Rich Future of the Social Sciences." *Science* 331 (6018): 719–21.
Kirkpatrick, R. 2012. *Harnessing the Power of Big Data for Global Development.* Paper presented at the European Evaluation Society Biannual Conference. Helsinki, Finland.
Lazer, D., R. Kennedy, G. King, and G. Vespignani. 2014. "The Parable of Google Flu: Traps in Big Data Analysis." *Science* 343 (6176): 1203–05.
Leonelli, S. 2014. "What Difference Does Quantity Make? On the Epistemology of Big Data in Biology." *Big Data & Society* 1 (1): 1–11.
Lermon, J. 2013. "Big Data and Its Exclusions." *Standford Law Review Online* 66:55–63.
Margetts, H. 2009. "The Internet and Public Policy." *Policy & Internet* 1 (1): 1–21.
Mayer-Schoenberger, V., and K. Cukier. 2013. *Big Data: A Revolution That Will Transform How We Live, Work, and Think.* Boston, New York: Houghton Mifflin Harcourt.
O'Reilly Media. 2011. *Big Data Now: Current Perspectives from O'Reilly Radar.* Sebastopol: O'Reilly Media.
Pawson, R. 2013. *The Science of Evaluation: A Realist Manifesto.* London: Sage.
Siegel, E. 2013. Predictive Analytics: Harnessing the Power of Big Data. *Analytics* (July–August): 38–42.
Sommer, P., and I. Brown. 2011. *Reducing Systemic Cybersecurity Risk.* Paris: OECD.

Swan, M. 2013. "The Quantified Self: Fundamental Disruption in Big Data Science and Biological Discovery." *Big Data* 1 (2): 85–99.

Taylor, L., R. Schroeder, and E. Meyer. 2014. Emerging Practices and Perspectives on Big Data Analysis in Economics: Bigger and Better or More of the Same? *Big Data & Society* 1 (2): 1–10.

Yudhoyono, S., E. Sirleaf, and D. Cameron. 2013. *A New Global Partnership: Eradicate Poverty and Transform Economies Through Sustainable Development. The Report of the High-Level Panel of Eminent Persons on the Post-2015 Development Agenda*. New York: United Nations.

2

What Is Big Data?

*Frédéric Lefebvre-Naré, Sebastian Lemire,
and Gustav Jakob Petersson*

Introduction

We live in a "datified" world. Every day billions of individual experiences and opinions are recorded and stored. The "Internet of Things," or the "pervasive Internet," offers an illustrative example: billions of people, as well as billions of connected things, sending small and irregular messages. We spend wickets, pay at checkouts, navigate by GPS, tweet, snapchat, point-and-click, browse, update, and like and unlike others and ourselves. We feed the Big Data river. Local computers and servers capture web pages we read, videos we launch, seconds we browse, and queries we make. Streams—even floods—of clicks and tags are connected every microsecond, tracing the products we buy, the purchases we make, the pages we visit, etc. Big Data is here, there, and everywhere.

To be sure, Big Data has become a fundamental aspect of everyday life. In this way, Big Data reflects a profound technological change in and of itself, producing new kinds of data, covering new life events, and opening the way to new uses of data. Yet, despite its prevalence and fundamental importance, using Big Data in program evaluation remains rare, as other chapters in this volume suggest. One barrier for the use of Big Data in the evaluation community may stem from a lack of understanding of what Big Data is, or is not. So what is this thing called Big Data? What is new and not so new about Big Data? And what types of Big Data might be relevant for evaluators? These are the questions that will guide this chapter.

What Is This Thing Called Big Data?

> *There's a lack of definitions around the most basic terminology. What is "Big Data" anyway? What does "data science" mean? What is the relationship between Big Data and data science?*
> —Cathy O'Neil and Rachel Schutt (2014: 2)

Definitions of Big Data abound. The Berkeley School of Information collected definitions of "Big Data" by forty-three "thought leaders in publishing, fashion, food, automobiles, medicine, marketing" (Dutcher, 2014). Looking across these definitions, we find at least five different ways of understanding the Big Data disruption:

1. *Big Data as a disruption to traditional data processing* (eighteen definitions). These definitions refer to different challenges: the amount of data, or the real time processing, or the diversity of sources, or the low density of these low-cost amounts of data. This is in-line with O'Neil and Schutt's (2014: 24) suggestion that

   > *Big Data... is a relative term referring to when the size of the data outstrips the state-of-the-art current computational solutions (in terms of memory, storage, complexity, and processing speed) available to handle it.*

   Most authors highlight the *technological gap*, others underscore the *new skills required* by these new data, and some even quote both.

2. *Big Data as data-driven decision making* (ten definitions). These definitions highlight the role of Big Data analytics and data visualization as new ways of "informing decision making with analytical insight derived from data" (John Akred cited in Dutcher [2014]).

3. *Big Data as continuous storing and processing of large volumes of data* (eight definitions). These definitions emphasize the ability to "capture and store data on a very large volume of actions and transactions of different types, on a continuous basis" (Rohan Deuskar cited in Dutcher [2014]). Within the perspective of handling data, definitions 2 and 3 are to be combined: handling data effectively means simultaneously effectively handling big amounts of data and making them operative in the physical or human world.

4. *Big Data as a cultural movement* (five definitions). These definitions liken Big Data to a new data analytic revolution, introducing both ethical challenges as well as huge opportunities. In the words of one "thought leader", "Big Data is now a cultural movement by which we continue to discover how humanity interacts with the world" (Drew Conway cited in Dutcher [2014]).

5. *Big Data as the absence of human interpretation* (two definitions). These definitions emphasize the absence or lack of need for human interpretation; "a cultural shift in which more and more decisions are made by algorithms" (Daniel Gillick cited in Dutcher [2014]).

To be sure, these definitions represent neither an exhaustive nor a conclusive list of definitions. What they do represent is an indication of the diversity of thought on what we mean by Big Data. While some definitions refer to the role or potential role of Big Data in society (e.g. Big Data as a cultural movement), others emphasize Big Data as a technological disruption that will change how we process and make use of data (e.g. Big Data as data-driven decision making). Big Data means many different things to many different people.

Noticeable by its relative absence in the above typology is any attention awarded to the critical characteristics of Big Data. With the exception of definitions emphasizing storage and processing capabilities, the proposed definitions are relatively silent on the defining features of Big Data, as opposed to those of other types of large-scale secondary data (e.g. census and register-based data). Toward specifying key features of Big Data, the following oft-cited definition by Gartner (2012) may be more useful: "Big Data is high *volume*, high *velocity*, and/or high *variety* information assets that require new forms of processing to enable enhanced decision making, insight discovery and process optimization."

These three fundamental features of Big Data deserve our attention. First and foremost, Big Data is characterized by high *volume*. This begs the question how high is "high" in the context of Big Data? There is no consensus or definitive answer to this question. This is perhaps because the question is a bit like asking: How long is a long piece of string? Well, it depends. In the context of Big Data, "high volume" is usually taken to mean too big to fit into the memory that traditional databases and computers use for processing.

To make matters more complex, however, there is also another important aspect of the size of Big Data, namely that at least some forms of Big Data encompass data on entire populations (as opposed to samples). As such, the "big" in Big Data may also refer to a completeness (or totality) rarely realized in other secondary data sets (however large).

Sometimes it is also highlighted that at least some forms of Big Data not only encompass data on many different individuals, potentially reducing difficulties of generalization from samples but also encompass a lot of information on every individual. This granularity of Big Data has made some observers draw a parallel to the invention of the microscope, which allowed researchers to look at the physical world in much greater detail (Taylor et al., 2014).

Another central component of Big Data is that of *velocity*. Big Data is generated, captured, processed, and made available in close to real time, providing a continuous stream of information. As just one example, Wal-Mart processes more than one million customer transactions, generating more than 2.5 petabytes of data every hour (Kitchin, 2014). The unprecedented velocity of Big Data stands in marked contrast to traditional data sources, which are often episodic and in effect delayed in time.

The third important characteristic of Big Data is that it is massive not only in scale but also in *variety*. Big Data spans from traditional data sources, digitized with intent, to passively generated data in the form of unintended digital traces left behind on the Internet. In this way, Big Data creates the potential to render into data many aspects of the world, which have never been collected or even considered as data before.

Finally, and advancing beyond the three Vs (volume, velocity, and variety) promoted by Gartner (2012), others have emphasized *veracity*, either as another defining characteristic of Big Data or as a challenge Big Data providers unavoidably face. Veracity is in the context of Big Data referring to data that may be structured or unstructured, uncertain, and imprecise. The importance of the veracity issue regarding Big Data stems in large part from the velocity and variety alluded to above, from the ways in which Big Data is generated—as opposed to traditional survey data that would be collected as part of a prearranged and controlled process.

In summary, the term Big Data is used in many different ways, mirroring a new world of data. In responding to the newness and at times the high-pitched hype surrounding Big Data, it might be worth reminding ourselves what is truly new about Big Data.

What Is New and What Is Not So New About Big Data?

Digitalization is nothing new. Since the early 1960s, an ever-increasing range of operations and activities has been digitalized, spanning financial, public service, and communication systems. Simply consider the inventory management of stores, online banking, government job portals, and so forth. Extracting meaning from large amounts of data, digging and sorting through data records in order to extract information, is also nothing new. Digging for informational gold nuggets, that is, "data mining," became fashionable in the 1990s. Similarly, the use of data to make predictions and provide insights for making data-driven decisions is nothing new in the context of social sciences. Since Sir Ronald Fisher's promotion of correlation-based statistical techniques in the 1920s, social scientists have pursued statistically significant correlations with equal amounts fervor and statistical conviction.

With these observations as our backdrop, it is perhaps no surprise that we may have a feeling of *déjà vu, déjà entendu* when we read and hear about Big Data. The stories about Wal-Mart predicting customer behavior—didn't we read similar stories in the data mining era (Fisk, 1997)? Didn't the debate on *open data* take place thirty years ago? This new job of *data crunching* that is required to transform mountains of raw data into sense and action—wasn't it already called so in the 1970s[1]?

Also the cultural and ethical debates surrounding Big Data have roots going decades back in time. Fiction authors assumed data collectors to have long-lasting memory, even at times when they had not so much. Well-known examples include Big Brother in George Orwell's "Nineteen Eighty-Four" (1949), Philip K. Dick's "Minority Report" (1956), and more recently Andrew Niccol's "Gattaca" (1997). These authors introduced data pervasiveness issues long before actual technologies met them. But for this very reason, such references may be misleading, as customary as they may be within present discussions of Big Data issues in mass media. The kind of data that are actually recorded, the way they are, and the way they can be processed and used, is quite different from what fiction authors imagined.

In this regard, the novelty of Big Data is perhaps best viewed as an unprecedented expansion of our technical abilities to capture, store, access, and make sense of new forms of data. Let us consider these in turn.

Large Storage and Processing Capacities

One novel aspect of Big Data, arguably a driver of the Big Data revolution, is the technological change dramatically reducing the unit cost for collecting, storing, and transmitting raw data. Following Bellity (2013), we understand the reduction of unit storage costs as the major driver for the rise of Big Data, much more that any increase in data demand or in data processing abilities. The low cost and high capacity for data storage is made possible by the way data are managed within information systems. As highlighted by Hal Varian (cited in Dutcher [2014]), Big Data moves from the (SQL) "standard relational database" to not only SQL (noSQL) and "data lakes." Admittedly, this sounds like a technicality, but the consequences are profound.

To understand why that is, let us first consider the structure of traditional databases. Their design involves a model that reflects the reality of the organization. Physical places are modeled by standardized addresses; families are classified by the profession of the head of the household; physical things on sale are referred to by product reference; and so on. This involves a complicated data structure, distinguishing mailboxes from other physical places, individuals from families, products from add-ons, and so on. Once you know the data structure, you can query the database in a structured way, that's what SQL means, "Structured Query Language." One severe drawback of structured databases is that any change in reality might make the database structure obsolete. Such databases are hardly adaptive to change. New information on a same reality—for example, a new mail address for the same person—will cancel and replace the previous one. For an relational database, the typical way to handle change is to keep record of the "cancel and replace" operation—in a log file, saved in the organization's data warehouse, usually with a "noSQL" structure.

Another view on the same reality consists in recording events when they take place, stacking the data available when they took place. The developments in the Big Data era took this direction: they give up modeling present realities, and rather record past and present events in a form that was relevant at the moment they happened. Such less structured data warehouses, where data aggregate and older data are very seldom moved or modified, are often called data lakes.[2] Giving up the advantages and restrictions of structured relational "SQL" databases, they are part of the noSQL family of database technologies.

Big Data, then, suggests a new, implicit, model of reality based on space and time and not on the internal structure of the organization. Altogether, a deep relationship exists between the way data is organized at the moment when it is stored, and the way it can be used, processed, and transformed into knowledge later on. Most events, if not all, are located in space and time. The data analyst can quite easily locate on a same space–time map, different kind of events: where people live and where their workplace is, where clients make purchases, and where they check in (e.g., in public transportation or the car park). Many applications of Big Data, such as predictive policing,[3] primarily consist in projecting organizational data onto a space–time grid.

New Algorithms to Access These Stored Data

Another driver is the enhanced processing and retrieval algorithms. During the 2000s, Yahoo!, Google, Amazon, and other giant IT companies created algorithms and software that are able to handle the massive amounts of data generated by their users. These algorithms accommodate not only mammoth data *volumes* but also processing *velocity* while reconciling data *variety* (Big Data stemming from users is heterogeneous data, issued by independent sources). The algorithms extract value from the data. They look for valuable correlations between operable variables on one hand, such as customers' address and their previous purchases, and outcome variables on the other hand, such as later purchases.

Looking for such correlation is nothing new, but a novelty is the unprecedented power of real-time processing algorithms. The overarching aim of these algorithms was that relevant data should be retrieved, processed, and used at the speed of the user's click. Big Data holds the potential to determine some automated actions much, much faster, and more efficient than human processing. To illustrate, in Stockholm county (Sweden): 9,500 volunteers agreed to receive a text message and a computer-generated phone call if they were located within 500 m from a suspected out-of-hospital cardiac arrest. In forty-four percent of reviewed out-of-hospital cardiac arrests, "one or more volunteers reached the location prior to ambulance arrival" (Fredman, 2012). This is Big Data: heterogeneous data oceans (geolocation data, phone calls data including emergency calls, and a small file of volunteers contact data) interfaced with real-life events (out-of-hospital cardiac arrest, call reception, and sending an ambulance), but processed much faster than human decision might do.

Another, and widely known, example is the Amazon recommendation feature. It was, in some sense, easier to design than the out-of-hospital cardiac arrest emergency feature, because online recommendations require no connection with the physical world and its inherent unpredictability. For this reason, e-commerce, as well as finance, may have been a step ahead in using Big Data technologies. Many other industries, such as consumer retail and health, became able to access data in a practical manner only in the 2010s.

The work of a powerful algorithm and its advantages may be illustrated with the highly renowned algorithm MapReduce, published in 2004 by Google. Mapping basically consists in cutting a job to be done, into smaller parallel independent tasks that can be sent to different processors or servers/disks. Mapping is recursive, meaning that the tasks can cut themselves into subtasks and so on. Reducing, recursively also, consists in combining the results of the tasks into a relevant output of the original job. For example, if you search a same word in different stacks of documents, each task might consist in taking out of one stack from the few documents with the best matching with the searched word, and the "reduce" step would consist in assembling and sorting this small selection. Such a way of doing is fully "scalable," i.e. if you have twice more documents, you just need twice more servers, and the job will not last significantly more.[4] Many "Big Data" management tools, such as the Apache open-source software framework Hadoop, created in 2005, implement MapReduce. But MapReduce is only one of several technologies for handling Big Data.

Another key aspect to understanding how value is extracted from Big Data is the very idea of "data users" (a plural). This is because the uses of a data stock do not depend that much on the design of the data flow or on the data extraction process. More importantly, data users behaviors can affect data flows. Search engines provide an easy example of this:

- Data design: the search company designs a search form allowing a user to access a database of documents.
- Data collection: when the user formulates searches and selects the relevant answers among those the engine returned, the form records these user-generated data.
- Data usage: the search company mines the huge stock of searches of returned answers and of selections by users, in order to make its search algorithms more effective as well as to target consumers.

The Emergence of Data Science

A new community of researchers is emerging, experts in the extraction of value from Big Data: The data scientists. However, data science, just like Big Data, comes with a number of definitions. Current definitions converge on two points:

- They define data science as know-how in the sense of "what it represents may not be science but more of a craft" (O'Neil and Schutt,

2014: 3), or just engineering, often emphasizing empirical tips rather than deploying theories.
- They locate data science at the meeting point of three sciences: computer science, statistics (or learning theory), and the science of what data are about—for example, social science, economics, ecology, and business, depending on the data sets. Sometimes "data science" has been understood as "data-based science."[5]

According to IBM (2014),

> *a data scientist represents an evolution from the business or data analyst role. The formal training is similar, with a solid foundation typically in computer science and applications, modeling, statistics, analytics and math. What sets the data scientist apart is strong business acumen [...] Anjul Bhambhri, vice president of Big Data products at IBM, says, "A data scientist is somebody who is inquisitive, who can stare at data and spot trends. It's almost like a Renaissance individual who really wants to learn and bring change to an organization."* (IBM, 2014)

Data science may still be considered to be in its infancy. Nonetheless, data scientists have proven that Big Data is of great value.

Big Data offers unprecedented avenues of new data. When "Big Data" records human behavior, reading data files is reading snippets of stories about people and trying to connect the dots. There are certainly evaluators who don't feel very comfortable neither with statistics nor with computer science. They might consider the growth of Big Data science as a major challenge. But evaluators can also see this situation as a major opportunity to bring their own knowledge and experience of figures, databases, and data as a contribution to this new science. To realize the potential, we must first appreciate the different types of Big Data that might be relevant in the context of evaluation.

Which Kinds of Big Data Are Relevant for Evaluators?

For evaluators, the conceptual diversity surrounding Big Data may serve as a two-edge sword. On one hand, the conceptual diversity may represent a challenge in terms of identifying what is and what is not relevant Big Data. Confusion may ensue. On the other hand, the conceptual diversity highlights the potentially broad range of data applications in evaluation in the Big Data era. To correctly realize the opportunities, however, distinctions are called for which can stimulate a debate on which types of Big Data are most relevant to evaluators.

Perhaps unsurprisingly given the conceptual diversity outlined above, many types of Big Data exist. A focus might be put on the originator of the data. Many authors, such as Hurwitz et al. (2013), distinguish between machine-generated and human-generated data and immediately point a hybrid category. The sensor is in almost all cases automated: it is a machine. But the recorded operations encompass human action. The distinction is, therefore, not that effective.

Another more helpful distinction typology is offered by Tata Consultancy Services (2013), who typifies Big Data according to two dimensions:

- Whether the data are **structured, semistructured**, or **unstructured**, for example, data in relational databases, bulletin board discussions, and videos on YouTube, respectively;
- Whether the data are **internal** or **external** to the organization, for example, messages to the after-sales service on one hand and tweets regarding the same products on the other hand.

The most common distinction is actually between structured and unstructured data, especially because different data structures demand different types of software and handling. Before going forward with this distinction, let us admit that even the border between structured and unstructured data is fuzzy. For example, the key/value storage in noSQL files handles structured and unstructured data together. And even the simplest structured table on Excel may include a column of "observations," that is, unstructured text. Indeed, the evaluator will often find that the most valuable pieces of information hided there and that using these observations requires to encode them, for example, into ad hoc (structured) categories.

Leaving the fuzziness aside, pushing ahead with the distinction between structured and unstructured data, allows us to classify data according to their kind of structure and identify the methodological and software tools that can manage them accordingly. From this perspective, meaningful kinds of Big Data and corresponding tools might be the following, with some overlap:[6]

Table 2.1. Data types and managerial tools

Types of Big Data	Analytical Approaches and Relevant Software Tools
"Rows and columns" tables and relational databases, where each field contains an information bit of a specified type on a specified individual (row) and on a specified topic (column): for example, the *wage* paid to *Mr. Smith* at the end of *April 2014* (quantitative variable); or the *department* *Mr. Smith* was employed at at the same time (categorical variable)	**Structured Query Language**(s) provide extraction, sorting, and computing features to process structured databases. Traditional **statistics and software** (SAS, SPSS, etc.) provide much more "univariate" or "multivariate" functions, especially on quantitative variables **Survey processing software** performs especially well to combine categorical variables **Business Intelligence or Business Analytics** software (Business Objects, Tableau Software, QlikView, etc.) typically cuts volumes they call "metrics," such as sales, according to categories they call "dimensions" **Data mining** looks for correlations or "association rules" within large sets of variables. Many disciplines developed **dedicated processing software** that suited better the kind of variables they had to handle (such as EpiInfo for epidemiology)
Texts	**Natural language processing** algorithms and software can either use prior knowledge of the language used, or not; for example, counting the number of tweets including #programevaluation does not require any knowledge of the language whereas sorting the tweets including the word "evaluation" also with abbreviations or misspelling requires such knowledge Texts **classification** algorithms provide huge opportunities for program evaluation. See below for some development

(Continued)

Table 2.1. (*Continued*)

Types of Big Data	Analytical Approaches and Relevant Software Tools
Images	**Pattern recognition**/image analysis techniques
	Movement detection in videos
Time series	**A broad range of mathematical tools**, strongly depending on data volume, itself depending on the sampling periodicity: 1 figure/year in economics, ±1,000/second in finance or in human movement analysis, etc.
Space-related data, for example, data about roads or jurisdictions	**Geostatistics**[7] process transforms and combines variables related to geographical coordinates
	Geographic information systems are best known for their visualization capabilities; some provide Business Intelligence features
Space–time positions, such as individuals' location data	**Geographic information systems** and other software allow plotting individual paths on maps—but it remains hard to sum up between individuals!
	Newcomers such as CitizenData (2015) develop dedicated database structures for "geo time series".
Network data, basically data about the links between pairs of elements in a population	Dedicated databases for network data— **"graph databases,"** such as Neo4j, are part of the "noSQL" movement
	Graphs visualization also requires dedicated software such as Gephi
...And others, including combinations of the above!	

Let us focus on two kinds of data that, despite intrinsic complexity, represent obvious opportunities for program evaluation: *natural texts* and data collected along *individual paths*.

Natural texts are probably the most common material that Big Data evaluators can have access to, together with structured tables. An unprecedented amount of qualitative data are today being archived, for instance, through Google's digitalization of nearly every single book ever written (Bail, 2014). Many algorithms and software prove very effective on classifying texts according to their own categories. Such software will classify the spontaneous messages about a given program according to the kinds of problems, issues, or perceptions that people share about this program. This approach is very effective regarding public programs targeting the general public and commented by enough people from this public. For example, one of the authors has used such software[8] to answer questions, such as

- What worries the French about the pension system and their own, present or future, pension?
- What are the main occupational safety and health issues in a very large organization?
- How have perceptions of a car-sharing service changed after it was effectively introduced?

These types of questions all hold evaluative relevance.

A simplified version of such questions received much attention during the last years: "sentiment analysis," consists in classifying texts according to their positive, negative, or neutral tone regarding their subject, for example, pension plans. But it is not "simple" at all to be relevant in classifying texts this way. Many texts will be positive, negative, or neutral; "positivity" is hardly a relevant category as far as people's spontaneous expression about a service is concerned. Many people will want to solve a problem related to this service (which does not imply they dislike it) or suggest solutions to the problem (which does not imply they like it). Algorithm will struggle to capture and classify such distinctions.

Recorded individual paths, a combination of rich encoded data and time-series, offer another opportunity for the Big Data-oriented evaluator. For example, when trying to evaluate employment policies based upon individual data, a person may experience a succession of bouts of employment with changing status, periods of unemployment, training sessions, and interspersed with various supportive services. A number of log files will exist in different places about the behaviors of the person before and after they received supportive services and about the use of physical and human means (beyond the money that pays them), which may be tracked minute after minute. Real-time analyses of these pathways, including the identification of potential causes and consequences, offer both challenges and opportunities. The most effective way to handle such data may often be to dive qualitatively into individual cases, in order to find an adequate way to summarize the data (e.g. at which time point should be set the "initial" and "final" dates) and to simplify drastically the paths, generally by cross-sectional views (initial vs. final situations).

What these examples illustrate is that Big Data expands the landscape of data many evaluations may now use. This may seem like a modest change, compared to the often bright and bold prophecies surrounding the era of Big Data, but it's actually a deep change: discovering, extracting, processing, analyzing, understating, and summarizing preexisting (huge, messy, biased, etc.) data require specific tasks and specific "data science" skills that may change the evaluators' job, the skill sets we may need in evaluation teams, and the ways in which we approach and carry out evaluations.

Concluding Thoughts

Big Data is defined in many different ways. High volume, high velocity, high variety, and high veracity are generally considered fundamental characteristics of Big Data. Although digging and sorting through data records in order to extract information and support decision making is nothing new, Big Data offers an unprecedented expansion of our technical abilities to capture, store, access, and make sense of new forms of data. Of particular interest to evaluators are natural texts and data collected along individual paths.

Notes

1. See for example LeCompte and Preissle (1977).
2. "A data lake is a large object-based storage repository that holds data in its native format until it is needed," Margaret Rouse cited in Devlin (2014).
3. See RAND Corporation (2013).
4. This scalability issue is often related to the shift from SQL relational databases, to other (admittedly more scalable) models, under the keyword "noSQL," but SQL databases can be distributed in clusters too. For discussions on the scalability issue, see for example http://programmers.stackexchange.com/questions/194340/why-are-nosql-databases-more-scalable-than-sql and a summary of arguments in Section 7.2 in Cattell (2010).
5. "The key word in data science is not 'data'; it is 'science'. Data science is only useful when the data are used to answer a question. That is the science part of the equation" (Leek, 2013).

6. O'Neil and Schutt (2014) developed approximately the same list (with "**sensor data**" as a distinct kind) and emphasized choosing adequate methods and algorithms depending on the kind of data.
7. See https://en.wikipedia.org/wiki/Geostatistics.
8. This is especially the open-source software IRaMuTeQ, based upon R packages. See for example Smyrnaios and Ratinaud (2013).

References

Bail, C. A. 2014. "The Cultural Environment: Measuring Culture with Big Data." *Theory and Society* 43: 465–82.

Bellity, E. 2013. "L'écosystème du 'déluge de données.'" *Variances*, 46. Accessed November 29, 2014. http://www.ensae.org/docs/2013164614_v46-focus1.pdf.

Cattell, R. 2010. "Scalable SQL and NoSQL Data Stores." Accessed November 28, 2014. http://www.cattell.net/datastores/Datastores.pdf.

Devlin, B. 2014. "In the Data Lake: Not Waving but Drowning." Presentation at Strata+HadoopWorld, 2014.

Dick, P. K. 1956. "Minority Report." In *Fantastic Universe*, edited by S. Merwin, B. Jones, and H. Margulies, King Size Publications.

Dutcher, J. 2014. "What Is Big Data?" Accessed November 29, 2014. http://datascience.berkeley.edu/what-is-big-data/.

Fisk (1997), "Beer and Nappies – A Data Mining Urban Legend, on Donald Fisk's website http://web.onetel.net.uk/~hibou/Beer%20and%20Nappies.html (retrieved on October 30, 2016)

Fredman, D. 2012. "Use of Mobile Phones to Dispatch Volunteers to Perform Early CPR, the First 303 Cases." Presentation at *The Boston Medicine 2.0'12 Congress*.

Gartner, 2012. "Big Data." Accessed November 29, 2014. http://www.gartner.com/it-glossary/big-data.

Hurwitz, J. S., A. Nugent, F. Halper, and M. Kaufman. 2013. *Big Data for Dummies*. Hoboken, NJ: John Wiley & Sons.

IBM. 2014. "What is a Data Scientist?" Accessed April 21, 2014. http://www-01.ibm.com/software/data/infosphere/data-scientist/.

Kitchin, R. 2014. "Big Data, New Epistemologies and Paradigm Shifts." *Big Data & Society* 1: 1–12.

LeCompte, M. D., and J. Preissle. 1977. "Data Crunching, or, What Do I Do with the Five Drawers of Field Notes?" Presentation at the meeting of *the Council on Anthropology and Education of the American Anthropological Association*.

Leek, J. 2013. "The Key Word in 'Data Science' Is Not Data, It Is Science." Accessed November 28, 2014. http://simplystatistics.org/2013/12/12/the-key-word-in-data-science-is-not-data-it-is-science/.

Niccol, A. 1997. *Gattaca*. Columbia Pictures.

O'Neil, C., and R. Schutt. 2014. *Doing Data Science*. Sebastopol, CA: O'Reilly Media.

Orwell, G. 1949. *Nineteen Eighty-Four*. London: Secker & Warburg.

RAND Corporation. 2013. "Predictive Policing: The Role of Crime Forecasting in Law Enforcement Operations." Accessed November 28, 2014. https://www.ncjrs.gov/pdffiles1/nij/grants/243830.pdf.

Smyrnaios, N., and P. Ratinaud. 2013. "Comment articuler analyse des réseaux et des discours sur Twitter: L'exemple du débat autour du pacte budgétaire européen." *tic&société* 7 (2): 120–47.

Tata Consultancy Services (data). 2013. "What Kinds of Digital Data Are Companies Using?" Accessed November 29, 2014. http://sites.tcs.com/big-data-study/kinds-of-digital-data/; still accessible September 21, 2015. https://web.archive.org/web/20130404093949/http://sites.tcs.com/big-data-study/kinds-of-digital-data.

Taylor, L., R. Schroeder, and E. Meyer. 2014. "Emerging Practices and Perspectives on Big Data Analysis in Economics: Bigger and Better or More of the Same?" *Big Data & Society* 1: 1–10.

3

The Current Use of Big Data in Evaluation

Steven Højlund, Karol Olejniczak, Gustav Jakob Petersson, and Jakub Rok

Introduction

This book is intended to discuss the implications of Big Data for evaluation. We wish to provide some inspiration for evaluators searching a way into the twenty-first century. To be able to do so, we need to have a sense of where the evaluation community stands today with regard to Big Data. However, we know of no previous study which investigates the current use of Big Data in evaluation. Furthermore, in order to learn more about where innovative evaluators may tap relevant experience, we also need to learn more about the use of Big Data in the social sciences more broadly. Extending the scope of our analysis is also important since it is a contested issue whether evaluation should be considered as a discipline of its own or should rather be seen as an activity that may be performed in various social scientific disciplines. This is to say that there is no clear boundary between evaluation and (other) social scientific disciplines.

This chapter, therefore, discusses, first, the present use of Big Data in the evaluation of public interventions and, second, the use of Big Data in the social sciences. Our prime interests have been to find out whether the use of Big Data is a new trend in evaluation, to get a first sense of how use could be stimulated further, and to provide inspiration for evaluators by highlighting innovative uses of Big Data.

In order to address these questions, we applied a two-step exploratory approach. To learn about the use of Big Data in evaluation, we conducted a survey with a community of evaluators on the professional network LinkedIn. This sampling strategy is based on the self-perceived adherence to the evaluation community by the respondent. The results of the survey are discussed in the "Survey on Big Data in Evaluation" section.

To learn about the use of Big Data in the social sciences, we conducted a systematic literature review of all academic papers published in the SCOPUS database. Thereby, we covered both evaluation journals and other social scientific journals. We assumed that if Big Data is used in evaluation, either by the community of evaluators or by other social researchers for the purpose of evaluation, the more interesting results of those studies would end up in scientific publications. Also, this approach allows us to learn from social scientists outside evaluation. The findings from this analysis are presented in the "Systematic Review on Big Data in Evaluation" section.

As was shown in the previous chapter, there is a wide range of definitions of Big Data. Therefore, in both steps of our analysis, we allowed evaluators and social scientists to judge themselves whether they used Big Data and tried to understand their understandings of Big Data.

Both steps of our analysis indicated a highly limited use of Big Data in evaluation and evaluation-like activities. In the "Conclusions" section, we discuss the possible implications of this situation for the community of evaluators.

Survey on Big Data in Evaluation

To be able to discuss the use of Big Data in evaluation, we need to have a sense of the latter concept itself. Evaluation is, however, sometimes described as "a semantic magnet" with no commonly accepted definition (Vedung, 1997). It is associated with a long range of different methodologies and approaches depending on the discipline, sector, culture, and country in which it is applied. We, therefore, choose to rely on an inclusive definition of evaluation as an "assessment of worth and merit" (Mark et al., 2006), while public interventions are interpreted broadly as public projects, programs, policies, or even regulations (Howlett, 2011; Tucker, 2005).

To analyze the use of Big Data in the evaluation community, it is necessary to reach out to a representative group of evaluators. Using an inclusive definition of evaluation means that evaluators may be found in many different sectors and disciplines. However, we assume that individuals make sense of themselves in relation to the concept of evaluation and in relation to one or more significant other(s) in a population of individuals that we can call "the evaluation community"

(Weick, 1995). This is to say that we rely on the self-identification of a group of professionals who define themselves as evaluators, making it possible to search for evaluators in professional networks (Furubo et al., 2002). We assume that they will accept our broad definition of evaluation.

Using LinkedIn to Reach Evaluator Communities

Evaluators partake in evaluation communities all across the world, and these communities are very different with regard to sector, organization, methodology, culture, language, evaluation principles, and so forth. So how can we sample from this plethora of communities?

We decided to conduct an e-survey disseminated via an online survey link to the LinkedIn groups listed in Table 3.1. The survey was conducted in May and June 2014. LinkedIn is a professional online

Table 3.1. Groups related to evaluation on LinkedIn

LinkedIn Group Name	Number of Users
Technical assistance consultancy network; EU, Worldbank, calls, grants, and international development	36,907
EC/EuropeAid Framework Contracts Projects	16,608
American Evaluation Association	14,813
European Evaluation Society	3,138
Evaluation jobs	3,020
Evaluators group	2,515
Monitoring and Evaluation Job/Consultancy	2,116
RealWorld Evaluation	1,168
Eastern Evaluation Research Society	1,137
Danish Evaluation Society	860
Independent Evaluation Group	802
Canadian Evaluation Society—Ontario chapter	776
Job evaluation	627
United Kingdom Evaluation Society	492
African Evaluation Association	407
Pakistan Evaluation Society	233
Total	85,619

network, similar to Facebook. However, LinkedIn facilitates interaction of a professional nature between individuals based on the users' profiles that are created like a curriculum vitae listing previous experiences, language capabilities etc. LinkedIn was founded in 2002, and by 2013, it had more than 259 million users all over the world. Through user-generated content, LinkedIn is more than a platform for recruitment. LinkedIn is free, and users can meet in professional groups that are started and maintained by the users themselves. Groups are used to share important content on a topic such as evaluation. In the groups, the users interact by asking questions to each other or sharing articles, job openings, tenders, or posting questions to like-minded.

On LinkedIn, there are multiple groups related explicitly to evaluation. Table 3.1 contains the groups found to identify and relate explicitly with evaluation.[1]

On LinkedIn, both established evaluation associations and groups, or organizations, of evaluators that only have an online presence are represented. This makes LinkedIn a valuable tool to sample evaluators. As can be seen from Table 3.1, LinkedIn makes it possible to sample more than 85,000 evaluators (with some doppelgangers) when sampling from the groups explicitly related to evaluation.

There are several further advantages of using LinkedIn. LinkedIn is global, allowing anyone identifying as an evaluator to sign up to evaluation groups. Second, membership of several LinkedIn groups is free. This inclusive nature of LinkedIn makes it easy to reach out to a broad range of evaluators. Third, disseminating survey links on LinkedIn groups is a cost-efficient way to collect data. Survey links can be shared among members and, thus, make it possible for like-minded to answer to the survey as well. As default LinkedIn sends group updates to the e-mail of the user. Group posts like the survey link used for data collection in this chapter are forwarded to the e-mail of the users. Fourth, LinkedIn seems to catch a broad range of people identifying themselves as evaluators. Although there may be a general conception that social networks are mainly used by young people due to their earlier adoption of technology, this is not the case with LinkedIn, probably because it is a professional network. As compared with users of other social networks, LinkedIn users are on average the oldest ones (forty-four years).[2] Neither is gender a manifest sample bias, though there is a small majority of female users on LinkedIn.[3] It should however be noted that LinkedIn is an English-based platform. Though local language editions exist and the users can choose their own language for their profiles, the platform started in North America and is predominantly used by North Americans. This is a bias that cannot be controlled for, and we, therefore, encourage other studies of countries and contexts where evaluations are not performed in English.

The Questionnaire

The questionnaire contained twenty variables that were both quantitative and qualitative variables (string, numerical, and categorical), including demographic characteristics of the respondents. An overview of the survey questions is provided in the appendix. The results of the survey are presented in the following sections.

Are Big Data Used in Evaluation?

Our survey indicates that Big Data is not yet reasonably described as a new trend in evaluation. A first striking finding pointing in this direction is the response rate; only 324 responses, corresponding to a response rate of less than one percent. Is this an indication that evaluators have very little experience of Big Data? Our survey also showed that half of the respondents did not know what Big Data was and they were, therefore, filtered out and guided to the exit page of the survey. Furthermore, approximately one out of ten (thirty-seven respondents) reported to have worked professionally with Big Data. However, we need to understand what the respondents understand by "Big Data." We, therefore, asked respondents to provide five words that they associate with Big Data (Q2) and to give an example of the Big Data that they have worked with (Q7), in order to gauge to what extent the respondent had actually worked with Big Data.

To determine if respondents understand the concept of Big Data, we had to use a yardstick to measure against. In this book, we leaned toward Douglas Laney's definition of Big Data as data of large volume, high velocity, and great variety (three Vs) (Laney, 2001). It is not a very precise definition (Chapter 2 by Lefebvre-Naré et al. in this book), but it highlights three important traits that all needs to be satisfied when talking about Big Data. First, Big Data is large. But what does that mean? Conventionally, large data are bigger than what can be handled on conventional personal computers and by conventional software packages such as Microsoft Excel (Beyer and Laney, 2012). Some sources define Big Data according to its *volume* excluding data below one terabyte (1,000 GB) (Zikopoulos et al., 2014). *Velocity* refers to how fast new data are added or existing data changed in the database. Thus, the data are increasingly collected typically through sensors, such as ATMs and electronic locks. Finally, *variety* refers to different types of data. Variety in data file types usually also require special database types such as clustering and batch processing systems like Apache Hadoop, SAP Hana, and several others.

To allow some discretion, we relaxed Laney's definition a bit to be volume as well as *either* variety *or* velocity. We did this as we quickly realized that none of the examples in the data completely met the three Vs definition proposed by Laney. Also, if volume together with another V is satisfied, then most people would consider that as Big Data. With regard to volume, the size should be close to one terabyte.

Drawing on the answers to Q2 and Q7 provided by thirty-seven respondents, we found a strong indication that fifteen respondents conceptually understood Big Data more or less in-line with the common definition (the three Vs) and technical requirements of Big Data in relation to database infrastructure. Though the three Vs were rarely referred to directly, several synonyms were used to describe the same phenomenon. One respondent that did not work with Big Data stated: "People are using the term, but rarely does the data satisfy the three 'V'-definition of Big Data." In Table 3.2, some examples from the data are provided to show the difference in words when the fifteen respondents describe Big Data compared to the rest of the thirty-seven respondents.

It should be clear from Table 3.2 that there is a difference between the two groups represented in the columns. First of all, volume is a relative thing but nevertheless the easiest to understand. Velocity is not met when large data in a database are analyzed if that data are not continuously updated. Similarly, surveys are rarely continuous events of data collection, but usually, they take place over the course of a fixed time period. After this period, the data are collected and analyzed without changing in size. Variety is probably the hardest to conceptualize and also the hardest to meet. Even large volumes of financial data that are continuously updated in relational databases might not meet this requirement because the data type could be the same throughout.

Some cases are borderline cases, and sometimes the examples provided by the respondents could be Big Data cases depending on the actual data set. However, some cases are also clearly not Big Data cases. Borderline cases include social media data, because querying tweets one time does not make Big Data. But if a large number of tweets on Twitter are analyzed over a long time, then that would constitute a

Table 3.2. Examples of words and examples used to describe experience with Big Data

	Big Data (Fifteen Respondents)	Not (Necessarily) Big Data (Twenty-Two Respondents)
Descriptive words (Q2)	Coding, data mining, multi-format, batch processing, four Vs, IT infrastructure, cloud, scalable database, Gartner, Internet of everything, Hadoop, distributed, R, unstructured database, algorithm, and many sources of data	Complicated data, administrative databases, in-depth analysis, triangulation, statistician, large data sets, survey, governmental databases, big sample sizes, and social media
Examples of use (Q7)	– Financial information – Real time population movement through mobile tracking – Electronic medical records	– School test scores – School enrollment data – Census data – Administrative data sets – Twitter data – Survey data of thirteen mio. US higher education students

Big Data analysis in combination with other types of data. Analyzing school test results for an entire country could also be Big Data if they are frequent, and the analysis is taking place over time and continuously.

Several respondents clearly stated the uncertainty about what Big Data is: "I guess I'm partially unsure of what Big Data IS. I've launched surveys to over 38k members. Is that Big Data?" Another respondent is also unsure about what Big Data is and its use:

> I'm honestly not sure if I have or not. I have used millions of records of state government administrative data to assess a program's utilization, however, I was able to do this using SAS and not some "data analytics tool" per se. For the most part, I don't know of 'Big Data' that are useful in general program evaluation work in the public sector (which is what I do).

In conclusion, we find that 0.5 percent of the sample (fifteen respondents) have used Big Data in their work. Even though sampling was not completely random, a ninety-nine percent confidence interval below one percent of the respondents (0.016; 0.076) signifies that the probability of observing more than 0.8 percent evaluators working with Big Data in the population is very slim.[4] Taking the sampling bias into account and the relaxed criteria for the definition of Big Data as well (see above), the true value in the population of evaluators is next to zero.

Why Is Big Data (Not) Used in Evaluations?

The findings presented so far raise the question why evaluators are slow to embrace Big Data. To answer this question, we asked the survey respondents to state why they work with Big Data as well as why not.[5] We also asked the respondents who worked with Big Data about the challenges and advantages with Big Data.

One hundred nine respondents answered why they did not work with Big Data. The results are somewhat surprising considering that respondents could check multiple answers. It is surprising that only one out of four considers the right competences to be a problem since Big Data requires highly specialized knowledge to work with. However, many supplementary comments (Q9) indicate clearly that respondents not working with Big Data are aware of the special skill set needed for Big Data analysis. One respondent stated that "manipulation of Big Data requires high levels of competence in statistical methods and software - this is often not readily available, above all in local communities." Another respondent replied that "I am a for profit sole proprietor evaluation and research consultant who works on a laptop and a desktop computer. I have neither access to nor computer capabilities to analyze 'Big Data' even if I wanted to do so."

The special skill set required to be able to analyze Big Data is the basis of a whole new title, namely, the "data scientist." The data scientist is a combination of a (backend) developer, a statistician and a user interface/visualization expert. Evaluators typically do not have all of these skills, and therefore, they depend on other people to analyze the data, which is a challenge both in terms of organization of work and culture. Big Data requires expensive and time consuming data mining and analysis that evaluation budgets normally would not cover. Moreover, clients are also not equipped with these skills in their organizations, and Big Data might therefore be something they have without knowing how to utilize.

In itself, it is also surprising that Big Data was not considered relevant to one-third of the respondents. Summing up on respondents' comments in relation to relevance, Big Data (if available) is often on indicator level, thus providing a very rich estimate on only one out of many indicators to be used to answer one (out of many) evaluation questions. The lacking skill set taken into consideration, Big Data is therefore not cost effective and not adding a lot of value to the typical evaluation that answers to questions on a much higher level. Take the example of an organizational evaluation, Big Data might be available in the form of electronic key card entries per employee combined with employee information. In itself, this information is very interesting, but does it link up with an evaluation criterion (such as efficiency) or an evaluation question? Most likely it does but only to a very limited extent and most likely only to a few indicators such as average work time per employee that could identify bottlenecks in the organization. Thus, some respondents argued that integrating Big Data in the work of evaluators is a considerable challenge—it take a lot of time to prepare and analyze but might eventually only elucidate one tiny element of the entire scope of an evaluation.

Approximately forty percent state that they do not work with Big Data since there is no Big Data of relevance: "I work in education. There are some Big Databases available but not Big Data as such. I have worked with databases of thousands of school pupils but not the entire school population."

Also the quality of the data is considered a problem in cases where data collection has stopped or where data points are redefined over time:

> *I work in international development, where data is often relatively poor quality or very patchy in relation to problems that often require quite contextualised and nuanced solutions. There are no shortage of blogs, etc. on Big Data, but I have seen little practical use of it to date in international development.*

Lack of resources seems to be another barrier hampering the use of Big Data. As one of the respondents put it: "Our stakeholders are not able to collect it due to resource constraints, and our organizational leadership has not felt it necessary to invest in the means to collect it." Another theme was data protection and privacy that are barriers for merging public databases and make data Big: "Big data is sensitive information and often data protection laws and policies hinder the access to and use of the data, in particular cross referencing different sources of Big Data." The issue of privacy, data protection, and risk of abuse of Big Data are themes in many of the respondents' answers. This is clearly a concern for most respondents to the survey.

Further hypotheses regarding why evaluators are slow to use Big Data emerged from the coding of the respondents' answers, including privacy, costs, time, and dependence on third parties in relation to managing the data. Issues of privacy of data subjects limit evaluators' access to data for several reasons. First, evaluators in some countries need approval from review boards to get access to personal information. Second, it can be compulsory for the evaluator to clean the data for personal identifiers, which takes a lot of time. Also, there is a strong ethical dimension to working with personal data that many of the respondents were aware of. Finally, working with Big Data often entails working with the holder or proprietary of the data. The evaluator depends on cooperation including explanations of the data (e.g. code books, time series, and file formats) and technical interfacing either through APIs or with direct access to the database. Usually, evaluators are not trained in IT on this level and will require close cooperation with data scientists on their own team as well as specialists with the organization that hosts the data and possibly with the client as well.

When asked about the advantages of Big Data, the respondents highlighted the speed of data analysis and collection. The data are already collected when the evaluator gets it. Also Big Data is very precise, reliable, and valid, as it can contain the data of an entire population instead of just a sample. Big Data is also real time, which allows excellent monitoring.

Summary

The findings of our survey indicate that the use of Big Data among evaluators is most limited. This is indicated already by the fact that the response rate was as low as one percent. Few of the respondents had themselves worked with Big Data. Out of 324 respondents, thirty-seven respondents reported to have worked with Big Data. Analyzing these examples in detail, it was clear that only fifteen respondents had in fact worked with Big Data.

Furthermore, among the respondents, the knowledge about Big Data seems to be limited. Conceptually, only very few respondents related Big Data with the three Vs definition proposed by Laney (2001). Mostly, respondents associated the term Big Data with large volumes of data but not with complexity and variety, and particularly not with velocity and real-time updating of data.

Some findings do shed light on difficulties associated with using Big Data in evaluation. For one, several respondents report a lack of available data. Respondents also do not find Big Data relevant, but this finding may mirror the small extent of knowledge on Big Data. Furthermore, respondents reported that clients do not demand evaluation solutions with Big Data. Somewhat surprisingly, skills were only considered a barrier to the use of Big Data by about twenty-five percent of the respondents. This finding is probably related to the misconception of Big Data and what it takes to analyze Big Data.

Others highlight that the use of Big Data is still in an explorative phase, and that role models are still lacking: "It's too early to adopt the use of Big Data. What's needed is demonstrations of how Big Data can be used for evaluation and this is currently lacking. The ideas and potential are there but as yet no compelling examples or case studies of use."

This respondent may find that present book provides some inspiring demonstrations of the use of Big Data in evaluation. Evaluators exploring the potential of Big Data could also look to other social science disciplines where Big Data has been of importance for evaluative work. The remaining part of this chapter, therefore, investigates the use of Big Data not only in evaluation but also in the social sciences more generally.

Systematic Review on Big Data in Evaluation

Good evaluative work with a use of Big Data is likely to sooner or later be published in academic journals or conference proceedings. Given that evaluation is frequently referred to as a meta- or trans-discipline, such work may be published in different kinds of social scientific journals. It could be found not only in an evaluation journal but also in any public policy journal or even in emerging Big Data journals. If evaluators have been slow to utilize Big Data, it may therefore be a good idea to look to other disciplines for inspiration.

As the second step of our study, we, therefore, conducted a systematic literature review of all academic journals accessible through SCOPUS database. This strategy allowed us to trace the work of social researchers and practitioners who do not identify themselves as a part of the evaluation community but nevertheless conduct evaluative work with a use of Big Data.

Using the SCOPUS Database to Map Research Articles on Big Data and Evaluation

The source of data for the systematic literature review was the SCOPUS database run by Elsevier (https://www.elsevier.com/solutions/

scopus). It is the largest abstract and citation database of peer-reviewed literature (including scientific journals, books, and conference proceedings). Compared to other databases focused on natural sciences (e.g. Web of Science), SCOPUS has substantial share of social sciences (actual proportions in SCOPUS are as follows: health sciences thirty-two percent, life sciences fifteen percent, social sciences twenty-four percent, and physical sciences twenty-nine percent). Since our scope of interest was realm of public policy, the choice of SCOPUS seemed valid.

SCOPUS covers over 21,000 peer-reviewed journals, which include all leading journals in the field of evaluation such as *Advances in Program Evaluation, American Journal of Evaluation, Educational Research and Evaluation, Evaluation, Evaluation Review,* and *Evaluation and Program Planning.* Database also covers a number of public policy journals possibly relevant to evaluation practice or Big Data use in public management (e.g. *Evidence and Policy, Public Policy Research, Public Administration Review,* and *Journal of Policy Analysis and Management*).

Our search query started with broad search of coexistence of just two terms in SCOPUS database: "Big Data" and "evaluation" to see the scale of the phenomenon and its trend over the past few years. Then, we have carefully constructed a detailed search query that would match the goal of our research. The search formula is presented in Table 3.3.

Based on the formula, we narrowed down our search to articles, conference proceedings, and work in press. We focused on those types of publications because, contrary to books, they are published much faster and they quickly pick up novel research topics. We were looking for articles that have "Big Data" and "public" terms in title, key words, or abstract. This guaranteed that "Big Data" was a key aspect of the particular work and that application of Big Data would be somehow related to public policy. An additional filtering term was "evaluat*," which covers all possible grammatical variations of evaluation inquiry. We approached it as broadly as possible, by looking for any reference to evaluation in the full text of the articles. So even if the author would not make evaluation a core aspect of its article, if he/she described any

Table 3.3. SCOPUS search formula

TITLE-ABS-KEY ("Big Data") AND TITLE-ABS-KEY (public) AND ALL (evaluat*) AND (LIMIT-TO (DOCTYPE, "ar") OR LIMIT-TO (DOCTYPE, "cp") OR LIMIT-TO (DOCTYPE, "ip"))

evaluative activity with Big Data in its article—it would be picked up by our search.

In the second step, we analyzed the content of all the articles found in order to assess their relevance for the topic. In coding, we used simple three-level scale to assess the relevance of the articles.

Findings—Overall Picture

The initial quick scan of coexistence of two terms "Big Data" and "evaluation" resulted in over 1,000 records. Starting from 2011, there is a booming trend in articles about Big Data, with the number of articles growing by the factor of 72 in just three years (Figure 3.1).

It has to be noted that the vast majority of these publications has little relevance to evaluation despite using the "e" word in text. It is often used in the context of either evaluating the particular Big Data method or assessing sets of data. More detailed search query formula (see Table 3.3) narrowed down the population from 1,117 to 160 articles. It is worth noting that this limited population is dominated by conference proceedings and working papers, and none of these articles comes from an evaluation journal.

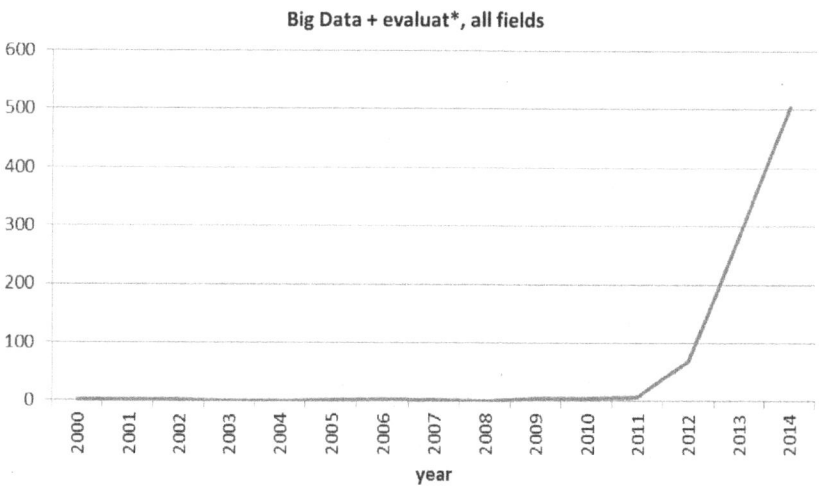

Figure 3.1. Trends in Publication of Articles about Big Data and Evaluation.
Notes: Data were collected on May 15, 2015. Articles published in 2015 were excluded from this figure.
Source: SCOPUS.

Further in-depth content analysis of the 160 articles showed that only thirty-five of them described some aspects of using Big Data in running public interventions. Within this group, only one article was an example of an evaluative inquiry, while the remaining thirty-four focused rather on the use of Big Data in planning, managing, or running public interventions.

These results raise two questions. What inspirations for evaluators may be found in the broader cluster of articles that seem to link Big Data with evaluation inquiries outside of the public policy sphere? And what can we learn from a small but more specific population of thirty-five articles that have been identified as relevant to the usage of Big Data for running and evaluating public interventions?

Articles on Big Data and Evaluation Without Reference to Public Interventions

Let us start with articles that have no description of the use of Big Data in public intervention, despite the fact that they reported (at least in verbal terms) some kind of evaluative exercise. Within that population, we identified four groups of contributions. We discuss them more in detail because some of them can be inspirational in thinking about evaluation research, even though their Big Data and evaluative components have no reference to public programs.

Articles from the **first group discuss technical issues** such as advances in certain methods or approaches (e.g. the article by Dewan and Jena [2015] on the emergence of new services that combines social, mobility, analytics, and cloud computing), results of evaluation of particular types of analysis (e.g. the article by Jia and Cristianini [2015] on tool for classifying gender from millions of images), and sources of data (e.g. the article by Tanasijevic et al. [2015] on critical assessment of evaluation mechanisms behind social media and biases that it can generate, an issue that relates closely to evaluation practice of online feedback platforms used in the evaluation of programs). Within this group, there are articles that could provide interesting methodological inspirations for crafting an evaluation study. For example, ideas for geotagging tweets, that is, assigning hundred millions of tweets to a particular geographical location (Compton et al., 2015), strategies of dealing with a variety of data (a key characteristic of Big Data) and mashing different sources of Big Data for the purpose of one analysis (Hendrik and Tjoa, 2014), and ways of conducting research with the use of apps and getting real-life data from people in their "natural habitat" (Poppinga et al., 2012). A critical evaluation of accuracy of traditional surveys showing how Big Data can correct misreporting of those surveys might be of particular interest to evaluators (Ansolabehere and Hersh, 2012). Finally, an appealing way forward is shown by exploring practical utility of the "folksonomy," that is collaborative tagging by particular community of users—practice that proliferated as a consequence of the growth of Web 2.0 communities. As authors explain, the behavior of users is highly influenced by the behavior of their neighbors or community members, and this can be utilized in constructing user profiles and understanding their needs (Xie et al., 2014).

The second big group of articles focused on sentiment analysis, a text analysis and computational linguistic of unstructured materials. It aims at revealing attitude of a speaker or a writer with respect to particular topic or situation. One of the most interesting examples was the analysis of impact of Fukushima disaster on how scientific knowledge has been used in media to tackle this crisis and construct different narratives (Lansdall-Welfare et al., 2015). In general, twitter feeds have been one of the dominant sources for sentiment analysis (e.g. Garg and Chatterjee, 2014). One of the most interesting examples of policy use of tweets was Big Data analysis of how police and other agencies used twitter to evaluate situation during the riot crisis (Procter et al., 2013). Most quoted, even in popular media, was the research done by Wojcik et al. (2015). Using three different Big Data sources (including tweets), they assessed relation between political declarations (liberals vs. conservatives) and displaying actual well-being. The authors found out that earlier research findings based on traditional self-reporting were wrong in suggesting that political conservatives are happier than political liberals. The former results turned out to be fully mediated by conservatives' self-enhancing style of self-reporting.

The third group of articles presents application of Big Data to the evaluation of health issues. There have been a number of inspiring articles on evaluating the impact on health through apps (from user perspectives, not particular government programs, e.g. Griffin and Jiao, 2015). Very inspiring idea was to use mining of the web posts to establish severe drug–drug interaction (Jiang et al., 2014). Also worth mentioning in that group is a visionary article on the perspectives for progress in epidemiology research and practice with a use of Big Data (Khoury et al., 2013).

In the final group, we put articles discussing challenges of Big Data. The key issue is privacy. Some authors show that the technologies coming with Big Data allow constructing very detailed user profiles from fragmented disclosures and default rules spread across the web (Porat and Strahilevitz, 2014). Big Data brings also dangerous potential in merging data sets that used to be discrete. For example, French (2014) argues that discourse on the data-driven, information revolution must be supplemented by a more modest discourse empirically rooted in the everyday, pragmatic realities of IT.

Articles on Using Big Data for Running and Evaluating Public Policies

Finally, let us look at the small population of articles that discussed the use of Big Data to design, implementation, and evaluation of public interventions. Within the group of thirty-five articles, there is a very clear dominance of three sectors: transport (ten cases), environment and planning (nine cases), and health (ten articles). There were also some examples from crisis and security management (two cases). The following sections will provide us with a closer look at the content of the three main fields.

Transport

Empirical studies in that field focus heavily on reacting to the changing needs of the users, by evaluating—on an ongoing basis—transport services and then immediately adapting them to new situations or changing behaviors. Concepts discussed here include integrated real-time mobility, event-driven architecture (e.g. Motta et al., 2013; Cai, 2014; Tao et al., 2014). Some of the articles go beyond exploring utility and focus on the efficiency criteria for evaluation of policy with Big Data (Fayazi et al. [2015] evaluated and improved fuel efficiency of public transport, using Big Data system that adapts the movement of buses across city to signal phases at intersections). Other articles explore real patterns of transportation behaviors to evaluate the effectiveness of public policies that were based on evidence from traditional econometric models (e.g. Li and Kauffman, 2012; Cai and Xu, 2013).

Environment and Spatial Planning

Somewhat overlapping with transport is a group of articles on environment and spatial planning. Environmental and spatial policies designed and evaluated with Big Data include metropolitan area service provision (Zheng et al., 2014), management of energy (Shahrokni et al., 2014; Bellini et al., 2014), and other natural resources

(Fang et al., 2014). Cao and Tang (2014) combined the assessment of needs with the evaluation of current policies by their users drawing on data derived from online discussion forums. It allowed them to quickly detect rising needs and big community issues.

Health

The key issue in this group is focused on prediction and prospective adaptation of actions, based on the evaluation of effectiveness of current interventions. A number of articles discuss public health surveillance system that identifies disease outbreaks using individual and population health indicators (see Lopez et al., 2015; Rexit et al., 2015). Some authors create health indexes based on emerging individual Big Data to assess and monitor whole communities (Velikic et al., 2012). That is a kind of a bottom-up approach, allowing to obtain a big picture out of myriads of individual pieces of information. Other health articles go in the opposite direction. Based on Big Data and evaluation of current services, they try to break it down to develop profiles that match individual users (Martin and Felix-Bortolotti, 2014). Finally, within the health group, there are articles that propose to use Big Data for the monitoring and evaluation of post-market drug regulatory process (scanning drug actual performance once it enters the market and have been used by population) (Bian et al., 2012; Abbott, 2013).

Summary

With the literature review, we found that there are virtually no examples of employing Big Data for purely evaluative exercise, understood as assessment of worth and merit of the particular public intervention, be it service, project, or program. However, one particular issue emerges across all articles and sectors. Working with Big Data seems to blur the lines between different stages of the policy cycle, which emphasize learning about interventions, such as diagnosis, monitoring, and evaluation. Big Data allows for prediction on an unprecedented scale, putting an emphasis on ex ante evaluation to satisfy the informational needs of policy stakeholders and target populations, making the traditional distinction between the stages of the policy cycle that seem artificial. What remains important is to search for solutions in real life, while continuously learning and adapting the particular intervention. And indeed, Big Data provides an opportunity to make this learning more agile, providing a source of an immediate feedback. Such data might be used in real time to identify policy issues, analyze their structure, design intervention, and observe and evaluate its impact.

Conclusions

This chapter has discussed the use of Big Data in the evaluations of public interventions and, more broadly, in the social sciences. Findings both from a survey to the community of evaluators and from a systematic review of publications by social scientists clearly indicate that Big Data is hardly used in the evaluation of public interventions. The findings from the survey indicate that Big Data, understood as large volume, variety, and velocity (Laney, 2001), is almost not applied by evaluators. Evaluators work with longitudinal survey research or queries in databases that are very large in scope but rarely large enough so that the term Big Data can rightfully be applied. Evaluators thereby seem slow to realize the opportunities associated with exploring the real-time data accumulated in ever greater volumes and which could be combined with other kinds of databases. Even more troubling, there is virtually no discussion about this emerging trend and its implications for the craft of public policy evaluation. The concept of Big Data seems not even to be known to the majority of evaluators. To put it simple, the issue of Big Data seems to be non-existing for evaluators. This situation, however, does not seem to be unique to evaluation. Also other communities, such as policy analysts, seem late in recognizing Big Data and only recently start the discussion about its game-changing implications (Pirog, 2014).

The findings of our survey suggest that there are a number of factors responsible for the virtual non-use of Big Data in evaluation, factors that must be considered broadly by the evaluation community. One of the main barriers is the lack of resources and/or skills needed to effectively apply Big Data. Evaluators, coming mostly from the social science background, lack the highly specialized "data scientist" type of skills. But our results suggest that there is an even more significant barrier, that is, the availability of relevant data. The notion that available Big Data is not suited to serve evaluation studies may however also mirror a lacking awareness of the possible uses of Big Data, particularly given the technical obstacle described above. Later chapters in this book point to the importance of managers of evaluation units both in forming teams including data scientists and in securing access to relevant data (Chapter 9 by Bohni Nielsen et al.). At the same time, however, other chapters show that Big Data may be valuable also for evaluation that cannot draw on the expertise of data scientists (Chapter 6 by Leeuw and Chapter 5 by Willemsen and Leeuw).

Another reported obstacle is a relatively small demand from clients, creating no incentive to devote resources either to develop these skills or to co-opt a "data scientist" to a research team. The role of commissioners to enhance the use of Big Data in evaluation is further explored later in this book (Chapter 10 by Forss and Norén). Chapter 10 reinforces our impression that commissioners are the key players to stimulate the innovative use of Big Data in evaluation.

Perhaps because Big Data applications in policy-related analyses are still a new phenomenon as indicated in our literature review, the topic is frequently described in technical language and dominated by fragmented, case-specific descriptions. Thus, accessing the knowledge that has been already generated in this field is challenging and time-consuming. This may add to evaluators' notions of limited relevance, resulting in a lack of recognition and/or understanding of the potential of Big Data. The literature review that we have conducted aims to overcome this barrier by giving an overview of a small, but growing, body of research using Big Data for evaluation. Presenting the scope and most interesting examples of Big Data applications for policy-oriented studies might be of particular help in addressing the awareness issue and, ultimately, in paving the way for increased uptake of Big Data in evaluation inquiries.

This rather troubling situation provides us with three implications for our community of evaluators. First, to start with an optimistic tone, there is an opportunity. Evaluators do not recognize Big Data, but it seems that the emerging Big Data community knows and understands little from the craft of public policy evaluation. Therefore, our community could benefit from combining the evaluation body of knowledge with this new, emerging trend of Big Data and perhaps extend the landscape of public policy. For example, our contribution could include issues on theory of change, social mechanisms, causality, side effects, and impact. However, one word of caution is needed here. Our sampling of literature covered established journals. There are some interesting works on Big Data application in public policies in emerging journals (not catalogued yet by SCOPUS) such as *Big Data* and *Big Data and Society*. It is highly possible that out there, Big Data analysts have been already conducting practical evaluation exercises without referring to our field, so our window of opportunity for innovation is limited.

Second, we have definitely much to learn both on the technical level (e.g. Big Data sources and their integration, analytical procedures, and algorithm development) and also on the conceptual level (e.g. logic of theory building from pattern recognition and dealing with hidden biases of apparently immense data). All of these aspects are beyond our comfort zone and most likely would require teaming up with people from the Big Data world.

The third point refers to a challenge of public policy making. As evaluators, we may need to rethink our role in public policy and move from non-involved assessors of worth and merit to co-designers and testers of policy. Big Data clearly follows the path similar of another recent development in the field of public policy—behavioral insight (see Haynes et al., 2012; Shafir, 2013; World Bank, 2015). They blur lines between design, monitoring, and evaluation. These types of researchers and analysts assist policy decision makers in theory building, often by searching for mechanisms through pattern recognition in data or in the psychological literature, testing policy prototypes with data (Big Data) or with pilot experiments (behavioral insight), and then adapting those prototypes and scaling them up to the full size interventions. In short, they design, test, evaluate, and adapt as they go! In our opinion, it is a game changer because it is highly pragmatic, user-oriented, and yet firmly grounded in data and research. It offers policy makers practical, research-based support during the ongoing policy process. Contrary to evaluation results that are postponed in time (especially ex post assessment), it offers just-in-time knowledge.

It is time for evaluators to start embracing the opportunities of Big Data, and we hope that this and the following chapters will provide some inspirations in that undertaking.

Appendix

This appendix consists of survey items used in the e-survey research and the explanation of relations between research questions and survey items (questions) (Tables A.1 and A.2).

Table A.1. e-Survey questions

Q#	Questions	Variable Type
Q1	Initially, we would like to know, if you have heard about Big Data?	Dichotomous
Q2	Write five words/concepts that you associate with Big Data.	Text

The Current Use of Big Data in Evaluation

Q3	Have you worked professionally with Big Data?	Dichotomous
Q4	In the last year, how often have you participated in the four activities described below and how many of those times did you make use of Big Data?	Ratio
Q5	In this period, have you used Big Data for other purposes than the ones specified above? If so, what purposes?	Text
Q6	In what types of evaluation studies have you used Big Data?	Nominal
Q7	Please describe the Big Data that you have worked with.	Text
Q8	Why have you not used Big Data in your professional work?	Nominal
Q9	Please elaborate your answer on why you did not use Big Data in your professional work.	Text
Q10	Please describe the challenges related to working with Big Data.	Text
Q11	Please describe the advantages related to working with Big Data.	Text
Q12	If you know of any relevant academic references or reports that you think we should cite, please write the reference or link here.	Text
Q13	In what type of organization do you work?	Nominal
Q14	What is your citizenship? (if dual citizenship, choose your most used citizenship).	Nominal
Q15	What is your gender?	Dichotomous
Q16	What is your age?	Ratio
Q17	What is your primary occupation?	Nominal
Q18	In what sector(s) do you work with evaluation?	Nominal
Q19	What is the highest level of education or schooling you have completed?	Ordinal
Q20	In case you have comments or suggestions with regard to this survey or this study on evaluation and Big Data, please provide them in the field below.	Text

Table A.2. Organization of questionnaire

Research Question	Survey Question
Are Big Data used in evaluations?/*If Big Data are used?* (+ *what is Big Data to you?*) To what extent are Big Data used in evaluations?	Q1–Q3 + Q7
How are Big Data used in evaluations?	Q4–Q7
Why are Big Data used in evaluations?	Q8–Q11
Other questions	
"Snowball questions"	Q12 + Q20
Demographic variables	Q13–Q19

Notes

1. The groups were found using the search terms "evaluation" in the LinkedIn search bar. Searches were made in German and French as well but did not result in any groups found.
2. Source: Google at http://royal.pingdom.com/2012/08/21/report-social-network-demographics-in-2012/. Accessed August 29, 2016.
3. Ibid.
4. 0 = not working with Big Data. 1 = working with Big Data. Confidence interval: (0.016; 0.076). Mean value = 0.046.
5. These questions (Q8 and Q9) were asked to respondents who stated previously (Q3) that they did not work with Big Data.

References

Abbott, R. 2013. "Big Data and Pharmacovigilance: Using Health Information Exchanges to Revolutionize Drug Safety." *Iowa Law Review* 99 (1): 225–92.

Ansolabehere, S., and E. Hersh. 2012. "Validation: What Big Data Reveal about Survey Misreporting and the Real Electorate." *Political Analysis* 20 (4): 437–59.

Bellini, P., M. Benigni, R. Billero, P. Nesi, and N. Rauch. 2014. "Km4City Ontology Building vs Data Harvesting and Cleaning for Smart-City Services." *Journal of Visual Languages and Computing* 25 (6): 827–39.

Beyer, M. A., and D. Laney. 2012. *The Importance of Big Data: A Definition*. Stamford, CT: Gartner.

Bian, J., U. Topaloglu, and F. Yu. 2012. "Towards Large-Scale Twitter Mining for Drug-Related Adverse Events." *Proceedings of International Conference on Information and Knowledge Management*, 25–32. Maui, HI, USA – October 29 – November 2, 2012.

Cai, D. 2014. "Demand Responsive Bus Transit with Real Time Planning and Visualization." *WIT Transactions on Ecology and the Environment* 179 (2): 959–65.

Cai, H., and M. Xu. 2013. "Greenhouse Gas Implications of Fleet Electrification Based on Big Data-Informed Individual Travel Patterns." *Environmental Science and Technology* 47 (16): 9035–43.

Cao, L., and X. Tang. 2014. "Topics and Trends of the On-line Public Concerns Based on Tianya Forum." *Journal of Systems Science and Systems Engineering* 23 (2): 212–30.

Compton, R., D. Jurgens, and D. Allen. 2015. "Geotagging One Hundred Million Twitter Accounts with Total Variation Minimization." *Proceedings – 2014 IEEE International Conference on Big Data*, IEEE Big Data 2014, 393–401.

Cousins, J. B., S. C. Goh, S. Clark, and L. E. Lee. 2004. "Integrating Evaluative Inquiry into the Organisational Culture: A Review and Synthesis of the Knowledge Base." *The Canadian Journal of Program Evaluation* 19 (2): 99–141.

Dewan, B., and S. R. Jena. 2015. "The State-of-the-art of Social, Mobility, Analytics and Cloud Computing an Empirical Analysis." *2014 International Conference on High Performance Computing and Applications*, ICHPCA 2014.

Fang, S., L. D. Xu, Y. Zhu, J. Ahati, H. Pei, J. Yan, and Z. Liu. 2014. "An integrated system for regional environmental monitoring and management based on internet of things." *IEEE Transactions on Industrial Informatics* 10 (2): 1596–605.

Fayazi, S. A., A. Vahidi, G. Mahler, and A. Winckler. 2015. "Traffic Signal Phase and Timing Estimation from Low-Frequency Transit Bus Data." *IEEE Transactions on Intelligent Transportation Systems* 16 (1): 19–28.

French, M. 2014. "Gaps in the Gaze: Informatic Practice and the Work of Public Health Surveillance." *Surveillance and Society* 12 (2): 226–43.

Furubo, J.-E., R. C. Rist, and R. Sandahl. 2002. *International Atlas of Evaluation*. London: Transaction Publishers.

Garg, Y., and N. Chatterjee. 2014. "Sentiment Analysis of Twitter Feeds." *Lecture Notes in Computer Science (including subseries Lecture Notes in Artificial Intelligence and Lecture Notes in Bioinformatics)* 8883: 33–52.

Griffin, G. P., and J. Jiao. 2015. "Where does Bicycling for Health Happen? Analysing Volunteered Geographic Information through Place and Plexus." *Journal of Transport and Health* 2 (2): 238–47.

Haynes, L., O. Service, and B. Goldacre. 2012. *Test, Learn, Adapt: Developing Public Policy with Randomised Controlled Trials*. London: UK Cabinet Office. Behavioural Insight Team. www.behaviouralinsights.co.uk

Hendrik, Anjomshoaa A., and A. M. Tjoa. 2014. "Towards Semantic Mashup Tools for Big Data Analysis." *Lecture Notes in Computer Science (including subseries Lecture Notes in Artificial Intelligence and Lecture Notes in Bioinformatics)* 8407 LNCS: 129–38.

Howlett, M. 2011. *Designing Public Policies. Principles and Instruments*. London, New York: Routledge.

Jia, S., and N. Cristianini. 2015. "Learning to Classify Gender from Four Million Images." *Pattern Recognition Letters* 58, 35–41.

Jiang, G., H. Liu, H. R. Solbrig, and C. G. Chute. 2014. "Mining Severe Drug-Drug Interaction Adverse Events Using Semantic Web Technologies: A Case Study." *Lecture Notes in Computer Science (including subseries Lecture Notes in Artificial Intelligence and Lecture Notes in Bioinformatics)* 8643: 628–38.

Khoury, M. J., T. K. Lam, J. P. A. Ioannidis, P. Hartge, M. R. Spitz, J. E. Buring, S. J. Chanock et al. 2013. "Transforming Epidemiology for 21st Century Medicine and Public Health." *Cancer Epidemiology Biomarkers and Prevention* 22 (4): 508–16.

Laney, D. 2001. *3D Data Management: Controlling Data Volume, Velocity, and Variety*. Technical Report, Stamford: META Group.

Lansdall-Welfare, T., S., Sudhahar, G. A., Veltri, and N. Cristianini. 2015. "On the Coverage of Science in the Media: A Big Data Study on the Impact of the Fukushima Disaster." *Proceedings – 2014 IEEE International Conference on Big Data, IEEE Big Data 2014*, 60–66.

Li, T., and R. J. Kauffman. 2012. "Adaptive Learning in Service Operations." *Decision Support Systems* 53 (2): 306–19.

Lopez, D., M. Gunasekaran, B. S. Murugan, H. Kaur, and K. M. Abbas. 2015. "Spatial Big Data Analytics of Influenza Epidemic in Vellore, India." *Proceedings – 2014 IEEE International Conference on Big Data, IEEE Big Data 2014*, 19–24.

Mark, M., J. Greene, and I. Shaw. 2006. "The Evaluation of Policies, Programs, and Practices." In *The SAGE Handbook of Evaluation*, edited by I. Shaw, J. Greene, and M. Mark, 1–30. Thousand Oaks, CA: Sage.

Martin, C. M., and M. Felix-Bortolotti. 2014. "Person-Centred Health Care: A Critical Assessment of Current and Emerging Research Approaches." *Journal of Evaluation in Clinical Practice* 20 (6): 1056–64.

Motta, G., D. Sacco, A. Belloni, and L. You. 2013. "A System for Green Personal Integrated Mobility: A Research in Progress." *Proceedings of 2013 IEEE International Conference on Service Operations and Logistics, and Informatics, SOLI 2013*, 1–6.

Pirog, M. 2014. "Data Will Drive Innovation in Public Policy and Management Research in the Next Decade." *Journal of Policy Analysis and Management* 33 (2): 537–43.

Poppinga, B., H. Cramer, M. Bohmer, A. Morrison, F. Bentley, N. Henze, M. Rost, and F. Michahelles. 2012. "Research in the Large 3.0 – App Stores, Wide Distribution, and Big Data in MobileHCI Research. MobileHCI'12." *Companion Proceedings of the 14th International Conference on Human Computer Interaction with Mobile Devices and Services*, 241–43.

Porat, A., and L. Jacob Strahilevitz. 2014. "Personalizing Default Rules and Disclosure with Big Data." *Michigan Law Review* 112 (8): 1417–78.

Procter, R., J. Crump, S. Karstedt, A. Voss, and M. Cantijoch. 2013. "Reading the Riots: What Were the Police Doing on Twitter?" *Policing and Society* 23 (4): 413–36.

Rexit, R., F. Tsui, J. Espino, P. K. Chrysanthis, S. Wesaratchakit, and Y. Ye. 2015. "An Analytics Appliance for Identifying (Near) Optimal Over-the-Counter Medicine Products as Health Indicators for Influenza Surveillance." *Information Systems* 48, 151–63.

Shafir, E., ed. 2013. *The Behavioral Foundations of Public Policy*. Princeton: Princeton University Press.

Shahrokni, H., F. Levihn, and N. Brandt. 2014. "Big Meter Data Analysis of the Energy Efficiency Potential in Stockholm's Building Stock." *Energy and Buildings* 78, 153–64.

Tanasijevic, S., K. Bohm, and K.-M. Ehrhart. 2015. "Behavioral Strategies in Online Forums with Different Feedback Types." *Proceedings – 4th IEEE International Conference on Big Data and Cloud Computing, BDCloud 2014 with the 7th IEEE International Conference on Social Computing and Networking, SocialCom*

2014 and the 4th International Conference on Sustainable Computing and Communications, SustainCom 2014, 555–63.
Tao, S., J. Corcoran, I. Mateo-Babiano, and D. Rohde. 2014. "Exploring Bus Rapid Transit Passenger Travel Behaviour Using Big Data." *Applied Geography* 53, 90–104.
Tucker, J. 2005. "Intervention." In *Encyclopedia of Evaluation*, edited by S. Mathison, 210. Thousand Oaks, CA; London: Sage.
Vedung, E. 1997. *Public Policy and Program Evaluation*. New Brunswick, NJ: Transaction Publishers.
Velikic, G., E. Sukic, T. Jevtovic-Stoimenov, M. F. Bocko, L. Stoimenov, and A. Pentland. 2012. "Ongoing Diagnostics Mapped: From an Individual to the Community Health Index." *HealthMED* 6 (9): 3152–57.
Weick, K. E. 1995. *Sensemaking in Organizations*. Thousand Oaks, CA: Sage.
Wojcik, S. P., A. Hovasapian, J. Graham, M. Motyl, and P. H. Ditto. 2015. "Conservatives Report, but Liberals Display, Greater Happiness." *Science* 347 (6227): 1243–46.
World Bank. 2015. *Mind, Society, and Behavior*. Washington, DC: World Bank Group.
Xie, H., Q. Li, X. Mao, X. Li, Y. Cai, and Y. Rao. 2014. "Community-Aware User Profile Enrichment in Folksonomy." *Neural Networks* 58, 111–21.
Zheng, Y., L. Capra, O. Wolfson, and H. Yang. 2014. "Urban Computing: Concepts, Methodologies, and Applications." *ACM Transactions on Intelligent Systems and Technology* 5 (3): 1–55.
Zikopoulos, P., D. deRoos, C. Bienko, R. Buglio, and M. Andrews. 2014. *Big Data beyond the Hype – A Guide to Conversations for Today's Data Center*. New York: MaGraw Hill Education.

4

Getting Started with Big Data: The Promises and Challenges of Evaluating Health-Care Quality

Maria Barrados and Jonathan I. Mitchell

Introduction

A preoccupation for many governments is meeting the demand of their citizens for quality health care that is efficiently and effectively delivered within available budgets. One of the approaches traditionally relied on in Canada and many other countries to support quality care is health-care accreditation. This quality assurance process is designed to examine the adherence to pre-existing standards of quality health care and often includes a specific commitment to continuous quality improvement (Hort et al., 2013).

The specific evaluative question being addressed by a number of international researchers (Barrados, 2013) is the effectiveness of accreditation in promoting the outcomes of quality of care. Most of the research has been conducted in acute care institutions (hospitals). The work to date has demonstrated the complexity of the question and the demanding data requirements.

These demanding data requirements can potentially be eased through using Big Data. In Canada, we have the advantage of large automated data systems, many of which would be considered Big Data. This chapter describes an approach that is being developed to get started using these Big Data, frequently designed for other purposes.

The challenge for the evaluator is how to make use of these new data sources in ways that differ from their past practices. Evaluators have extensive experience in the collection of data from primary sources, both quantitative analysis and qualitative analysis, as well as meta-analysis. They are often reluctant to turn to secondary data sources preferring to generate their own data for their specific evaluation. In this way, they seek to control the validity and reliability risks associated with using data collected for other purposes.

The Evaluation Tradition

Alkin and Christie in their work on evaluation theory describe the main branch of evaluation as research guided by research methods. Much of the preoccupation of this branch of evaluation has been with the application of experimental design and quasi-experimental design in the tradition of Campbell and Stanley (1966). The explicit approach is designed followed by collecting valid and reliable evidence and complimenting qualitative methods with quantitative methods. Rossi and Freeman (1985) described theory evaluation as "involving a detailed program theory that is used to guide the evaluation" (Alkin and Christie, 2004: 26); in other words, the evaluation is driven by theory.

The experimental design is the dominant paradigm, but others in the research tradition have argued for the use of quasi-experimental design and using a priori knowledge and theory to build evaluation models (Chen and Rossi, 1983: 300). Whichever approach is taken, there is a consistent concern with internal and external validity (extent that the result can be generalized) and data reliability. To deal with the issues of data reliability and validity, evaluators are more comfortable in designing and collecting their own data rather than relying on secondary data sources.

In this respect, Big Data is no different than other secondary data sources. In this tradition, evaluators would develop a design and determine whether there are existing data available or whether new data need to be collected. However, the size, volume, and variety of Big Data provide data as has not been seen before. These features also require greater computing and analysis capacity.

The Shifting Paradigm

Big Data in and of itself provide an opportunity. The management literature has coupled discussion about Big Data with Big Data analytics. The power and usefulness of the data depend on the ability to take massive amounts of electronic information produced every minute and harness that information to inform decisions.

> *If a business can harness the data itself - capture it, distill it, identify the patterns it unveils - than the organization can use the findings hidden within to make smarter, more informed decisions. ... When companies can make more evidence-based decision making, they can better position themselves to drive foundational shifts in a profitable direction. (Lutes, 2014: 13–5)*

The authors go on to caution that the use of Big Data analytics requires a knowledge of what is used and how it is analyzed, need to be driven by the question that is being asked and can accordingly be targeted. Furthermore, they argue that Big Data analytics is only useful if they drive value for the organization.

McKinsey & Company has provided a number of examples of what they term "advanced analytics." In their analysis of the insurance industry, they make the following observation:

> *The proliferation of third-party data sources is reducing insurers' dependence on internal data. Digital "data exhaust" from social media and multimedia, smartphones, computers, and other consumer and industrial devices—used within privacy guidelines and assuring anonymity—has become a rich source for behavioral insights for insurance companies, as it has for virtually all businesses. (Clarke and Libarikian, 2014)*

McKinsey also cautions to make sure to focus on business value. A new type of specialist is required in advanced business analytics bringing together the diversity of information in an ever changing technological context in real time. They distinguish between a "black box" data-modeling process (pure statistical analyses of large amounts of data) and "smart box" filled with the knowledge of experienced practitioners. The "smart box" is the way to get the tools that staff will trust and use. "Smart box" analysis is consistent with the evaluation approach of using models to develop the empirical questions to be addressed.

The possible computing barriers also appear to be breaking down with increasing power of computers and the availability of IBMs' supercomputers online. IBM has invested heavily in business analytics that has culminated in providing broader access to its technology. They have, for example, established a partnership with the Mayo Clinic to analyze some 8,000 active clinical trials and 170,000 worldwide in cancer therapy (Pilieci, *Ottawa Citizen*, 2014).

The distinction from business applications between Big Data and Big Data analytics is important for evaluators. Data in and off itself gain its greatest value for evaluators when it is thought of in terms of analytics—the measures and indicators that are drawn from Big Data that help answer evaluation questions.

Evaluators tend to favor collecting the data that they need to answer their evaluation questions rather than rely on already collected data or secondary data. As Morra Imas and Rist (2009: 310) point out, using secondary data is less expensive and faster than collecting original data. However, secondary data have the disadvantages of potentially not being exactly what is needed, may be difficult to obtain and may be hard to verify validity, reliability, and other coding or algorithm problems. What we find today, however, is that we have so much more data being collected and coming available through open sources. It is no longer a debate of the appropriateness of using census data (Coleman, 1969) but how to take advantage of all the data now available.

There is a needed paradigm shift because the amount of Big Data and associated analytics behooves evaluators to consider it as important as primary data sources. Big Data needs to be queried with the evaluation question with all the methodological cautions of the discipline's tradition. By looking into existing data and analytics, evaluators can potentially save significant time and resources to produce more timely evaluations.

The traditional logic model provides the framework that sets out the inputs, activities, outputs, and outcomes—immediate, intermediate, and ultimate. It is necessary to think not only of the intended but also of the unintended outputs and particularly outcomes. The framework for determining what has to be measured and evaluated is a part of the evaluation tradition.

As the literature attests, the task of identifying valid and reliable measures for the outputs but particularly the outcomes is an ongoing challenge. The availability of much more data should make it easier to find appropriate measures and also has the advantage of identifying other unanticipated effects. Innovative approaches to searching through the data to identify reasonable and appropriate measures will need to be developed.

However, the sheer volume will mean not only looking at Big Data but also looking at Big Data analytics and drawing on different expertise to do it. The increasingly large, complex, and often messy Big Data will require the expertise of data scientists and computer specialists to develop the algorithms to draw meaningful measures out of these complex data sets. For many evaluators, the Big Data derivative, Big Data analytics, offers the most promise. The Big Data analytics would have had the work done by data scientists and subject area specialists. The evaluators either develop Big Data analytics, which can be difficult, time consuming, and potentially costly, or draw on Big Data analytics developed by other experts. The latter approach presents clear advantages as is illustrated in the following sections.

The opportunity to use "real time" data also raises the very attractive possibility of having results that are more current and more relevant to present circumstances. This answers an often heard criticism that evaluations take too long and are dealing with the circumstances of eighteen to twenty-four months before.

The Challenge of Evaluating the Effectiveness of Hospital Accreditation

Health care can be delivered by the public or private sector or in combination, but the preoccupation with quality care and patient safety (not doing harm) remains the same.

The approach to support the quality improvement of care in many countries has been accreditation.

Accreditation is used not only in health care but also in many other industries; it essentially follows a process of determining (Braithwaite et al., 2011)

1. Whether organizations satisfy pre-existing standards.
2. Are regularly examined and continuously improve.
3. [Assess] extent to which customer satisfaction is met or enhanced.

The standards set out the definition of safe, quality care, and how it should be managed.

The results of standardizing surgical procedures in the United States in the early 1900s were sufficiently persuasive to result in the creation of accreditation bodies of the full continuum of health care in Canada, the United States, and Australia. However, the body of evidence demonstrating its effectiveness is being developed.

Accreditation of health care is based on the premise that adherence to evidence-based standards will result in an improved quality, safety, and efficiency in the delivery of health care (Nicklin, 2015). There is a great deal of variation internationally how accreditation programs operate (Scrivens, 2002).

Braithwaite et al. (2005) in their discussion article for the Australian Council for Safety and Quality conclude that: "there is little empirical evidence on whether accreditation is a cost-effective strategy for raising the performance standard." (21)

Nor is there much empirical evidence on long-term improvement. The evidence is surprisingly limited on overall effectiveness. The most extensive work has been done in Australia where their accreditation programs go back to the 1970s. There are now questions being raised about the increasing cost and complexity of compliance with standards, the resultant increase in costs, and the lack of public accountability (Hort et al., 2013).

The literature shows a number of different approaches that have been taken.

Literature Reviews

Accreditation Canada, encouraged by its Board, also did a review of the available evidence on the effectiveness of accreditation in 2008 (Nicklin, 2015). It was found that "few studies have attempted to draw causal inferences about the direct influence of accreditation on patients' health outcomes."

Specific Case Studies

Lanteigne (2008) examined two organizations that had gone through one accreditation cycle (about three years) using the Canadian methodology and concluded that there had been improvement in their systems and practices and that they had resulted in strategic and operational change.

Meta-analysis

Greenfield and Braithwaite (2008: 172–83) undertook an extensive review of over 3,000 abstracts, sixty-six studies that empirically examined accreditation. The results were classified into ten categories. They concluded that it is a complex picture. There were consistent findings that accreditation supported promoting change and professional development, but for the remaining categories, there were either inconsistent or insufficient findings.

The meta-analysis of past studies attempts to generalize across different methodologies with highly varied research contexts. There are important variations by country, health-care setting, and accreditation programs. As well, there is no consistent use of empirical analysis and empirical design. The meta-analysis and individual case findings do

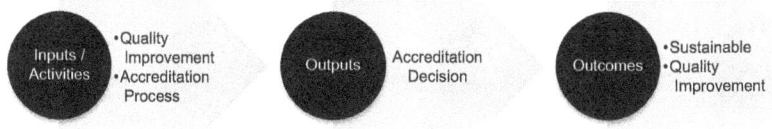

Figure 4.1. Evaluation Model. Inputs: quality improvement and accreditation; activities: associated with the full accreditation cycle; output: accreditation certification; and outcomes: quality improvement, long-term sustainability, and long-term improvement.

show that there is value in results from the accreditation process but did not find empirical results on long-term effects.

Large Scale Empirical Studies

Internationally researchers, particularly in Australia (Braithwaite et al., 2005) and Europe (Shaw et al., 2014), are undertaking studies requiring the development of new research tools and data collection to assess the effectiveness of health-care accreditation. Most have involved extensive collection of new data for a sample of health organizations. The implicit evaluation model being tested is shown in Figure 4.1.

Ovretveit and Staines (2007) argue that there is an expected linear correlation between quality improvement work and patient results. Furthermore, their research suggests that there is a threshold before the results are seen. Hence, an initial period where there is no correlation is followed by a linear correlation.

Shaw et al. (2014) in the DUQuE study of 210 European hospitals concluded that third-party review, whether by ISO or accreditation, improved performance. However, since accreditation has been specifically designed for health care, it was not surprisingly found to have a greater positive effect on clinical practice. Shaw et al. (2014) used a model of accreditation impact on change management, as shown in Figure 4.2.

The analysis in 2014 was carried out in 291 services in seventy-three acute care hospitals. These services managed acute myocardial infarction, hip fracture, stroke, and obstetric deliveries. The analysis tested for health outcomes in the clinical practice areas instead of the whole hospital.

The results showed the benefits of accreditation more in acute myocardial infarction and stroke than in deliveries and hip factures. The study authors concluded that "accreditation and certification are

Figure 4.2. A Model of Accreditation Impact on Change Management. Input: absence or presence of accreditation; activities: change management activities; and outcome/impact: (1) organization and culture, (2) professional practice and clinical procedure, and (3) improved health outcomes.
Source: Shaw et al. (2014).

positively associated with clinical leadership, systems for patient safety and clinical review, but not clinical practice." (Shaw et al., 2014: 100)

Braithwaite and colleagues are undertaking a large study to determine whether accreditation makes a difference to quality and performance. They have a design of twelve separate studies each with its own design and data collection to address its specific questions. Results are being published as components as they are being completed. As shown in Figure 4.1, they are exploring both the factors that result in effective processes leading to accreditation and the resultant impact.

What Does Big Data Offer?

It has proven difficult to empirically demonstrate the effectiveness of accreditation of acute care institutions (hospitals). The literature has few examples of using Big Data and Big Data analytics to tackle the question. An interesting example is found in Figure 4.3 on research in Taiwan examining quality improvement pre- and post-accreditation (methodology in Figure 4.1). Data used included indicators of the Taiwan Quality Indicators Project.

In Canada, there is a widespread interest in answering the question of cost effectiveness of health-care accreditation. There are also large data sets that have been built for many different purposes often for acute care. Following from the literature, an approach to getting started to answer the effectiveness question with data is explored.

Canada has a single insurer system that provides universal healthcare insurance and coverage to all Canadians for doctors and hospital-based care. Each of the ten provinces and three territories operates an insurance system that provides for portability across the country. Some health-care delivery systems are under the jurisdiction of the federal government: Aboriginal Health Services, Corrections and

Taiwan has a national health insurance system, semi-voluntary requirement for hospital accreditation and a national accreditation body, The Taiwan Joint Commission on Hospital Accreditation.

A pre- and post-accreditation study of seventy-seven hospitals to assess the influence of accreditation on sixteen quality indicators was carried out from 2007 to 2011. Data were drawn for the accreditation process (including surveys) and the Taiwan Quality Indicators Project.

No significant difference was found in many quality indicators. However, significant differences were found in the unscheduled readmission rate within fifteen days for the same diagnosis (Lee et al., 2014), from 1.63% (twelve months before) to
- 1.35% (−17.5%, index month);
- 1.23% (−24.7%, three months after);
- 1.18% (−27.9%, six months after).

Figure 4.3. The Influence of Hospital Accreditation on Quality and Hospital Management in Taiwan.

Canadian Forces. Each Canadian and Canadian resident has a unique health-care insurance number. These systems have primarily been used for financial purposes.

McKinsey (Biesdorf and Niedermann, 2014) in their analysis of health-care's digital future described the adoption of IT in health care as not unlike other industries. First, IT was used for accounting and payroll, followed later by more integrated systems including electronic health records with extensive infrastructure. Now, there is a greater digitization in health care. Canada has followed a similar path but at different rates through the various health systems.

Accreditation Canada is a not-for-profit independent organization that provides national and international health services organizations with quality-focused, comprehensive accreditation services. Accreditation Canada has been accredited by the International Society for Quality in Health Care and has supported organizations in improving health-care quality since 1958.

All 600 Canadian hospitals with very few exceptions are accredited by Accreditation Canada. Information on the Accreditation Canada's Qmentum accreditation program, the health-care organizations accredited by Accreditation Canada, as well as national reports of findings from the Accreditation Canada program is available at www.accreditation.ca.

Accreditation Canada has extensive data holdings on the results of their accreditation work including data on performance against approximately seventy national standard sets, results of self-assessment surveys, and accreditation decisions over time.

Statistics Canada, the Canadian Statistical Agency, has been building data sets related to health care and the health of Canadians from administrative data, and hospital medical records made up of many individual transactions and specialized data collection often in the form of surveys. Increasingly, data collection is automated as electronic health records and electronic medical records are being introduced and widely used. Much of the responsibility for the collection and analysis of health data has been turned over to the Canadian Institute for Health Information (CIHI). CIHI is an agency that has the single focus on health information and serves both federal and provincial interests.

Over the years, CIHI has gained experience in using large data sets from Canadian hospitals that include the coding of individual patient records. Initially, the coding of patient records was slow and often incomplete. Now, however, both the quality and the timeliness of the data have improved in the acute care sector. A focus on data quality and re-abstraction studies has resulted in data of higher quality that is needed to derive reliable indicators. Timeliness of the data reporting has also improved. For example, emergency department findings from patient-level data for the fiscal year ending 31 Mar 2014 were released in October 2014 (CIHI, 2014). Data from Canadian hospitals are available, see www.yourhealthsystem.ca. There are other bodies that capture data on health care and its use such as jurisdictional Health Quality Councils and other health-care providers. There are also numerous sites on social media that provide ratings on hospitals and care providers.

There have been cautions in the literature about relying on administrative data because of the lack of standardization in both the collection and coding of information. Efforts to use administrative data to compare hospital performance have been examined in Europe. From a sample of randomly selected hospitals in seven European countries, Groene et al. (2014) concluded that hospital administrative data did not seem to be an appropriate source of information for the comparison of hospital performance in the European Union.

Canada has the advantage of having one national accreditation body that holds the accreditation data in the acute care sector as well as the long standing work of its national statistical agencies responsible for health statistics. There are extensive data holdings on the accreditation process and results, and there are result measures available from CIHI. These data sources suggest that data collected could populate some of the models already described in the literature. Certainly, given the large amounts of data being collected in Canada and its increasing availability before new data collection is considered, existing Big Data and analytics need to be explored.

How to Proceed?

Particularly with the availability of large data sets, the temptation might exist to take a "data mining approach." The volume and complexity of the different data sets make that not very realistic. Data mining of large data sets also raises the uncomfortable possibility of meaningless correlations as argued by Petersson et al. in Chapter 1.

A theoretical approach is advocated, which sets out the implicit or explicit models to be tested. Hence, a first step is a review of the literature and an assessment of evaluations to date to determine what is known about causal theories and evaluation approaches in the area. As is shown in the proceeding sections, an international literature exists on the effectiveness of health-care accreditation in acute care institutions, and different evaluations have been undertaken.

Data needs are defined by evaluation questions and theoretical considerations. Once a theoretical framework and models have been established, the available data sets and analytics need to be closely examined to determine whether the appropriate measures are available. As a first step, a thorough and careful inventory of available data needs to be made. Preliminary work was undertaken to inventory the data available at Accreditation Canada and CIHI. It was concluded that there were sufficient data to test some of the models from the literature in the Canadian setting.

The advantage of using data from Accreditation Canada and CIHI is that the data sets are known and the analytics are well documented. Data from other sources such as patient comments via social media will require more wide ranging searches and investigation of methodology. This would be especially true for Big Data analytics without clear, transparent methodologies.

The amount of work involved in working with Big Data that has been managed or analyzed by others can potentially be quite large, often requiring a level of data science expertise that evaluators may not have. Evaluators will need to assess their skills and the skills of their team to determine how it needs to be supplemented.

Big Data analytics, on the other hand, from established organizations, such as national statistical agencies and agencies dealing with the analysis and statistics of a particular area, would be much easier to assess, since these agencies provide detailed methodologies with their work. Again, the evaluator would need to assess their capacity to properly evaluate the methodologies provided.

Further considerations relate to the required expertise to manage and manipulate the data sets. For example, with the proposed data and application of a causal model, data from institutions will need to be matched or linked. It was determined that it was possible to match 96% of the hospitals, providing the feasibility of linking outcome data from these Canadian "Big Data" with the Accreditation Canada data collected through the accreditation process.

With the potential sources for data identified, the accessibility of the data and whether special arrangements or conditions have to be met need to be determined. With health-care data, the concern to protect the privacy of health information is always paramount. With the accreditation data while there are no individual patient records, however, individual responses to surveys need to be protected. Some institutions expect that confidentiality of their accreditation results is maintained, and Accreditation Canada maintains a proprietorial interest in the data. While there is a movement to have more data openly available, some potential data may have access restricted. Depending on the restriction, there may be special arrangements that can be made, such as de-identification of the data, or it may not be possible. Preliminary discussions about access have been held.

The approach being taken in the example of the effectiveness of hospital accreditation is to rely on the analytics as much as possible that have already been generated if they are viewed as valid and reliable. Ideally, some initial exploratory work can be done on the data to understand the statistical features, its validity in relation to the concepts, and its reliability. Significant analytic and statistical expertise to match the data sets would be required. The initial work can inform the type of resources required and its associated costs. For previously unanalyzed

Big Data, the resource requirements will be much more unknown but will likely require the skills of data science specialists.

While a theoretical approach is advocated, there may be more than one way to measure a concept. A degree of flexibility and an iterative manner needs to be maintained to identify reasonable indicators for the concepts to be evaluated. This will allow a determination of what data elements provide reasonable indicators of the concepts and how much substitutability is possible.

After an initial examination, we have concluded that the potential exists in the Canadian case. Data on accreditation and the practices of health-care organizations would stem from the data sets generated as a part of the accreditation process, namely the ratings of surveyors as they perform the independent third party accreditation on-site surveys. Data on outcomes would be derived from CIHI data. Data analysis would be done using randomized organizational identifiers, hence protecting individual records. Only meta-data would be published.

A number of logistical issues such as obtaining the resources and expertise to carry out the work still have to be worked out. Data science specialists will be needed to do the required data matching and manipulation. Once the working data set is established, the more traditional approach to statistical analysis familiar to evaluators could be used.

Conclusion

This chapter explored the use of Big Data to address a specific evaluative question. The data sets that were identified came from more traditional sources such as statistical agencies. This is not to suggest that there are no other useful sources drawn from the automation of our everyday life that evaluators could explore, as suggested in some of the other chapters.

The availability of Big Data and Big Data analytics offers the possibility of doing evaluations more efficiently and cost effectively by saving the time and resources to collect new data. It also offers the possibility by having much more data available that are generated in real time. By relying on analytics generated by others, such as a statistical body, data for evaluation will now be available much more quickly. By using larger amounts of data more efficiently, there will also be an increased opportunity to derive additional benchmarking data and to obtain greater insight into the predictive factors for achieving quality health care.

References

Alkin, Marvin C., and Christina A. Christie. 2004. "An Evaluation Theory Tree." In *Evaluation Roots: Tracing Theorists Views and Influences*, Ch. 2, edited by Marvin Alkin, 11–58. Thousand Oaks, CA: Sage.

Barrados, Maria. 2013. "Assuring Quality Care in Publicly Managed Organizations: The View from Canada." *Presented at the International Research Society for Public Management (IRSPM) Conference 2014*, Carleton University, Ottawa, April 9–12, 2014.

Biesdorf, Stefan, and Florian Niedermann. 2014. "Health Care's Digital Future." *McKinsey & Company Insight*. Accessed August 17, 2015. www.mckinsey.com/Insights/

Braithwaite, Jeffrey, Johanna Westbrook, Brian Johnston, Stephen Clark, Mark Brandon, Margaret Banks, Clifford Hughes, et al. 2011. "Strengthening Organizational Performance through Accreditation Research – A Framework for Twelve Interrelated Studies: The ACCREDIT Project Study Protocol." *BioMed Central Research Notes* 4: 390.

Braithwaite, John, Judith Healy, and Kathryn Dwan. 2005. "The Governance of Health Safety and Quality." A Discussion Paper. Commonwealth of Australia.

Campbell, Donald T., and Julian C. Stanley 1966. *Experimental and Quasi-Experimental Designs for Research*. Chicago: Rand McNally.

Canadian Institute for Health Information (CIHI). 2014. "Emergency Department Highlights in 2013–2014." Accessed August 17, 2015. https://secure.cihi.ca/free_products/NACRS_ED_QuickStats_Infosheet_2013-14_ENweb.pdf

Chen, Huey, and Peter H. Rossi. 1983. "Evaluating with Sense: The Theory-Driven Approach." *Evaluation Review* 7: 283–302.

Clarke, Richard, and Ari Libarikian. 2014. "Unleashing the Value of Advanced Analytics in Insurance." *McKinsey & Company Insight*. Accessed August 17, 2015. www.mckinsey.com/Insights/

Coleman, James S. 1969. "The Methods of Sociology." In *A Design for Sociology: Scope, Objectives and Methods*, Monograph No. 9, edited by Robert Bierstedt, 86–114. Philadelphia: American Academy of Political and Social Science.

Greenfield, David, and Jeffrey Braithwaite. 2008. "Accreditation Research: A Systematic Review." *International Journal for Quality in Health Care* 20 (3): 172–83.

Groene, O., S. Kristensen, O. A. Arah, C. A. Thompson, P. Bartels, R. Sunol, N. Klazinga, et al. (2014). "Feasibility of Using Administrative Data to Compare Hospital Performance in the EU." *International Journal for Quality in Health Care* 26 (Suppl 1): 108–115. doi:10.1093/intqhc/mzu015.

Hort, Krishna, Hanevi Djasri, and Adi Utarini. 2013. "Regulating the Quality of Health Care: Lessons from Hospital Accreditation in Australia and Indonesia." The Nossal Institute for Global Health Working Paper Series, 28. Accessed August 17, 2015. http://ni.unimelb.edu.au

Lanteigne, Giles. 2008. "Etudes de cas sur l'impact de l'integration du programme d'Agrément Canada sure le changement et l'apprentissage organisationnel: la Health Authority of Anguilla et la Ca'Foncella Ospetale di Treviso." Departement de l'administration de la Sante, Faculté de Médicine. Thèse présentée à la Faculté des études supérieures en vue de l'obtention du grade de Philosophiae doctor (Ph.D.) en Sante publique. August 2008.

Lee, Wui-Chiang, Shing Liao, Hung-Jung Lin, and Tsung-Hsien Su. 2014. "The Influence of Hospital Accreditation on Quality and Hospital Management in Taiwan." Presentation at ISQUA, Rio de Janeiro 2014, Session A4, 1280. Accessed August 17, 2015. www.isqua.org.

Lutes, Jim. 2014. "Big Data Bring Big Risks and Bigger Opportunities." *Director Journal.* March/April, 13–15.

Morra Imas, Linda G., and Ray C. Rist. 2009. *The Road to Results.* Washington: The World Bank.

Nicklin, Wendy. 2015. "The Value and Impact of Health Care Accreditation: A Literature Review. Updated April 2015." Accreditation Canada. Accessed August 17, 2015. www.accreditation.ca.

Ovretveit, John, and Anthony Staines. 2007. "Sustained Improvement? Findings from an Independent Case Study of the Jonkoping Quality Program." *Quality Management in Health Care* 16 (1): 68–83.

Pilieci, Vito. 2014. "IBM Opens Up Access to Its Supercomputer." *Ottawa Citizen,* September 14, A2.

Rossi, Peter H., and Howard E. Freeman. 1985. *Evaluation: A Systematic Approach.* Third edition. Beverly Hills, CA: Sage.

Scrivens, E. 2002. "Accreditation and Regulation of Quality in Health Services." In *Regulating Entrepreneurial Behaviour in European Health Care Systems,* edited by R. Saltman, R. Busse, and E. Mossalios. Philadelphia: Open University Press. Accessed August 17, 2015. www.euro.who.int.

Shaw, Charles D., Oliver Groene, Daan Botje, Rosa Sunol, Basia Kutryba, Niek Klazinga, Charles Bruneau, et al. 2014. "The Effect of Certification and Accreditation on Quality Management in 4 Clinical Services in 73 European Hospitals." *International Journal for Quality in Health Care* 26 (s1): 100–7.

5

Big Data, Real-World Events, and Evaluations

Frank Willemsen and Frans Leeuw

Introduction

Big Data consists of (call) logs, mobile-banking transactions, and online user-generated content, such as blog posts, social media, sensor apps, online searches, and satellite images, including all the data that one holds in e-mails, weblogs, intranets, extranets, etc. Usually Big Data is not collected by researchers but generated by machines, networks, and human interaction on systems like social media. They are "born digital." However, Big Data can also be "produced" by digitization of existing material like legal documents, video's, audio tapes, pictures, archives, company administrations, health reports, censuses, etc.

Bail (2014) described a bit of the background of this development. The central topic is that huge amounts of text-based information about behaviors, attitudes, rules, institutions, decisions, and emotions are now available that were unthinkable twenty years ago. "Between 1995 and 2008 the number of websites expanded by a factor of more than 66 million, recently surpassing 1 trillion" (Alpert and Hajaj, 2008). Although sociologists were concerned about digital divides in years past, these inequalities appear to be steadily decreasing (DiMaggio, 2001). According to a 2012 survey, roughly half of all Americans visit a social media site such as Facebook or Twitter each day, producing billions of lines of text in so doing. These trends are markedly higher among younger people, suggesting these trends may only continue to grow over time. Most of the text from social media sites is readily accessible via simple computer programs. Yet the outgrowth in text-based data on the Internet is not limited to social media sites. Screen-scraping technologies can be used to extract information from any number of Internet sites within time frames that are only limited by digital storage capacity. And the potential to collect such data is not only tied to the future, but also the past. Since 1996, the Internet Archive has been storing all text from nearly every website on the Internet. The outgrowth of text-based data is also not confined to the Internet. Thanks to new digital technologies from fields as diverse as library science and communications, an unprecedented amount of qualitative data is being archived. Google alone has already created digital copies of nearly every single book ever written in collaboration with more than 19 million libraries worldwide. Academic data warehouses such as LEXIS-NEXIS or ProQuest now contain digital copies of most of the world's journals, newspapers, and magazines. The Vanderbilt Television News Archive contains copies of most major newscasts produced since 1998. An unprecedented amount of text-based data that describe legislative debates, government reports, and other state discourse is also now available on websites such as the National Archives of the United States and Great Britain.

Data on other OECD countries are available and show for some countries (Western/Northern Europe) similar trends. For the developing world, the UN Global Pulse organization's White Paper "Big Data for Development: Challenges & Opportunities" describes the spectacular increase in use of mobile phones/smartphones that produce massive data sets.

> *The spread of mobile-phone technology to the hands of billions of individuals over the past decade might be the single most significant change that has affected developing countries since the decolonization movement and the Green Revolution. Worldwide, there were over five billion mobile phones in use in 2010, and of those, over 80% in developing countries.... Across the developing world, mobile phones are routinely used not only for personal communications, but also to transfer money, to search for work, to buy and sell goods, or transfer data such as grades, test results, stock levels and prices of various commodities, medical information, etc. (Global Pulse White Paper, 2012: 9)*

Big Data is characterized by three or five Vs: high volume, high velocity, high variety information, high veracity, and high volatility. It is "an evolving term that describes any voluminous amount of structured, semi-structured and unstructured data that has the potential to be mined for information. Although Big Data doesn't refer to any specific quantity, the term is often used when speaking about petabytes and exabytes of data." Big Data usually includes data sets with sizes beyond the ability of commonly used software tools to capture, curate, manage, and process the data within a tolerable elapsed time. A number of open source processing frameworks have become entrenched in the Big Data arena. They are designed to handle the large volumes inherent in Big Data that are not easily stored in traditional databases.

Although there is no doubt that the Internet (of things), smart apps, sensors, and wearables are creating a world in which Big Data is everywhere and highly relevant for evaluation, there are also a couple of challenges to address. Hartford (2014: 17) has formulated a few in his article "Big data: are we making a big mistake?"

> *Because found data sets are so messy, it can be hard to figure out what biases lurk inside them – and because they are so large, some analysts seem to have decided the sampling problem isn't worth worrying about. It is. .... An example is Twitter. It is in principle possible to record and analyze every message on Twitter and use it to draw conclusions about the public mood. (In practice, most researchers use a subset of that vast "fire hose" of data.) But while we can look at all the tweets, Twitter users are not representative of the population as a whole. (According to the Pew Research Internet Project, in 2013, US based Twitter users were disproportionately young, urban or suburban, and black". .... "N = All" is often a seductive illusion. (ibid: 18).*

A second challenge Big Data have to deal with is this. "Big data do not solve the problem that has obsessed statisticians and scientists for centuries: the problem of insight, of inferring what is going on, and figuring out how we might intervene to change a system for the better" (Hartfield, 2014: 19).

Finally, a third challenge is how to deal with theories about behavior in the Big Data world. Some are arguing that there is no need for theories, others argue the opposite, by saying that in order to move from correlations to causality, theories will always be needed.

In this chapter, we present several real-world examples showing the relevance of working with Big Data, while in the final section, we hold a plea for the importance of Big Data when doing evaluations of (real-world) policies and programs. In doing so, we have also tried to refer to some of the challenges outlined above.

Real-World Example One: Consumer Confidence and Social Media Data

In September 2014, Daas and Puts of Statistics Netherlands (CBS) published an article in the *Statistics Paper series* of the European Central Bank. They studied the relationship between changes in consumer confidence and Dutch public social media messages, and they revealed a strong association between consumer confidence and the sentiment in public Facebook and Twitter messages. At Statistics Netherland (CBS), changes in consumer confidence are traditionally measured on a monthly basis. Consumer confidence is based on the sentiments of households about the economic climate in general and about their own financial situation. Every month, Statistics Netherlands conducts the *consumer confidence survey* among 1,000 households. They are asked five questions (two general economic questions and three about the personal financial situation) and may answer positively, negatively, or neutrally. The indicators are calculated by subtracting the percentage of pessimists from the percentage of optimists.[1] Consumer confidence is the average net result for all five questions (Figure 5.1).

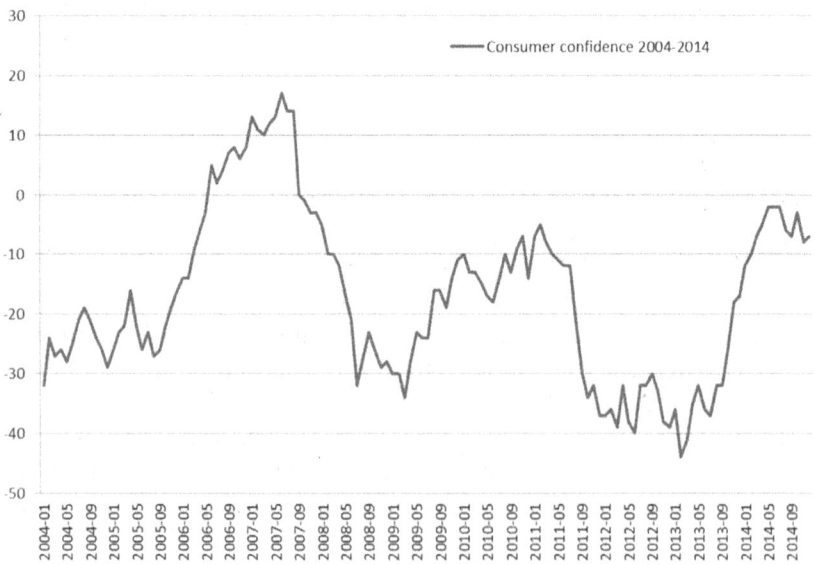

Figure 5.1. Consumer Confidence 2004–2014.

Daas and Puts (2014) set themselves to find out about the correlation between the findings shown in Figure 5.1 and the data from a second source, social media messages. They hypothesized that by analyzing these data, information could be obtained by describing consumer confidence but in a much faster and less expensive way. In the Netherlands, there are several companies collecting social media data on a daily basis; one of them is Coosto. This company supplies software tools that allow businesses to gain insight into the social web and to gain some control over social media. Based on the acquired analyses and insights, businesses can respond to relevant messages via their webcare suite. Coosto boasts a search engine in which billions of documents are stored. The archive goes back to 2009, and web spiders are continuously crawling over more than 400,000 online sources.[2] Important sources are the most popular social media platforms in the Netherlands, such as Twitter, Facebook, LinkedIn, and Google+. Around 2.5 million new Dutch messages are added every day to the Coosto databases.

One of the key features in the Coosto analytic toolkit is the automatically determined sentiment of the messages in their database. This is done by checking whether a message expresses a positive or negative opinion. On an individual level, such a classification will contain errors, but since the researchers were mainly interested in measurement on a aggregated level (days, weeks, or months), these errors will (probably) cancel each other out because of the enormous number of messages produces every day (Daas, 2014: 6). Daas and Puts used the Coosto interface to find out how many messages were posted in several time periods on various social media platforms and for how many messages a positive or negative sentiment was assigned. The average sentiment was calculated by subtracting the percentages of messages classified as negative from those classified as positive. Average sentiment was then compared with consumer confidence obtained from the Statistics Netherlands household surveys.

What Are the Results?

Figure 5.2 shows the development of daily, weekly (dot), and monthly (square) aggregates of social media sentiment from June 2010 until November 2013. In the inset, the development of consumer confidence is shown for the same period.

This study reveals that there is a very strong association between changes in the sentiment of Dutch social media messages and consumer confidence (up to $r = 0.9$). This is predominantly affected by

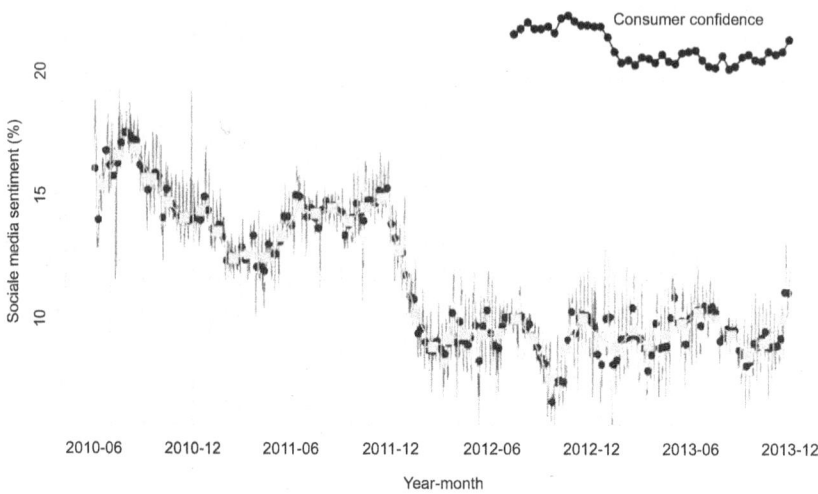

Figure 5.2. Social Media Sentiment and Consumer Confidence.
Source: Daas and Puts (2014: 9).

changes in the sentiment of all Dutch public Facebook messages. The inclusion of various selections of (public) Twitter messages improved this association. Not only sources correlate highly, but time series also cointegrate,[3] meaning that both are affected by an identical underlying phenomenon. It may be that changes in consumer confidence precede changes in social media sentiment. The researchers estimate that the social media sentiment lag is most likely in the order of seven days.

The very strong correlation between the data collected through a traditional survey carried out by Statistics Netherlands with all its checks and controls, and the Social Media data may point toward similar applications in other policy fields. One of the options currently under exploration deals with comparing findings on victimization and perceptions of crime measured through annual victim surveys in the Netherlands and social media data on these topics, collected on a daily basis.

Two Other Real-World Examples: Global Influenza and Bankruptcy in the Netherlands

In the first example, researchers used data from several social media platforms to model a phenomenon that is measured by monthly household surveys. In this example, we wanted to show how data from official registers correlate with (variations in) web search volume.

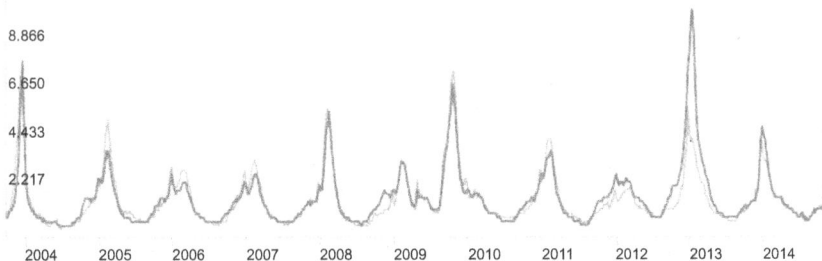

Figure 5.3. US Flu Activity. Influenza estimate: ◆, US data; ◆, Google Flu Trends estimate.[10]

Google Search Queries: The Google Flu Trend

"As people increasingly turn to the Internet for news and information, it is interesting to study online activity at any moment in time as a snapshot of the collective consciousness, reflecting the interests, concerns and intensions of the population" in a country (or language group) (Goel et al., 2010: 17486). In the Netherlands, almost every household has the opportunity to go online; the Dutch Internet penetration was ninety-five percent in 2013 (CBS, 2013). Google's search engine has a market share of around ninety-three percent in the Netherlands. This could make variations in Google's search query volumes a useful data source. Since almost every Dutch citizen contributes (the Internet population has become increasingly less biased in the last years), the external validity is strong; results can be generalized better to the world at large.

A well-known example of this way of working is the Google Flu Trends (GFTs), a tool that provides real-time estimates of flu incidence in several countries. Early detection of flew activity can reduce the impact of both seasonal and pandemic influenza. One way to improve early detection is to monitor online Google health-seeking behavior. Because the relative frequency of certain queries is highly correlated with the percentage of physician visits of patients with influenza-(like) symptoms, Google Flu can estimate the current level of influenza activity, with a reporting lag of about one day (Ginsberg et al., 2009). Traditional surveillance systems that rely on both virologic and clinical data publish findings with a one- to two-week reporting lag.

Figure 5.3 shows that estimates based on Google search queries are very closely matched to traditional flu activity indicators. Not only flu activity is modeled, web search query data were found to be capable of tracking dengue activity in Bolivia, Brazil, India, Indonesia, and Singapore. While traditional dengue data from official sources are often not available until after some substantial delay, web search query data are available in near real time (Chan et al., 2011).

Some GFT Problems

The initial 2009 Google article stated that the GFTs predictions were ninety-seven percent accurate compared with data from the US Centers for Disease Control and Prevention (CDC). In February 2013, *Nature* reported that GFTs predicted more than double the proportion of doctor visits for influenza-like illnesses than the CDC (Butler, 2013) (see Figure 5.3). It appeared that there were several problems, one of them being the instability in predictions due to *algorithm dynamics* affecting Google's search algorithm. Search patterns are based on thousands of decisions made by engineers and programmers and by millions of online choices of consumer. Another problem could be the media-stoked (of media-driven) panic in 2012–2013's flu season. A third problem is that people go for flu-related Google searches but don't know right from wrong regarding the diagnoses of (symptoms of) the flu (Butler, 2013). Searches for "flu" or "symptoms of flu" therefore may cause reporting of disease symptoms *similar to the flu, while in reality they are not caused by the flu.*

In our opinion, an important and more fundamental cause underlying these problems is that analyzing Big Data is often done without referring to one or more theories capable to understand and explain (search) behavior. The Google team used as much as fifty million search terms and let the algorithms do the work (Harford, 2014); it seemed not to be bothered to develop hypothesis on search terms that might be correlated with the spread of the disease and terms that are in some ways comparable but are definitely *not* correlated with the disease.

Improving the accuracy of the prediction can not only be done by using theories about (search) behavior. What also happened is that "by combining Google Flu Trends and lagged CDC data, as well as dynamically recalibrating GFT, the performance of GFT or the CDC alone [could] substantially [be] improved" (Lazer et al., 2014). In other words, combining traditional and "new" data, and using theoretical insights may result in better, more robust models and predictions (Mohebbi et al., 2011). In-line with this approach, we set ourselves to the challenge to develop another Google trend, based on Big Data, by doing exactly as suggested.

Google Correlate and Bankruptcy

We started with Google's online, automated method for query selection that does not require prior (i.e. theoretical) knowledge. This tool is Google Correlate and is free of charge available.[4] The tool determines which queries best mimic the data; these search queries can then serve to build an estimate of the true value of the phenomenon. Google Correlate searches millions of candidate queries in order to find the best matches for a targeted timeseries.[5]

To show how well this tool can work, we use bankruptcy time series of Statistics Netherland as an example. When a company, institution, or natural person is no longer in a position to meet their financial obligations, in the Netherlands, they—or one or more of their creditors—may file for bankruptcy at a District Court level. The number of bankruptcies pronounced per month partly depends on the number of days that the District Courts are in session during that month and may fluctuate strongly from month to month. See Figure 5.4 for the Statistics Netherlands (administrative) data.

Figure 5.4 shows that the start of the global financial crisis had a very serious impact on the number of bankruptcies in the Netherlands. Beginning with the bankruptcy of Lehman Brothers September 14, 2008, the financial crisis entered a critical phase marked by failures of prominent banks and efforts by the American and European governments

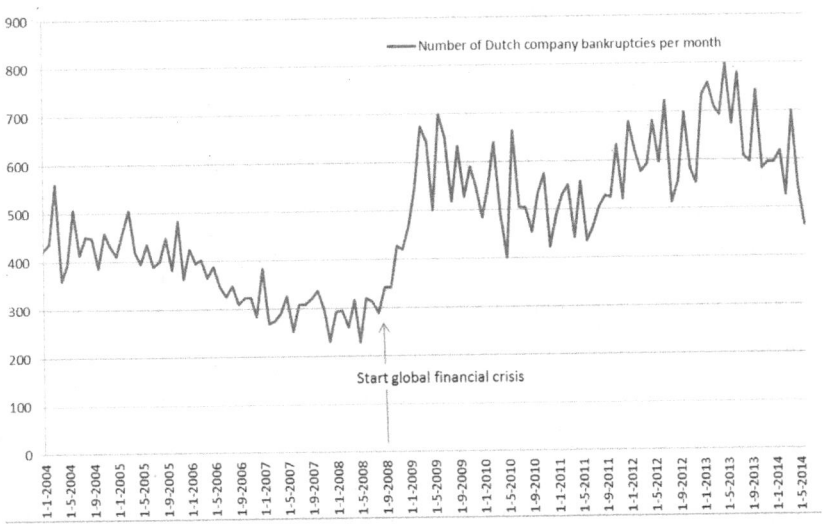

Figure 5.4. Business Bankruptcy Per Month in the Netherlands (2004–2014).

to rescue financial institutions. This reduced the possibilities for companies to obtain new loans to continue their businesses.

Google Correlate uses the same methodology and data as GFTs, so we uploaded the bankruptcy time series into the Google Correlate spreadsheet. We uploaded two variables only, a date (month and year) and the number of bankruptcies for every month, while no labels or relevant file names were attached. Next, correlation coefficients (r) were calculated between the time series and the frequency time series for every query in the Google database.

Google Correlate employs an approximate nearest neighbor algorithm over millions of candidate queries in an online search tree to produce results in seconds.

The queries that Google Correlate shows are the ones with the highest correlation coefficient (see Table 5.1).

The Dutch queries in Table 5.1 are most highly correlated with the uploaded target pattern (bankruptcy). This is rather amazing because almost all queries (except the one we labeled "to excel") have a direct link with the time series used in this example.

We then turned to the question what the role of a small-t theory may be in understanding this finding. Our small-t theory, that is to say, expectations about how the world works and what is needed to understand phenomena of interest (Lempert, 2010: 887) argues that employees of companies with severe financial problems are using these search terms to find relevant information, *even before bankruptcies*

Table 5.1. Top queries for bankruptcy time series in Google Correlate

Correlation (r)	Query (in Dutch)	Translation
0.900	WW-uitkering	Unemployment benefits
0.872	WW	Abbreviation for Dutch unemployment legislation
0.857	Berekenen WW	Calculate unemployment benefits
0.856	To excel	To excel
0.848	Doorstart	Relaunch (of a business)
0.847	Credios	Dutch debt collection agency
0.847	Uitkering	Unemployment benefits
0.844	Faillissement	Bankruptcy
0.842	Hoogte WW	The amount of the benefit

are pronounced at a District Court. The small-t theory also suggests that the global financial crisis causes two other mechanisms: the *fear of becoming unemployed* and a *lack of financial resources.* The first mechanism causes more queries for "unemployment benefits" and lookalike terms, the latter for more bankruptcy (terms). Linking our small-t theory's behavioral mechanisms with the global financial crisis makes the Google findings understandable (Figure 5.5).

Variation in the queries could predict the number of bankruptcies in the near future,[6] for which clues are also found in Figure 5.6. It shows that the query with the highest correlation "WW-uitkering" has the same shape as our uploaded time series from Statistics Netherlands (=representing the administrative and "real" numbers of bankruptcies). Remarkable is the fact that the query also acted very well in times of very serious changes (i.e. the sudden start of the global financial crisis in September 2008).

Having found correlated queries that can be related to a small-t theory (and therefore "make sense"), our next step was to export the normalized scores of these queries and use them to build *new predicting models* in SPSS. To judge the predictive power of these models, we have to make sure that models that contain query data predict *better* than simple autoregressive models.[7] To find this out, we used the stationary bankruptcies trend from January 1, 2004, to October, 1, 2008. We then tried to predict the next four months (when the numbers of bankruptcies in reality exploded) with a regular autoregressive integrated moving average (ARIMA)[8] model (Figure 5.7a) and a similar time series model to which we added normalized query data from Google Correlate (Figure 5.7b). The figures show that the forecast (behind the dotted line) of the second model is much better than the forecast using the regular ARIMA model.

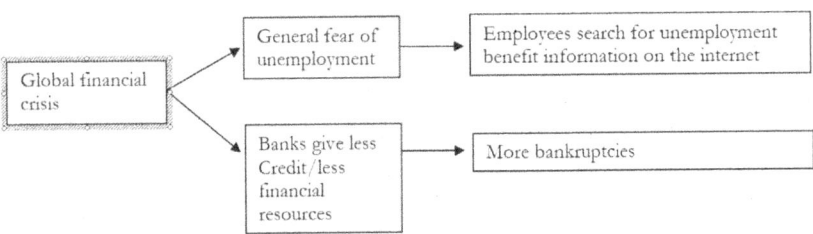

Figure 5.5. Linking Small-T Theory's Behavioral Mechanisms with the Global Financial Crisis.

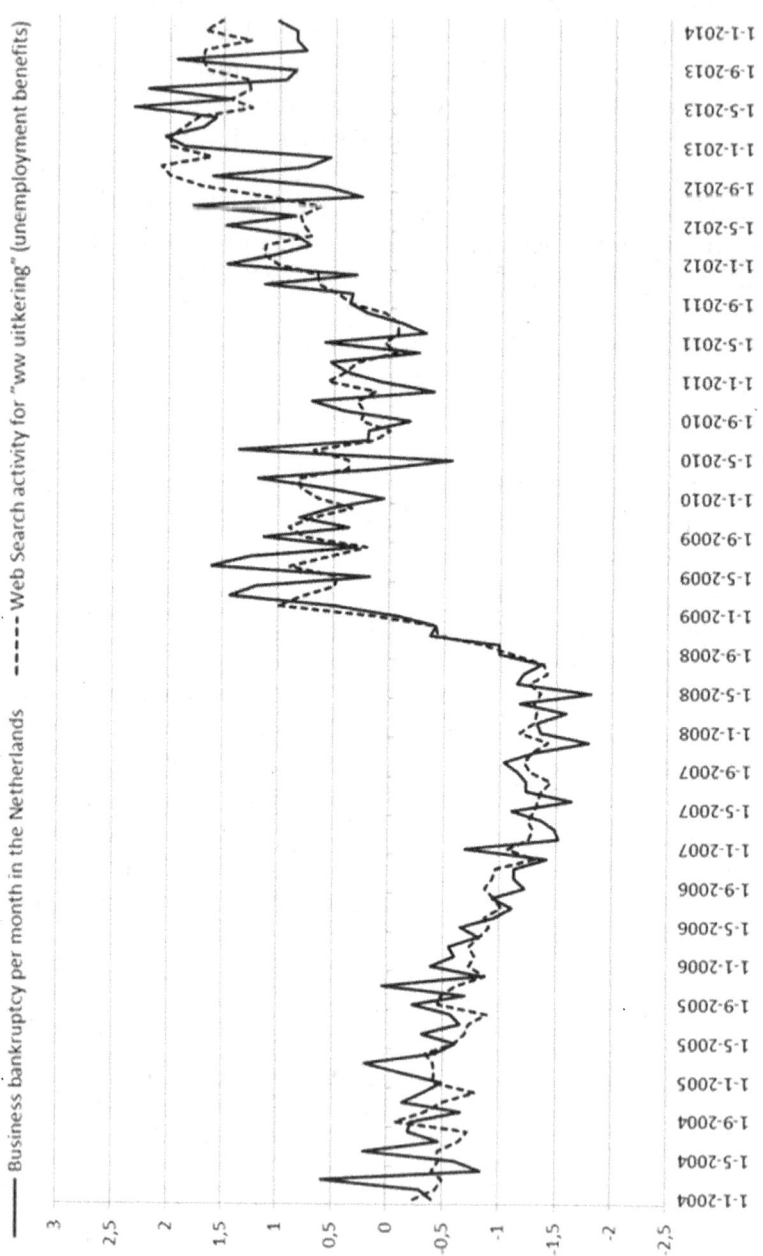

Figure 5.6. User-Uploaded Activity for Business Bankruptcy Per Month in the Netherlands and Web Search Activity for "WW-uitkering" (Unemployment Benefits), Normalized Scores ($r = 0.900$).

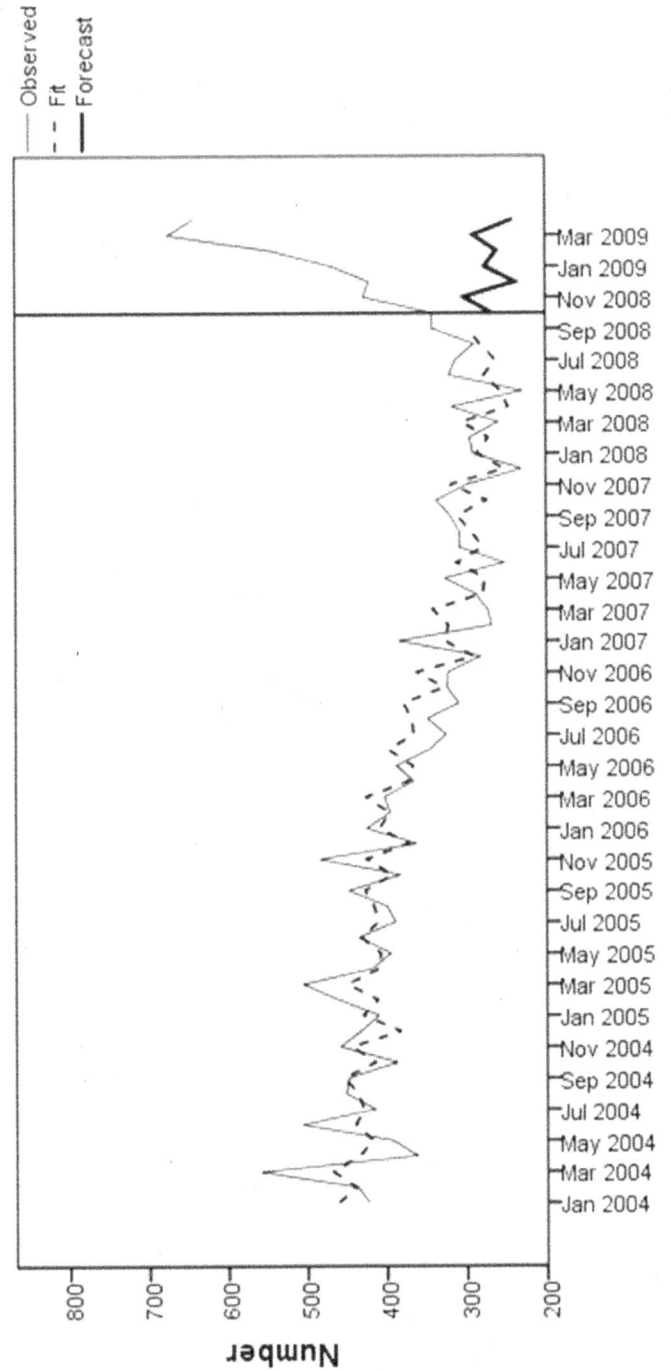

Figure 5.7a. Regular ARIMA Model (Historical Bankruptcies Data Only).

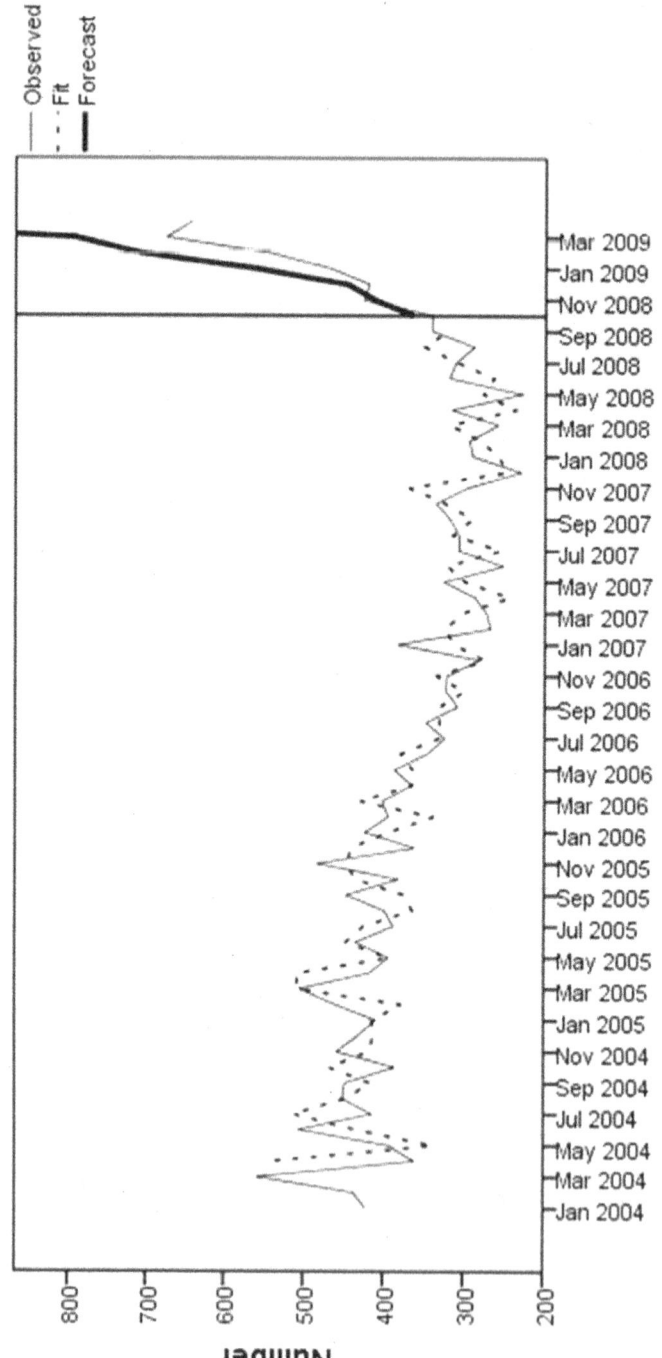

Figure 5.7b. ARIMA Model + Normalized Query Data as an Independent Variable.

To summarize

- combining traditional data and "new" query data can result in better models and predictions;
- working with a small-t theory is important because it addresses the why question (why has this happened) and it helps the persons who forecast to understand which mechanisms may be involved.

It is our assertion that by working along these lines, this will help to protect Big Data analysts from making the same mistake that was made with GFTs.[9]

Preventing the Big Data Hype by Comparing and Mixing Types of Data

The examples presented above do not fall prey to the Big Data Hype, claiming that working with Big Data is the only route to follow in future research (also known as *Big Data Hubris*). Although we are convinced that "there are huge scientific possibilities in Big Data, we have to take care of issues of [the role of theories], measurement, construct validity and reliability and dependencies among data" (Harford, 2014). Space and time prohibit us to discuss these issues more in depth. Therefore, we focus on two ideas coming from social science research.

The first idea is how to find small-t theories to help understand correlational query findings regarding social processes. The answer has two parts. The first is to open the black box of the empirical correlations by searching for mechanisms that may or may not play a role. See the example we discussed above. Astbury and Leeuw (2012) described how such a process works. The second is to use knowledge repositories consisting of reviews and synthesis of research on these mechanisms. Examples of repositories are the Campbell Collaboration, Eppi, 3ie, corrections and several "clearing houses" on education, labor, social security, and economic development.

The second idea focuses on articulating the (implicit) *measurement theory* when working with Big Data. A measurement theory describes the assumptions about the (different) ways through which data are collected or, in the Big Data world, "come to us." An example may help. The measurement theory that underlies survey methodology is something like this:

- people most of the time speak the truth and share that with the data collector,
- people know right from wrong,

- people are capable of remembering what happened a year or two years ago,
- people operate mostly without serious cognitive distortions, and
- what is measured is "as it really is (or was' at the time of measuring) (see Berka [1993] for background information on measurement and test and scaling theory).

We have not yet seen articles on the measurement theory (or theories) underlying the different types of Big Data (analysis) except for Patty and Penn (2014). These authors suggest the following:

> *Social scientists commonly construct indices to reduce and summarize complex, multidimensional data. Examples include assigning texts to topical categories, converting roll call matrices into "ideal points," producing brain images from raw fMRI data, various node- and edge-indices in network analysis, and the wide array of composite indicators that seek to distill potentially thorny concepts such as income inequality, democratization, civic competence, and environmental responsibility into a list of numbers. The benefits of these indices are clear: a single number is simple to interpret, and such indices can facilitate communication between scholars, policymakers, and the public on important issues. Moreover, indices make it possible to track the absolute and relative performance of objects over time. And importantly, indices lend themselves to empirical study as both dependent and independent variables, as they can be readily incorporated into a regression.*

They go on by arguing that

> *the task of data reduction increasingly necessitated by modern work in political science—particularly in areas popularly associated with "Big Data" such as networks, text analysis, and genetics—and the concomitant interface of theory and data implied by these endeavors, can be productively enhanced by concepts derived from a vein of theoretical social science called social choice theory. Social choice theory is principally concerned with aggregation: the creation of a measure of some underlying concept (e.g., social welfare, majority will, inequality, power) from a set of potentially heterogeneous inputs (e.g., individual preferences, ballots, incomes, relative capabilities).*

The reason we bring this to the floor is that according to some Big Data analysts like Anderson (2008), working with theories (and the scientific method) is "obsolete." We hope to have made clear that this is not a fruitful position.

The Relevance of Big Data for Evaluation

Let's go back to the example of the forecasting of bankruptcies in the Netherlands. We showed that by using Google search data, based on queries that made sense, we were capable of making better predictions of what would have happened than by extrapolating only.

The relevance for evaluations of this type of work is, we believe, high.

- First, given the increased interest in "real-time" evaluations and "rapid evaluation and assessment methods" (Sandison, 2003; Trotter et al., 2001), working with Big Data (analytics) almost is real time. A real-time evaluation feeds back its findings for immediate use, while the program is still being implemented.
- Second, as the example on bankruptcies shows, several predictions on what the (near) future will bring can be developed and tested by using social media and Google search engine data. This can happen almost on a day-to-day basis.
- Third, the costs of this kind of data are very small compared to the costs when doing interviews. Finally, we foresee that it may be possible to use Big Data to carry out impact evaluations of digital policies and programs. Examples are evaluating not only digital programs to reduce or prevent digital piracy behavior (of books, music, movies, and 3D devices) (see Chapter 6 by Bastiaan Leeuw) but also digital polices to curb trade in digital pornography, DDOS attacks, and others.

Notes

1. For more detailed information in English, see: http://www.cbs.nl/enGB/menu/themas/dossiers/conjunctuur/publicaties/conjunctuurbericht/inhoud/conjunctuurklok/toelichtingen/ck-03.htm.
2. http://www.coosto.com/uk/about-coosto.
3. Two or more predictive variables in a time-series model are cointegrated when they share a common stochastic drift. Variables are considered cointegrated if a linear combination of them produces a stationary time series.
4. http://www.google.com/trends/correlate.
5. For more information about the algorithms which power Google Correlate, see Vanderkam, Robert Schonberger, Henry Rowley. *Nearest Neighbor Search in Google Correlate*. http://www.google.com/trends/correlate/nn-search.pdf.
6. We didn't have the opportunity to study cointegration between both time series in the same way as Daas and Puts did in our first example.
7. An "example" of such a model can be found when predicting the weather in Las Vegas. In that city, the sun is shining more than 320 days a year. The model that uses "today's weather" is almost always an adequate forecast for tomorrow.
8. In statistics and in particular in time-series analysis, an ARIMA model is a generalization of an autoregressive moving average model. These models

are fitted to time-series data either to better understand the data or to predict future points in the series (forecasting). ARIMA models form an important part of the Box–Jenkins approach to time-series modeling. In our example, we used IBM Expert Modeler that automatically evaluates a range of seasonal and nonseasonal autoregressive (p), integrated (d), and moving average (q) settings and seven exponential smoothing models.
9. Nevertheless, it must be taken into account that while doing this work, we tested dozens of other time series hoping to find high and sense making correlations in Google Correlate. "Bankruptcy" was by far the best but time series like the number of monthly divorces, unemployment, stock prices, or the number of asylum requests per month performed poorly. The consumer confidence time series that was modeled successfully in our first example (using Coosto data) didn't have relevant correlations in Google Correlate.
10. http://www.google.org/flutrends/intl/en_gb/about/how.html.

References

Jesse Alpert and Nissan Hajaj, "We Knew the Web Was Big…" Official Google Blog, July 25, 2008. Accessed January 2012. http://googleblog.blogspot.com/2008/07/we-knew-web-was-big.html.

Anderson, C. 2008. "The End of Theory: The Data Deluge Makes the Scientific Method Obsolete." In *WIRED MAGAZINE*. http://archive.wired.com/science/discoveries/magazine/16-07/pb_theory.

Astbury, B., and F. L. Leeuw. 2010. "Unpacking Black Boxes: Mechanisms and Theory-Building in Evaluation." *American Journal of Evaluation* 31 (3): 363–81.

Bail, C. A. 2014. "The Cultural Environment: Measuring Culture with Big Data." *Theory and Society* 43.

Berka, K. 1993. *Measurement. It's Concepts, Theories and Problems.* Dordrecht: Kluwer.

Blok, A., and M. A. Pedersen. 2014. "Complementary Social Science? Quali-Quantitative Experiments in a Big Data World." *Big Data & Society* 1 (2).

Butler, D. 2013. "When Google Got Flu Wrong." *Nature* 494: 155–6.

Chan, E. H., V. Sahai, C. Conrad, and J. S. Brownstein. 2011. "Using Web Search Query Data to Monitor Dengue Epidemics: A New Model for Neglected Tropical Disease Surveillance." *PLoS Neglected Tropical Diseases* 5 (5): e1206. doi:10.1371/journal.pntd.0001206.

CBS. 2013. "Steeds Vaker Laptop, Smartphone en Tablet in Huis." *CBS Webmagazine*, Donderdag. Accessed November 28, 2013. . http://www.cbs.nl/nl-NL/menu/themas/vrije-tijd-cultuur/publicaties/artikelen/archief/2013/2013-3926-wm.htm.

Daas, P., and M. Puts. 2014. "Social Media Sentiment and Consumer Confidence." *Statistic Paper Series No 5*. https://www.ecb.europa.eu/pub/pdf/scpsps/ecbsp5.en.pdf.

DiMaggio, P., E. Hargittai, C. Coral, and S. Shafer. 2001. *From Unequal Access to Differentiated Use: A Literature Review and Agenda for Research on Digital Inequality.* Report prepared for the Russell Sage Foundation.

Harford, T. 2014. "Big Data: Are We Making a Big Mistake?" *Significance*. http://www.ft.com/cms/s/2/21a6e7d8-b479-11e3-a09a-00144feabdc0.html#axzz30INfAyMi.

Ginsberg, J., H. Matthew, R. Mohebbi, S. Patel, L. Brammer, M. S. Smolinski, and L. Brilliant. 2009. "Detecting Influenza Epidemics Using Search Engine Query Data." *Nature* 457: 19.

Global Pulse White Paper. 2012. "Big Data for Development: Opportunities & Challenges.". Accessed May 2012. http://unglobalpulse.org/projects/BigData-forDevelopment.

Goel, S., J. M. Hofman, and S. Lahaie. 2010. "Predicting Consumer Behavior with Web Search." *Microeconomics and Social Systems.* New York: Yahoo Research. http://www.pnas.org/content/107/41/17486.full.pdf+html.

Lazer, D., R. Kennedy, G. King, and A. Vespignani. 2014. "The Parable of Google Flu: Traps in Big Data Analysis." *Science* 343 (6176): 1203–5. http://www.sciencemag.org/content/343/6176/1203.

Lempert, R. 2010. "The Inevitability of Theory." *California Law Review* 98: 877–906.

Miller, G. 2012. "The Smartphone Psychology Manifesto." *Perspectives on Psychological* 7: 221. http://pps.sagepub.com/content/7/3/221.

Mohebbi, M., D. Vanderkam, J. Kodysh, R. Schonberger, H. Choi, and S. Kumar. 2011. *Google Correlate Whitepaper.* http://www.google.com/trends/correlate/whitepaper.pdf.

Patty, J. W., and E. M. Penn. 2014. "Analyzing Big Data: Social Choice & Measurement." *PS 2015.* http://journals.cambridge.org/download.php?-file=%2FPSC%2FPSC48_01%2FS1049096514001814a.pdf&code=8ee56bdfb-cd3061a388169c5ae3c5095.

Sandison, Pet. 2003. *Desk review of Real Time Evaluation Experience.* UNICEF.

Trotter, Robert T. II, Richard H. Needle, Eric Goosby, Christopher Bates, and Merrill Singer. 2001. "A Method-ological Model for Rapid Assessment, Response, and Evaluation: The RARE Program in Public Health." *Field Methods* 13 (2): 137–59.

6

Using Big Data to Study Digital Piracy and the Copyright Alert System

H.B.M. Leeuw[1]

Introduction

In recent years, policy makers have increasingly begun to rely on so-called "e-interventions" or "web-based interventions." These interventions stem from a variety of policy fields, such as health care and education. A few examples can be used to depict this variety. E-interventions can be found in relation to weight loss programs for pregnant or postpartum women (Fernandez et al., 2015), an e-learning program to reduce substance abuse (Schweizer et al., 2014), online monitoring and notification systems meant to reduce instances of online copyright infringement (Arnold et al., 2014), and an Internet-based cognitive behavioral theory intended to prevent and reduce depression among adolescents (Lillevoll et al., 2014). While these interventions vary significantly in terms of the policy tools used, all e-interventions share one commonality: they are all Internet-supported interventions (Barak et al., 2009) and, in varying degrees, deal with behavior that takes place in the digital environment.

The availability of the Internet has allowed for innovations in the design and implementation of interventions, as e-interventions allow for innovative ways in which policy makers can attempt to change the behavior of a target population. But it can be argued that the evaluation of such interventions is still often done through rather traditional methods, such as by using self-administrated questionnaires[2] and by conducting experiments (Doumas et al., 2009; Lillevoll et al., 2014). While these methods are robust and have proven merits, they suffer from a degree of artificiality, focusing on stated behavior but not necessarily observing actual behavior of the target population. Additionally, these more traditional approaches to policy evaluation are rather costly and time-consuming (Ludwig et al., 2011).

Yet, the capabilities of the Internet allow for a different approach in measuring the effects of some of these e-interventions. Imagine that an e-intervention is attempting to, through a specific website, inform unemployed individuals on the available online tools meant to help them with their job search. Individuals who would be interested in these tools would search for and visit this website. Search engines such as Google record the search behavior of its users, and search traffic would likewise increase. This stored data can be used to analyze changes in online search behavior. Analyzing such a data set can be labeled as being an example of Big Data as a data source. In this manner, it is possible to quickly examine the specific effects of an intervention. But, in using such an approach, the question emerges whether changes in search behavior can be attributed to this e-intervention or whether other variables or factors may have contributed to them.

This contribution sets out to analyze online search behavior following the implementation of such an e-intervention. The goal is not just to make observations on changes in online behavior but also to consider whether the applicable e-intervention contributed to these changes. The selected intervention is the *graduated response* (colloquially known as the three- or six-strike rule), which was implemented in the United States[3] in 2013. It is intended to reduce instances of digital copyright (or digital piracy[4]), which has proven to be a persistent digital deviance. The graduated response implemented in the United States is known as the Copyright Alert System (CAS).

The CAS and Digital Piracy

The CAS is a monitoring and notification system through which Internet Service Providers monitor whether or not one of their subscribers engage in digital piracy. If a subscriber is found to be infringing on copyrighted content, they will start to receive a series of warnings, each voiced more sternly than the last. Should subscribers persist in their behavior after repeated warnings, they are sanctioned through measures such as a disconnection from the Internet, account downgrading, or bandwidth throttling. This is done on behalf of the content owners, who state that digital piracy has negative economic consequences for the creative industries and society as a whole.

Proponents of this intervention claim that it will be successful in reducing digital piracy and that initial outcomes are encouraging (Center for Copyright Information, 2014) but have not presented any conclusive evidence that this intervention is indeed succeeding in its set out goal. While some limited evidence from other countries suggest that a graduated response system can have the desired effect (Danaher et al., 2014), no definitive conclusions have been made on the effectiveness of the graduated response in general or the CAS specifically.

Proponents of the CAS often cite its necessity. It is argued that music, movie, and software piracy are not only common but also harmful to the economic well being of the creative industry and society. The creative industry argues that piracy results in significant losses to their revenue, often ranging in billions of US$. In turn, these losses supposedly lead to job losses in the various industries affected by digital piracy. While these statements have been met with academic scrutiny (Aguiar and Martens, 2013; Barker, 2012; Hammond, 2014; Ma et al., 2014), demonstrating that these proposed negative consequences are far from certain, governments and stakeholders are trying to limit, inhibit, or deter digital copyright infringements. The CAS represents just one effort to reduce or deter digital piracy, but it is clearly under-researched. Given this fact, as well as the previous observation that it is labeled as an e-intervention, it is a suitable test case to examine the underlying search behavior. The assumption is that, if the CAS has an effect on digital piracy behavior, this should be reflected in the underlying search behavior. This is due to the fact that the measures used by the CAS trigger a deterrent effect. Subscribers who previously searched for pirated content might no longer do so out of fear of being punished. This means that search queries used to search and download pirated content should decline after the implementation if the intervention is to have the desired effect.

The role of search engines, such as Google, is important in the context of digital piracy. Though only around twenty percent of the users of infringing content use such search engines to find pirated content (MPAA, 2013), this is a significant part of all infringing traffic. Therefore, search engines support a significant part of all infringing behavior. Should changes in this traffic be observed following the implementation of the CAS, it can be assumed that this reflects changes in digital piracy behavior as a whole. These insights can be used to generate insights into the effects of the entirety of the CAS as an antipiracy intervention.

Three hypotheses are used to further shape and direct the current research. These focus on specific aspects of the possible outcome(s) that the CAS measure can have. The first deals with search queries that are used to search for pirated content on P2P[5] networks. As the CAS directly and only focuses on this type of piracy (Bridy, 2012), a change in these queries might suggest that the measure has had an impact on this type of digital piracy. An increase might mean that the measure is counterproductive, as this can reflect an increase in piracy-related search behavior.

> *H1: Search queries directly related to P2P piracy have decreased.*

A second hypothesis is related not to piracy queries but rather to queries that demonstrate a user's intention to search for and use content through legal venues (such as iTunes, Netflix, and Spotify). Any increases noted here might suggest that the CAS has had a potential effect of increased interest in legal content, especially if paired with a decrease in piracy-related search queries.

> *H2: Search queries directly related to acquiring content in a legal manner have increased.*

The third hypothesis deals with the notion that the CAS measure might result in a "diffusion of benefits," suggesting that its effect might extend to other types of digital piracy (such as cyberlockers). However, an increase in these queries might refer to the displacement of piracy: P2P piracy has become too risky, forcing individuals to look for other venues and opportunities as their inherent motivations have remained unchanged. Should a high level of displacement be found, a more critical perspective on the CAS is required, as such side effects are not be desired.

> *H3: Search queries directly related to other types of piracy have decreased.*

Methodology

By using Big Data as a data source to measure changes in search behavior, this contribution provides insights into the effect of the CAS.

The CAS currently has been rolled out by the five major Internet Service Providers across the United States. This means that a comparison between individual states within this jurisdiction cannot be made. This is an inherent limitation to this approach and influences any claims on the causal relationships between changes in search behavior and the implementation of the CAS.

The recent work of Ayers et al. (2011a, 2011b, 2012, 2013, 2014) has inspired and shaped the methodology applied in this contribution. Ayers et al. (2014) studied tobacco-related online search queries after the implementation of a specific intervention (a tax increase) designed to reduce smoking. They ranked and analyzed the specific search queries according to their relative increases, while at the same time considering the changes in absolute search volume.

There are a number of factors that require caution when interpreting the findings that stem from this data set. The way in which the CAS has been implemented does not allow for a proper control group within the United States. It is possible that other variables might have caused the observed changes. The nature of the data simply does not allow for the exclusion or consideration of such variables. But the data set does possess certain strengths when compared to other sources of data. It first allows for multiple measurements as data are gathered preceding and following the implementation of the intervention. It is also easy, freely accessible, and relatively quick to use. In theory, a geographically based, control groups can be used. These strengths and weaknesses are considered when estimating the contribution that the CAS has had on online search behavior.

Data Collection

To perform this analysis, data from Google Trends have been downloaded and used. The starting point is the so-called root terms.[6] These have been inputted manually into the database. It was then subsequently possible to automatically generate the top ten most related search terms for each of these root terms. Subsequently, the next top ten of each of these queries was generated, further boosting the total amount of queries. For the analysis, data for each search query were downloaded. As directed by the hypotheses, these search queries were clustered into three groups: P2P piracy, non-P2P piracy, and legal content. After data cleaning and checking for missing or duplicate queries, 115 unique and relevant queries remained and were usable for analysis. The data were captured prior to the implementation of the graduated response (forming the baseline) and following the implementation thereof. To allow for both short- and long-term analyses, queries were captured both on a daily basis (for one month prior to implementation and one month following implementation) as well as on a weekly basis[7] (for one year prior and postimplementation). For the daily captured queries, not all 115 queries yielded sufficient volume, reducing the queries to seventy-two for the daily analysis. Both short-term (February and March 2013) and long-term (February 2012 up to February 2014) search queries are therefore examined.

The goal is to compare the relative mean search volume (RSV) prior, during, and after the implementation. This was done for each of the retained search query. Subsequent modeling of the differences per period was accomplished by searching for the largest (relative) spike in search volume, which was done through a percentage increase. It was possible to rank the queries in order of change. In addition to depicting the overall changes per cluster, each individual query is examined for changes prior to and following the implementation of the CAS.

Observed Effects of the CAS

Changes are observed following the implementation of the CAS. The RSV of search queries for P2P piracy was lower in the month of March, particularly during the first half of this month when compared to the queries recorded in February. While search queries dealing with legal content initially depicted an increase, the changes decreased over time. By the end of the month, these search queries no longer depicted either a decrease or an increase, indicating zero effect of the intervention for these queries on the short term. The trends for search queries related to the alternative types of piracy demonstrated any significant change following the implementation of the CAS. Overall, it seems that the search queries dealing with P2P piracy have indeed been reduced directly following implementation (Figure 6.1).

An analysis of each individual query depicts a clear short-term decrease in −12.66 percent in P2P piracy-related search queries and a very small effect for queries that involve legal content (+2.33 percent). Search behavior related to alternative ways to pirate depicted a relatively minor increase (+6.49 percent) on closer examination, as opposed to what the trends initially depicted. This possibly indicates some degree of displacement to other methods of pirating content.

More interesting are the long-term effects of the CAS implantation as these allow for a better assessment of whether or not this implementation has resulted longer term or persistent changes in

Using Big Data to Study Digital Piracy and the Copyright Alert System

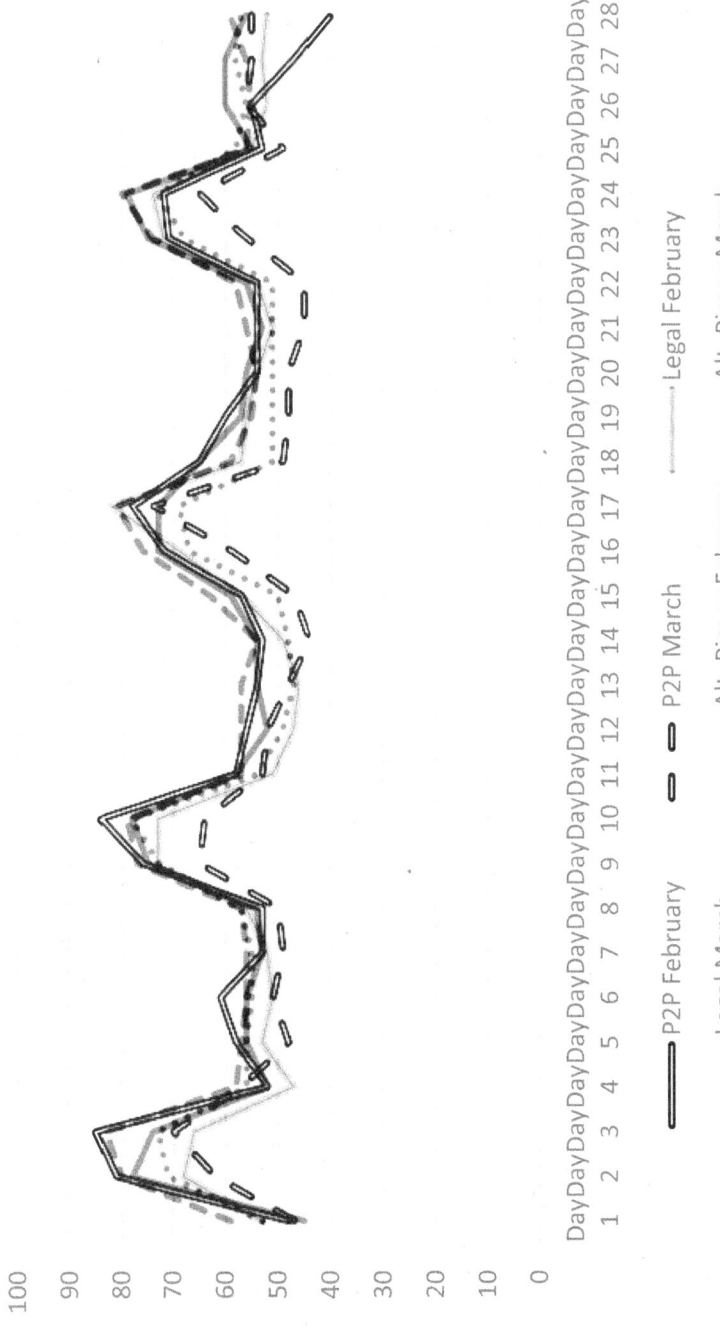

Figure 6.1. Short-Term Changes in the RSV of Search Queries (USA).

online behavior. The queries dealing with P2P piracy in 2013–2014 are significantly lower when compared to 2012–2013 baseline, potentially indicating that users have used these types of queries to a lesser degree after the CAS implementation. The differences between these periods become less sizeable as time passes. A full year after the implementation of the CAS, the differences are only relatively minor. This might suggest that there has been an initial effect of the CAS implementation but that this weakens over time. The legal and alternative search queries depict similar trends (Figure 6.2).

The observed changes are reflected in the individual search queries. P2P-related queries have the most significant reduction (−22.51 percent), while the increase in legal queries (+9.92 percent) and the reduction of alternative piracy queries are smaller (−11.65 percent). P2P queries related to specific P2P websites[8] have reduced the most.

Collectively, there are clear indications as to whether or not the implementation of the CAS resulted in changes in online search behavior related to digital piracy. P2P-piracy queries have definitely decreased, both for shorter and longer periods of time. Though less pronounced, the other clusters also depict the desired changes. For legal queries, there is a noticeable increase following implementation, though this effect diminishes over time. Alternative piracy queries likewise demonstrate changes in the volume, and the effects seem to be persistent. There is some evidence to argue that the CAS has had some desired effects and that some of these are maintained over a longer period of time.

Attribution of the Findings

The question remains whether these observations can be attributed in earnest to the CAS. It has already been stated that the manner in which Big Data is used in this contribution entails some limitations as to how these findings can be attributed. As other variables or causes of the changes are not controlled for, any observed change can be the consequence of this intervention, but it can also be the result of these confounding causes. Furthermore, these results only inform us on the search behavior itself and can therefore only be used as an indicator for changes in actual piracy behavior, even if only for those instances of piracy during which search engines are used. Other studies that used a related methodology have remained relatively silent about this causality issue. While Ayers et al. (2014) do identify some limitations to this research method (such as the lack of forecast-ability and the

Using Big Data to Study Digital Piracy and the Copyright Alert System

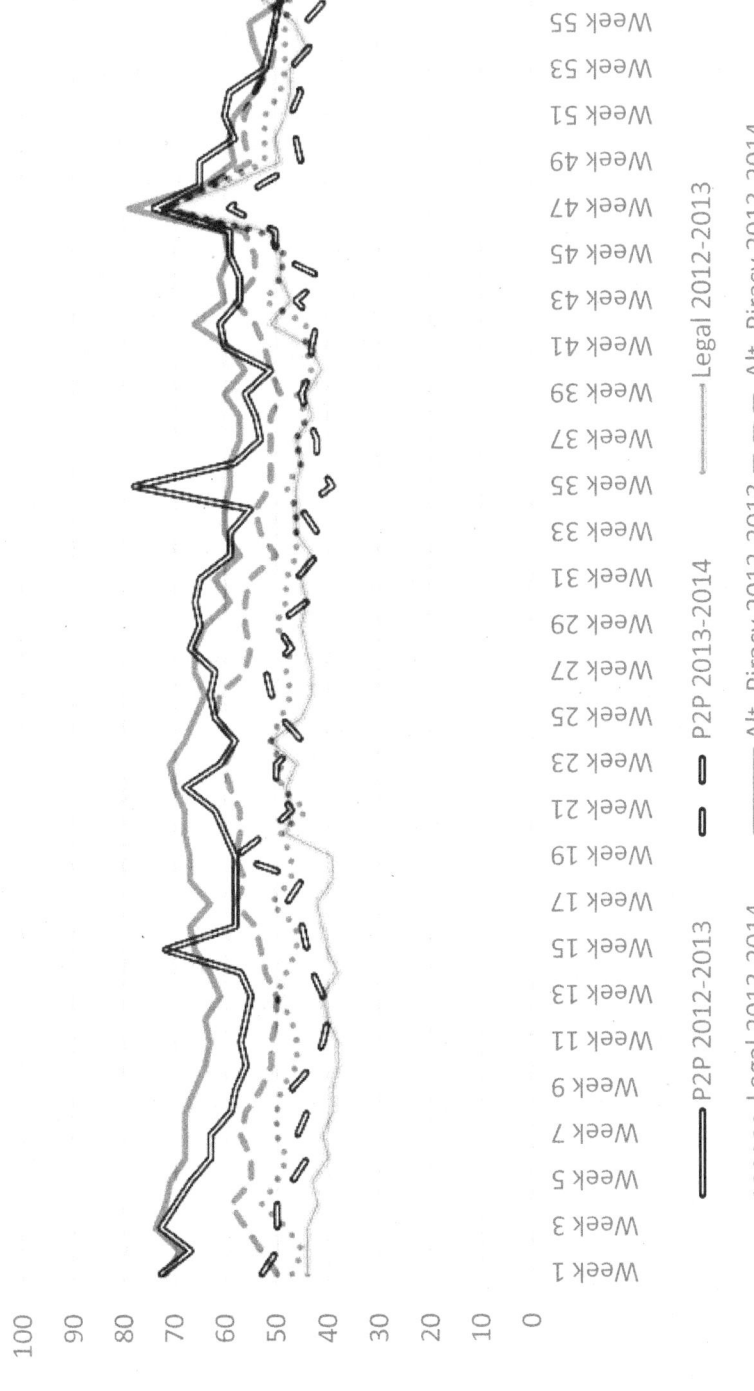

Figure 6.2. Long-Term Changes in the RSV of Search Queries (USA).

need for Internet access), little is said about the attribution, though it is hinted that, due to the large number of queries, the effect of an implementation becomes clearer. Based on the current examination, this is a reasoning that cannot be followed as this would propose that by simply having a larger data set results in clear effects, even though this does not solve the issues discussed earlier (cf. Chapters 5 and 13).

Two possible techniques can be used to shed additional light on the possible impact of the CAS and might improve the strength and reliability of the findings presented so far. These techniques can be seen as extensions to the method that has been used here. The first technique would be to compare the results of this study with a so-called counterfactual. The second is to use insights from the field of contribution analysis to (theoretically) explain why such an intervention has or has not contributed to the observed change.

Using a Counterfactual: Canada as a Comparative Case Study

While a true control group is not present in this study, it is possible to compare the findings to those of a different country or jurisdiction that has not implemented the CAS (or a similar graduated response) but is otherwise comparable to the United States. The jurisdiction that comes closest to the United States in terms of Internet access and access to digital content and sociodemographic variables is Canada. What is lacking, however, is an intervention similar to the graduated response.[9] While Canada is not an identical to the United States, it might be sufficiently similar for it to be used as a counterfactual. A second study was performed. This study examined the same queries in the Canadian context, during the same period of time, again using Big Data as a source of data. If the search queries from Canada do not demonstrate similar changes in online search behavior, this can provide additional reasons as to why the observed changes in the United States can be attributed to the CAS. Finding similar changes would be a reason to be more skeptical that the CAS has really caused any (persistent) change in behavior. Canadian data were captured solely for the longer period of time as the long-term search queries are most relevant to understand the effects of the implementation of the CAS.

The results paint a relatively clear picture: the changes observed, at least in relation to the changes in P2P piracy-related queries, are not unique to the US context. While the RSV in Canada is slightly lower from the beginning, clear decrease is noted, seemingly matching the decrease observed in the United States. As in the United States, the reduction in Canada decreases over time. Analyzing the individual queries shows, however, that the decrease is somewhat smaller when compared to the United States (−15.97 percent compared to −22.51 percent) (Figure 6.3).

The search queries dealing with legal content are examined, which depict a similar image. In both countries, an initial increase is noted, but over time, the effect diminishes. The analysis of the individual queries reveals that the overall increase in RSV is greater than in the United States (+24.31 percent compared to +9.92 percent) (Figure 6.4).

When it comes to alternative queries, the changes in RSV again follow a similar pattern in Canada. Initially, it seems that the decrease is more significant in Canada despite the fact that no intervention is in place. As in the United States, the effect decreases over time, but as opposed to the United States, these seem to be somewhat more persistent. However, the effect is slightly smaller than in the United States (−9.78 percent compared to −11.65 percent) (Figure 6.5).

This counterfactual depicts that search behavior dealing with P2P piracy has decreased in Canada as well. The two remaining clusters also change in a manner similar to the United States. Interestingly, the legal content queries have increased to a greater degree in Canada. As suggested, if similar changes to the various search queries were to be observed in Canada, it becomes more difficult to conclude that the implementation of the CAS has led to their reduction. In fact, if the Canadian counterfactual is any indication, it might even be concluded that the CAS has not had the intended effect on digital piracy and that the observed changes could have occurred naturally.

Contribution Analysis Applied to the CAS

There is an alternative manner to attempt to assess whether or not the attribution of these findings to the CAS can be established: the contribution analysis. The main focus of this approach is to verify the theory of change behind an intervention as well as considering the other factors that can influence this change (Mayne, 2008: 1). This method consists of six steps in order to make statements on the contribution that the intervention has had. For the purpose of this contribution, the focus is placed on understanding whether the assumptions made by the intervention are sound, whether any evidence can be presented that confirms their validity and whether any other factors exist that may have influenced the change.[10]

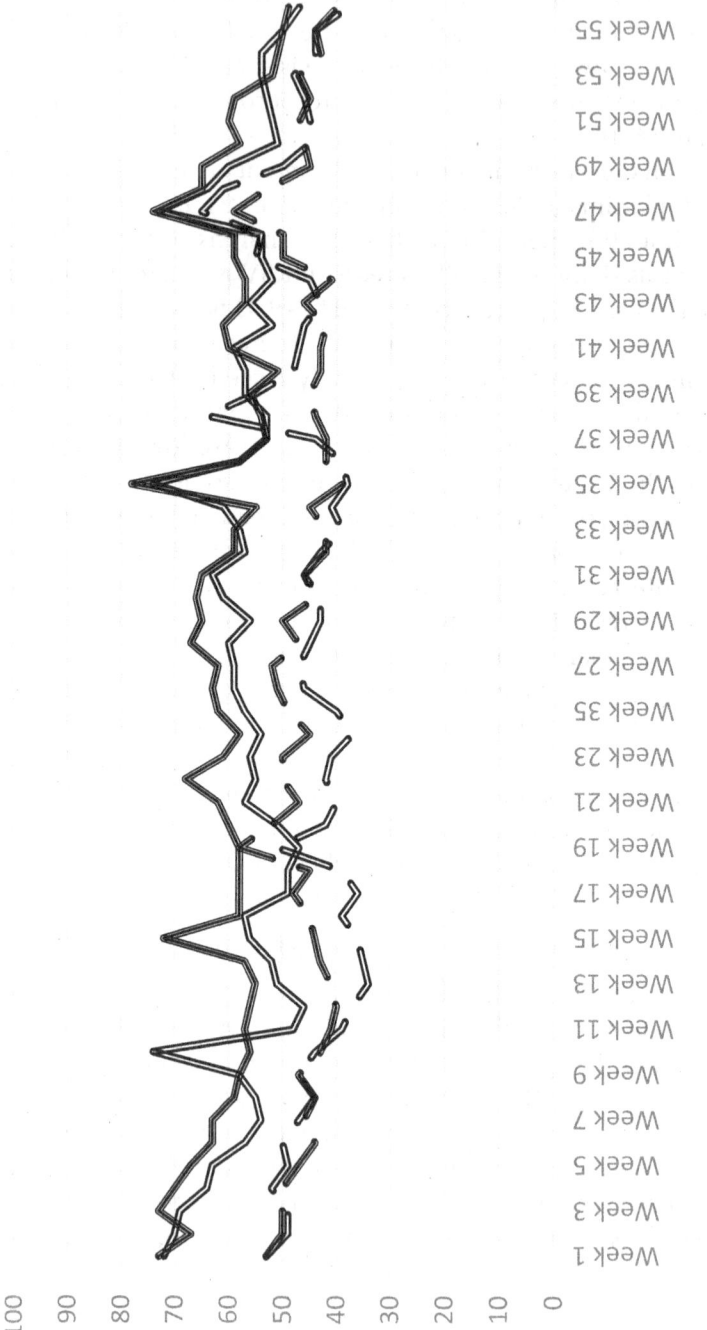

Figure 6.3. Comparison of RSV of P2P-Queries Between the USA and Canada.

Using Big Data to Study Digital Piracy and the Copyright Alert System

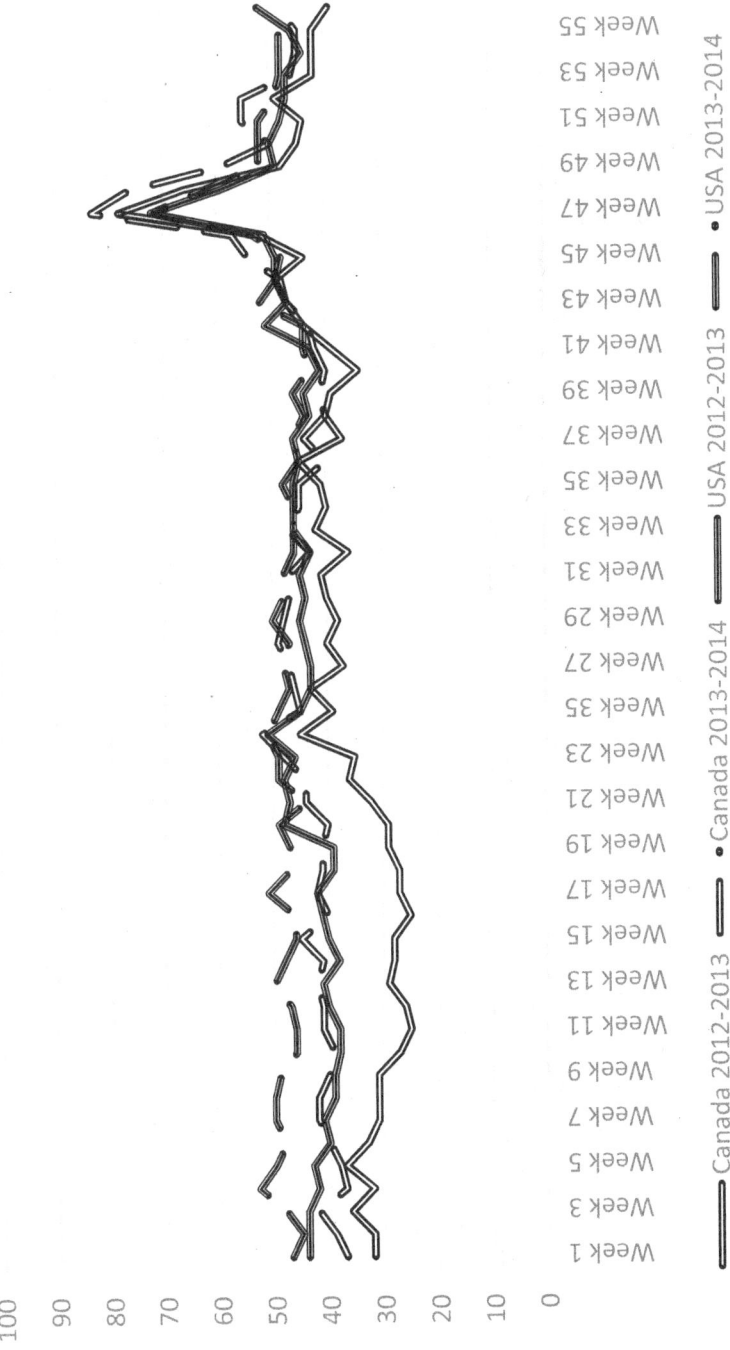

Figure 6.4. Comparison of RSV of Legal Content Queries Between the USA and Canada.

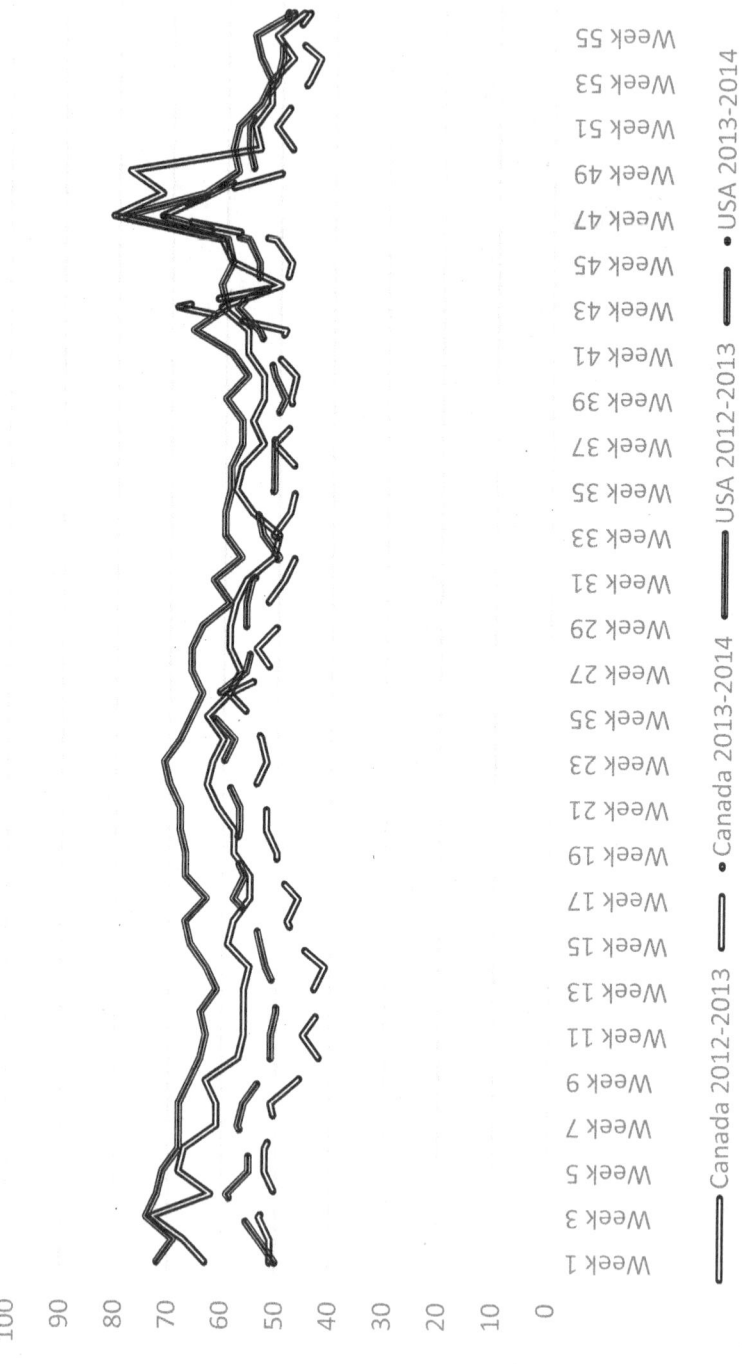

Figure 6.5. Comparison of RSV of Alternative Piracy Queries Between the USA and Canada.

Assumptions Underlying the CAS

At its core, the main assumption as to why the CAS is supposed to cause a change in piracy (search) behavior is the fact that repeat "offenders" are penalized by, for example, reducing the user's Internet speed. The effect of such a measure might mean that individuals who are considering to pirate content are deterred by the associated risk of this behavior.

Evidence on This Assumption

An intervention that relies deterrence needs to consider two important aspects: the severity and the certainty of the potential punishment. If these aspects are insufficient or perceived to be too low, it is unlikely that individuals are deterred. Is it likely that the CAS meets these requirements? While the CAS does not allow for fines or even criminal law sanctions, it can result in a significant reduction in the Internet speed, for a longer period of time. As having access to high speed is often seen as important to many individuals, reducing this speed can be seen as a sufficiently severe punishment. However, it is dubious that such punishment is significantly certain. There exists a "tipping point'" when it comes to the degree of certainty needed for the deterrent effect to take place (Loughran et al., 2012: 716). A number of studies have suggested that this tipping can be found at around 0.3–0.4 (or thirty to forty percent) (Brown, 1978; Chamlin, 1991; Loughran et al., 2012; Tittle and Rowe, 1974; Yu and Liska, 1993). During the first ten months after the implementation of the CAS, around 1.3 million alerts were sent. Per year, this comes down to around 1.5 million notices (Center for Copyright Information, 2014). On an Internet population of around 254 million, this is still quite low (0.59 percent), assuming that these alerts are all going to different individual subscribers. The number of sent notices will be doubled in the coming years. This would result in a 1.18 percent chance that the user receives a notice and sanctions. More or less one out of every hundred subscribers is likely to be sanctioned. On top of this, it is relatively straightforward to evade detection by using anonymity software or proxies, which will mask the user's identity. This might provide an explanation why the CAS is not likely to have caused changes in online search behavior as the certainty of punishment is simply too low.

Alternative Explanations

But then why do both countries demonstrate changes in piracy-related search behavior? Which factor or variable might be present in both countries that would trigger these changes? To provide a preliminary answer to these questions, a few directions can be presented. Each of these directions will be briefly focused upon to explain why each can have caused to noted changes in both countries. These serve as examples and are not fully fleshed out.

Direction I: A natural decline of digital piracy due to the availability of more, cheaper and better legal content

Between 2012 and 2014, a significant improvement in the way through which legal content can be enjoyed can be noted. While iTunes has been available for some time, other services, such as Spotify, Netflix, and Steam have had an important impact in the ease, speed, and affordability through which individuals can enjoy music, movies, and video games. It has never been easier to legally enjoy such content, it is not unlikely that this has had an impact on the frequency in which individuals will search for and use pirated content. In both the United States and Canada, the availability of these legal options is more or less similar, though certain services, such as Spotify, have been introduced in Canada at a later point in time.

Direction II: Digital piracy has become more perceived as being immoral

For years, both the creative industries and governments have attempted to dissuade individuals from pirating content. This is done in a variety of ways, but often attention is given to the immorality of the behavior. For example, the comparison between digital piracy and theft is often made.[11] The goal of such an approach is to change individual's attitudes and intentions toward piracy. While changing attitudes is difficult, it is possible that prolonged exposure to the message that piracy is "wrong" has begun to be reflected in the behavior of individuals, possibly resulting in a decrease in search volume toward digital piracy.

Direction III: Variations in content quality affects piracy behavior

One of the most important aspects that will determine whether or not an individual will pirate content is whether he/she has a desire to obtain and enjoy content in the first place. In turn, this desire is shaped by the currently available content. The release of popular or highly anticipated movies, music, or video games can have a significant impact on the search behavior of individuals. The question is, therefore, whether or not this applies to the years 2012, 2013, and 2014?

These three directions would require additional (empirical) validation in order to further substantiate whether these (or others) are indeed variables that (aid in) explain the apparent changes in online search behavior.

Discussion and Conclusion

A clear benefit of using Big Data as a source of data is that it examines actual (search) behavior rather than intentions. This allowed for some observations to be made on the potential effects that the CAS might have had on piracy-related online search behavior in the United States.

But attributing these observed changes to the CAS is problematic. The manner in which the search queries are gathered by Google means that other contributing variables to these changes cannot be excluded, requiring a complementation of the approach used. One option used was to examine Canadian search behavior that led to the conclusion that the implementation of the CAS has most likely not directly resulted in a change in online search behavior. Insights from the field of contribution analysis likewise cast clear doubts on whether or not the CAS has caused the changes in search behavior.

These observations raise the question as to what use the methodology used in this contribution has for the wider field of policy evaluation. It is first important to note that there are clear benefits to using Big Data as a data source in order to determine whether specific types of (online) behavior have changed following the implementation of an intervention. The ease of use and the speed of the data collection as well as the ability to observe online behavior both prior and following implementation and select data based on the location of the individual are all clear benefits.

The major issue remains the fact that any findings cannot be automatically attributed to the relevant intervention. Evaluators will need to be aware of this inherent limitation. If a method similar to the one used in this contribution is applied to other e-interventions, evaluators will need to combine methods and data sources in order to be able to reach more robust statements. Two examples used in this contribution are the use of a counterfactual and contribution analysis. Though limited applications of both methods have been applied, they have allowed for a better assessment of the possible effects of the CAS (e.g. that the noted changes in search behavior might not be due to the implementation of this measure). Other data sources can also be used. Sales data on legal content consumption can be analyzed before and after the implementation of the CAS. Any effect of the CAS could be reflected there as well.

Does this method have a place in the toolset of the evaluator? Perhaps it can best be understood as taking a position that is similar to the "Mechanism Experiment" (Ludwig et al., 2011). While the methods substantially and methodologically differ significantly, both can arguably be used to relatively cheaply and quickly, screen-specific interventions. If changes in online behavior are revealed through the Big Data analysis, a further, more robust, empirical examination may be warranted. On its own, it cannot be seen as serving as a tool for data analysis, and at the same time, it is not really a design that allows for a better assessment for understanding the impact of policy. The fact that additional methods are needed in order to able to reach this conclusion underlines this conclusion.

For evaluators however, the lesson to be learned is that relevant and interesting insights can be obtained by using Big Data as a source even though it cannot be used as the sole method to make statements about the effectiveness or impact of policy. It is also important to note that the data used in this contribution can be classified as being secondary data. Evaluators need to consider the fact that such data were initially collected for a different purpose. Still, within the context of e-interventions, Big Data as a source provides evaluators with an additional tool that can be used to analyze changes in online behavior.

Notes

1. This contribution was made possible through the financial support of the Horowitz Foundation for Social Policy.
2. Though the questionnaires are often done in an online manner.
3. Having previously been implemented in a number of countries such as France. Currently, the United Kingdom is considering implementing this intervention.
4. Defined in this contribution as "The act of illegally downloading digital goods (including software, documents, movies and music) by individual end-users that are actively protected by copyright law."
5. Referring to a peer-to-peer system.
6. A root term refers to an initial search query from which further search queries can be generated. For example, the root term "The Pirate Bay" would generate related queries such as "pirate bay torrent" and "free torrent movies." The other root queries selected were "free music download," "free movie download," "free video games download," "free software download,"

"torrent," "free e-book download," "free online streaming," "piracy," "P2P file sharing," "six strikes," "Netflix," "Spotify," "Steam," "iTunes," and "piracy illegal."
7. Data were captured from February 2012 to February 2013 and from February 2013 to February 2014.
8. Such as Mininova, Isohunt, and The Pirate Bay.
9. Instead, Canada uses a "notice-and-notice" system, which does not include enforcement tools to be used against individual users.
10. A full-fledged contribution analysis will not be performed however, due to the limits of this contribution.
11. MPAA (2005) "Piracy, It's a Crime" https://www.youtube.com/watch?v=HmZm8vNHBSU (accessed August 26, 2016).

References

Aguiar, L., and B. Martens. 2013. "Digital Music Consumption on the Internet: Evidence from Clickstream Data." *JRC Technical Reports*. Luxembourg: Publications Office of the European Union.

Arnold, M., E. Darmon, S. Dejean, and T. Penard. 2014. *Graduated Response Policy and the Behavior of Digital Pirates: Evidence from the French Three-strike (Hadopi) Law*. Accessed August 26, 2016. http://papers.ssrn.com/sol3/papers.cfm?abstract_id=2380522.

Ayers, J., B. Althouse, J. Allem, D. Ford, K. Ribisl, and J. Cohen. 2012. "A Novel Evaluation of World No Tobacco Day in Latin America." *Journal of Medical Internet Research* 14 (3): 1–8.

Ayers, J., B. Althouse, J. Allem, N. Rosenquist, and D. Ford. 2013. "Seasonality in Seeking Mental Health Information on Google." *American Journal of Preventive Medicine* 44 (5): 520–5.

Ayers, J., B. Althouse, K. Ribisl, and S. Emery. 2014. "Digital Detection for Tobacco Control: Online Reactions to the 2009 U.S. Cigarette Exicse Tax Increase." *Nicotine & Tobacco Research* 16 (5): 576–83.

Ayers, J., K. Ribisl, and J. Brownstein. 2011a. "Tracking the Rise in Popularity of Electronic Nicotine Delivery Systems (Electronic Cigarettes) Using Search Query Surveillance." *American Journal of Preventive Medicine* 40 (4): 448–53.

———. 2011b. "Using Search Query Surveillance to Monitor Tax Avoidance and Smoking Cessation following the United States' 2009 'SCHIP' Cigarette Tax Increase." *PLOS ONE* 6 (3): 1–7.

Barak, A., B. Klein, and J. Proudfoot. 2009. "Defining Internet-Supported Therapeutic Interventions." *Annals of Behavioral Medicine* 38 (1): 4–17.

Barker, G. 2012. "Evidence of the Effect of Free Music Downloads on the Purchase of Music CDsd in Canada." *Review of Economic Research on Copyright Issues* 9 (2): 55–78.

Bridy, A. 2012. "Graduated Response American Style: 'Six Strikes' Measured Against Five Norms." *Fordham Intellectual Property, Media & Entertainment Law Journal* 23 (1): 1–67.

Brown, D. 1978. "Arrest Rates and Crime Rates: When Does a Tipping Effect Occur?" *Social Forces* 57 (2): 671–82.

Center for Copyright Information. 2014. *The Copyright Alert System: Phase One and Beyond.* Accessed August 26, 2016. http://www.copyrightinformation.org/wp-content/uploads/2014/05/Phase-One-And_Beyond.pdf.

Chamlin, M. 1991. "A Longitudinal Analysis of the Arrest-Crime Relationship: A Further Examination of the Tipping Effect." *Justice Quarterly* 8 (2): 187–99.

Danaher, B., M. Smith, R. Telang, and S. Chen. 2014. "The Effect of Graduated Response Anti-Piracy Laws on Music Sales: Evidence from an Event Study in France." *The Journal of Industrial Economics* 62 (3): 541–53.

Doumas, D., L. McKinley, and P. Book. 2009. "Evaluation of Two Web-Based Alcohol Interventions for Mandated College Students." *Journal of Substance Abuse Treatment* 1 (1): 1–14.

Fernandez, I., S. Groth, J. Reschke, M. Graham, M. Strawderman, and C. Olson. 2015. "eMoms: Electronically-Mediated Weight Interventions for Pregnant and Postpartum Women. Study Design and Baseline Characteristics." *Contemporary Clinical Trials* 43: 63–74.

Hammond, R. 2014. "Profit Leak? Pre-Release File Sharing and the Music Industry." *Southern Economic Association* 81 (2): 387–408.

Lillevoll, K., H. Vangberg, K. Griffiths, K. Waterloo, and R. Eiseman. 2014. "Uptake and Adherence of a Self-Directed Internet-Based Mental Health Intervention with Tailored E-Mail Reminders in Senior High Schools in Norway." *BMC Psychiatry* 14 (1): 14–25.

Loughran, T., G. Pogarsky, A. Piquero, and R. Paternoster. 2012. "Re-Examining the Functional Form of the Certainty Effect in Deterrence Theory." *Justice Quarterly* 29 (5): 712–41.

Ludwig, J., J. Kling, and S. Mullainathan. 2011. "Mechanisms Experiments and Policy Evaluations." *Journal of Economic Perspectives* 25 (3): 17–38.

Ma, L., A. Montgomery, P. Singh, and M. Smith. 2014. "The Effect of Pre-Release Movie Piracy on Box-Office Revenue." Accessed August 26, 2016. http://papers.ssrn.com/sol3/papers.cfm?abstract_id=1782924.

Mayne, J. 2008. "Contribution Analysis: An Approach to Exploring Cause and Effect." *ILAC Brief*, 16.

MPAA. 2013. *Understanding the Role of Search in Online Piracy.* Boston: Millward Brown Digital.

Schweizer, H., C. Hayslett, N. Bansal, S. Ronco, and R. Schafer. 2014. "Effective Alcohol, Tobacco and Other Drug Intervention and Prevention Using Online Game-Based, E-Learning: An Evidence-Informed Program That Works." *International Journal on E-Learning* 13 (3): 335–74.

Tittle, C., and A. Rowe. 1974. "Certainty of Arrest and Crime Rates: A Further Test of the Deterrence Hypothesis." *Social Forces* 54 (4): 455–62.

Yu, J., and A. Liska. 1993. "The Certainty of Punishment: A Reference Group Effect and Its Functional Form." *Criminology* 31 (3): 447–64.

7

Protecting America's Biggest Sporting Spectacle

Jonathan D. Breul

Imagine this scenario: in the course of one hour this week, four different people involved in the Super Bowl set-up require emergency medical assistance, all for nausea and all in separate incidents. It could be that the some vendor is serving bad food or it could be a complete coincidence. But it could also be sign of some sort of criminal or terrorist act aimed at America's biggest sporting event. For the people in charge of public safety at and around MetLife Stadium in East Rutherford, NJ, USA, home to the 2014 National Football League (NFL) championship game, discovering the cause of four similar ambulance calls would be an extremely urgent matter (Terdiman, 2014).

Just a few years ago, it would have been next to impossible for security personnel to make the connection between four emergency medical services calls like that in real time. There was no technology available then, which could bring separate events to their attention and help them easily track what was happening in each case, or how, or if, they were connected. But in January 2012, Indianapolis prepared to host Super Bowl XLVI, the precise scenario played out one afternoon in the Super Bowl Village.

Gary Coons was the incident commander for that year's game. He was in charge of a massive security apparatus working to protect the Super Bowl and the tens of thousands of people in town for the game and the week of partying preceding it. Everywhere he went that week, he could monitor the event's critical infrastructure, as a wide variety of local sensors, 911 call systems, and even game-oriented social media fed information into a software package that Coons and many other security personnel could monitor in real time via smartphone or iPads (Terdiman, 2014).

Coons was able to use a Big Data system that made it possible to recognize the common thread between the four emergency calls in short order and to take action as fast as possible. He deployed a joint team that included fire hazmat specialists, support teams, and a biological hazardous materials specialist, all on the chance that something serious was happening. Fortunately, the four nausea cases turned out to be unrelated. But without technology and Big Data, "we would never have been able to pick up on having those four incidents at the same time in the same location" (Terdiman, 2014).

What Is Big Data?

In information technology, Big Data is defined as a collection of data sets so large and complex that it becomes difficult to process using on-hand database management tools or traditional data processing applications. The challenges include capture, processing, storage, search, sharing, analysis, and visualization. There is the "four Vs" corollary to this definition (i.e. volume, velocity, variety, and veracity), which is covered in Chapter 1 of this book (Joltsik, 2013).

What is security analytics? First, security analysis is the examination of a multitude of phenomena for the purpose of detecting and/or responding to security incidents (Joltsik, 2013). A security analytic is a deduction based upon the results of interactions of multiple simultaneous security phenomena. The thing that Big Data security analytics technology allows us to do is capture more data and turn large, disparate and unstructured data volumes into comprehensive and actionable information.

Big Data Takes Over the Big Game

In the first week of February 2014, Super Bowl XLVIII was held in the New York–New Jersey metropolitan area, presenting security officials with a far greater logistical challenge than anything Gary Coons had to manage. The Super Bowl has long been considered a terrorist target, and those concerns were elevated this year with the event hold in the New York region (Boyle and Haggerty, 2009). This Super Bowl was the first since the Boston Marathon bombings in April 2013, and it came amid considerable attention on the potential threats in Russia for the Winter Games in Sochi.

The Super Bowl was designated a Level One National Security threat by Department of Homeland Security, signifying that Homeland Security Presidential Directive 5 was in effect. This means that the federal government grants itself the power to intervene with and lead all security operations over a given event and its surrounding region (Police State USA, 2014).

The game was played at MetLife Stadium in New Jersey's Meadowlands, not even ten miles from Manhattan. They were expecting about 80,000 patrons and another 10,000 stadium employees (Gehlken, 2014). The stadium's location near a major airport and busy commuter train lines presented security challenges. Unlike audiences for other championship games, spectators of Super Bowl XLVIII relied heavily on mass transit (Perez, 2014). Because of this, the deadly bombings in the southern Russian city of Volograd raised worries (Hays, 2014).

New Jersey had its share of logistical challenges, with MetLife Stadium becoming a fortress for the game. To enter the stadium, fans lined up outside security screening tents, where they went through metal detectors. Fans were not allowed to bring much with them: a clutch and a small, clear plastic bag were permitted, but authorities discouraged fans from bringing much of anything. Rows of law enforcement vans lined the parking lot, and dogs checked cars, vans, and buses as they entered.

Protecting New York City, with its eight million residents, crowded streets and high profile, was an even larger chore. In the week leading up to it, the presence of police was highly visible in Midtown Manhattan where police lined the fan zone known as Super Bowl Boulevard, a thirteen-blocks running through Times Square. In addition to the actual game, more than two-dozen Super Bowl special events took place, according to the new police commissioner, William Bratton (Kouri, 2014).

Advanced Planning

Planning for the Super Bowl commences years in advance with site visits, consultations, and observations at prior Super Bowl venues. In every sense, the Super Bowl is a premier national and international event that involves 365 days of discussion and planning (Connors, 2007). Another benefit of starting the planning early is that by having agencies work together over a period of time on a project like this, agencies develop trust and confidence in one another, which is helpful from an operational standpoint.

The terrorist attacks of September 11, 2001, significantly modified the planning process for communities hosting a Super Bowl. Resources required to provide a secure environment and to position agencies to respond to emergencies increased dramatically. Officially, joint security task forces as notable and wide-reaching as the multi-agency Super Bowl group do not like to show their whole hand, but the layers of multiple agencies provided a "show of force like something in the military" according to the agents involved. "People would probably be surprised to know how much could be done in a matter of minutes. You're talking hundreds of law enforcement and armored vehicles on the field in around three minutes. And you're in live contact with every local and regional agency as well as the military. It's a full command post" (Godfrey, 2014).

While there was no specific threat posed to the game, security planning was prepared for bombings and shooters. "I would list them in priority order being a suicide bomber, a vehicle laden with explosives and a mass shooter or mass shooters similar to the Kenyan mall or Mumbai incidents," said Ed Hartnett, former head of the New York Police Department (NYPD) Intelligence Unit (Police State USA, 2014).

The NFL, MetLife Stadium, New Jersey Transit, and the New Jersey State Police collaborated for months. The NYPD drew on its experience securing the annual New Year's Eve celebration in Times Square, the New York Marathon, the U.N. General Assembly, and other high-profile events (Hays, 2014). Just like the teams on the field, "we have been practicing all year," said Aaron Ford, special agent in charge of the Federal Bureau of Investigation's (FBI) Newark office (Gehlken, 2014).

Beyond requiring procedures and traffic patterns for fans, staff, and public safety personnel, a globally watched event in a public venue has its own security challenges. Technology allowed security organizers to bring public and private video feeds into a centralized control room. This enabled greater collaboration, more contextual analysis, and a quicker, orchestrated, and more appropriate responsive to any situation (Nilsson, 2014).

A twenty-four-hour FBI command center monitored the latest counterterrorism intelligence, said Aaron Ford. Measures were taken to protect power grids and to make sure, there was plenty of backup energy in case of another blackout like the one last year at the game in New Orleans, said Jeffrey Miller, the NFL's head of security (Hays, 2014). Ford said the agency had been working with local and state officials for the past two years, calling it "an unprecedented collaboration" (Corcoran, 2014).

Wayne Hasenbalg, president of the New Jersey Sports and Exhibition Authority said that the 15,000 game-day workers—from security to guest services to food-and-beverage personnel—were required to be identified by early October 2013 to allow sufficient time for federal background checks. If a hot dog vendor called in sick, the only potential replacement was someone who had already passed a background check (Brennan, 2014).

Putting the Plan into Action

As is the case for other major sporting events, securing the Super Bowl is a complex and nerve-racking task that involves the coordination of many law enforcement agencies, the use of technologies like cameras and radiation detectors, and the identification of troublemakers. "Everything as an air, land, and sea concept," said Lieutenant Colonel Edward Cetnar of the New Jersey State Policy, who is in charge of security at the game itself. He had twenty-seven security subcommittees which include members of DHS, the FBI, and the NYPD (Police State USA, 2014).

On the Ground

Super Bowl security, which includes the game and the week of surrounding events, required a joint effort across two states, an unusual pairing for an event. New Jersey and New York agencies worked together, and representatives described the pairing as seamless and without ego (Gehlken, 2014). "In all, one hundred local and federal agencies, divided into twenty-seven committees, participated in Super Bowl planning operations for at least the past year," said Col. Rick Fuentes, New Jersey State Policy superintendent (Gehlken, 2014).

The security was two-fold, according to former police counterterrorism unit commander, Steve Knudsen. "There will be anti-terrorism operations which are clearly visible. And then you'll have counterterrorism which is usually classified and covert, such as intelligence gathering, undercover detectives and scout-sniper teams that include the 'spotters' and the 'shooters,'" said Det. Knudsen (Kouri, 2014). The NFL hired at least 4,000 private security officers to help out (Meminger, 2014).

New Jersey State Police assigned up to 700 troopers at the stadium, with a security center set up in a hollowed-out building across a highway from the stadium that's slated to become a mammoth retail and entertainment complex (Hays, 2014). The perimeter of the stadium was patrolled by helicopters in the sky and gunboats in the water, armed with heavy weapons, thermal cameras, radiation detectors, and other high-tech gadgets. Roughly 3,000 security guards and 700 cops were inside the stadium. Special Weapons and Tactics team were present at the game and high-altitude sniper nests were set up above the fans, where sharpshooters peered down at the crowd with high-powered rifles (Police State USA, 2014). Newark Liberty International Airport was crawling with bomb-sniffing dogs (Police State USA, 2014).

The police presence was truly massive. Mobile Command Units were parked on almost every block. NYPD mobile watchtowers were set up along sidewalks. Roughly 200 "temporary" surveillance cameras were installed to monitor Super Bowl fans, in addition to 2,000 permanent ones already in place (Police State USA, 2014).

NYPD used its teams of officers to stop, board, and inspect subway trains. Officers examined bags and other containers carried by passengers entering the subway system to detect explosives (Kouri, 2014). Squads of the Emergency Service Units officers with heavy weapons, canines, and side officers from the Intelligence Division or the Counterterrorism Bureau conducted patrols at City landmarks, critical infrastructure, and transportation hubs (transit stations/ferry terminals) (Kouri, 2014). Cops were using radiation-detecting helicopters, K-9 teams, and elite, heavily armed Hercules squads to monitor the crowds (Celona and Schram, 2014).

The stadium itself was transformed into a more secure environment (Brennan, 2014). There was a vehicle and cargo inspection system. "It's basically an MRI for shipped stuff that's in an undisclosed area near the stadium. That's where any truck that delivers anything for the Super Bowl was screened, said Frank Supovitz, NFL vice president of events" (McManus, 2014). "We are x-raying every piece of equipment, every cargo, every beverage, seat cushion, every piece of merchandise, food… everything that is going in the stadium has to be x-rayed before it goes in," said Kevin McCabe, Chief of the US Customs and Border Protection agency (Police State USA, 2014). The parking lots of the stadium were lined with license-plate scanners to log every vehicle that arrived. The vehicles could then be searched. Federal agencies declared that they were searching every truck that arrived—no probable cause needed (Police State USA, 2014).

The federal Department of Homeland Security (DHS) deployed air marshals and behavioral detection officers, radiological detection teams, and random baggage checks at transit hubs as security measures (Perez, 2014). The Transportation Security Administration (TSA) deployed its Visible Intermodal Prevention and Response, or VIPR, teams. Composed of air marshals, transportation security inspectors, and behavioral detection officers, the teams will work at train hubs, particularly New York's Penn Station and Secaucus Junction, TSA spokesman Ross Feinstein said (Perez, 2014). The FBI added more analysts, weapons of mass destruction specialists, and other agents to assist local authorities. Customs and Border Protection officers scanned cargo entering the stadium, looking for drugs and weapons. They also helped secure air space over the game. Immigration and Customs Enforcement officers targeted counterfeit vendors selling fake Super Bowl memorabilia (Perez, 2014).

In the Air

A no-fly zone was imposed for ten miles in every direction around the stadium and was enforced by armed Blackhawk helicopters. The gunships were prepared to shoot down violators of the no-fly zone. Even Air Force F-16s were patrolling the no-fly zone. Pilots and maintainers from the Atlantic City Air National Guard unit, the 177th Fighter Wing, showcased F-16s Fight Falcons, explaining that the jets could respond, intercept—and if necessary shoot down—potential aerial threats within mere minutes (Kreft, 2014). If fact, any one of dozens of Aerospace Control Alert units can and likely would have responded with this kind of security if a legitimate threat arose (Kreft, 2014).

On the River and Marshlands

Maritime defense was also particularly important. The US Coast Guard helped local authorities secure canals and rivers that pass next to the stadium complex. Both teams stayed in hotels along the Hudson River, the same body of water that many fans traversed via automobile, bus, and train on game day. This was a perfect opportunity for the New Jersey State Police to show off a $1 million, state-of-art patrol and transport vessel purchased with Federal Emergency Management funds. The state police deployed one of their two Moose boats to transport security personnel, including its special operations teams, along the Hudson. The Moose—so-called because it is made by Petaluma, California-based Moose Boats Inc.—is a 13.4 meter diesel water jet-propelled aluminum catamaran that can reach about eighty kilometers per hour and stop "on a dime" (within a length and a half of itself) (Kraft, 2014).

The Big Data and Technology That Make It Work

An ecosystem of law enforcement, federal agencies, industry partners, smartphones, tablets, and more was built around one of the biggest events of the year. The undertaking involved an immense amount of information shared among numerous partners, from first responders reporting suspicious activity to movements of team buses. All of that information streamed into a command center, where the information was prioritized by analysts and a full picture of Super Bowl situational awareness was displayed on a centralized screen—or on the smart phones or tablets of those accessing the data from the ground (Corrin, 2014). "The idea is to collaborate among lots and lots of agencies and partners," said Anthony Beverina, president of public safety and commercial business at Haystax Technology, which provided threat-detection technology and cloud services (Corrin, 2014).

Big Data and cloud power played a role in keeping things safe. There were approximately forty different agencies, plus all the NFL and other commercial entities, working to make sure everything went well during Super Bowl week. A specially designed public information cloud was in use that pulled in the huge flow of raw data to help deliver meaningful information that enabled the various entities to collaborate, detect threats, and thwart potential issues (Booker, 2014).

The public information cloud helped New York and New Jersey security officials navigate massive amounts of data in order to find any possible threat. Just a few years ago, this would have been impossible (Terdiman, 2014). It is designed to pull in a huge flow of raw data—things like camera feeds, radiological monitors, radio-frequency identification and global positioning system (GPS) systems, and social media—and algorithmically bring the most important data points to the top. In other words, it is designed to find the needle in the haystack (Terdiman, 2014). Super Bowl XVLIII presented security officials with a far greater logistical challenge than anything Coons had to manage. Haystax's latest technology was at the center of it all, providing everyone from the incident commander in charge of securing the event down to hundreds of other essential security personnel with the ability to see what is happening on the ground (Terdiman, 2014).

All of the monitoring generated a massive amount of raw data. Without a way to deliver meaningful information to the people responsible for security, detecting threats would be meaningless. Big Data and technology—built around patented risk management algorithms that fuse lots information—hundreds and hundreds of feeds—and assemble them to find important risk elements (Terdiman, 2014). The goal of the system was to algorithmically surface the most important data points and deliver them to right decision makers. Much of that data was coming from automatic systems. But more was coming from personnel deployed at points around the area, sending back reports from their mobile devices. They were taking pictures of security infrastructure, cases of trespassing, unexpected protests or flash mobs, and more. Anthony Beverina, Haytax's president of public safety and commercial business explains: "We will process all that through our engine, and we will find through our algorithms know that's important based on what they know. We will present that to an analyst and that analyst says, 'I think there's a potential problem here'" (Terdiman, 2014).

The software pooled together data from thousands of law enforcement personnel reporting incidents and observations through an app, in addition to other tools like traffic cameras, Twitter posts, and GPS. It then prioritized the information based on importance. Analysts also filtered by information type, like only viewing suspicious package reports. All the most recent or most important pieces of information were plotted on a map that included Northern New Jersey and New York City (Farmer, 2014). In the weeks surrounding the big game, the map and incident reports were also available to cooperating agencies and other interested parties like New York Mayor Bill de Blaiso. In an environment like the New York–New Jersey area, with millions of people within a short distance of MetLife Stadium, the amount of potential input is mind-boggling (Terdiman, 2014). The immediacy of the available data has become better and better, but there's still a long way to go. There is still no system that makes it easy to stick together video and imagery using their time stamps. It has to be done by hand (Farmer, 2014).

The Role of Evaluators

What role do evaluators have in this Big Data story? Quite a bit, as it turns out. The Department of Homeland Security's *Homeland Security Exercise and Evaluation Program* (HSEEP) (Department of Homeland Security, 2013) provides a set of guiding principles and overall methodology for the management, design and development, conduct, evaluation, and improvement planning of exercises and events. Chapter 5 of the DHS manual, titled *Evaluation*, provides the approach to evaluation planning and conduct through data collection, analysis, and development of individual organizations' and jurisdictions' after-action reports as well as an overall report.

Evaluation maintains the fundamental link between the event and improvement planning. Evaluation is necessary to measure the success of the implementation and the security plans. After the event ends and the crowds exit, a debriefing and preparation of an after-action report begins. Supervisors and representatives from all law enforcements agencies and key partners are interviewed and asked to prepare daily critiques of operations so that details are not forgotten. The after-action reports include critiques of all operations including field operations, access point, personnel, logistics, equipment, communication, and training. The reports include deviations from the event security plan as well as recommendations what to keep, what to change, and how and why the changes should be made. The aim is to impart the lessons learned for the safety and security for future Super Bowls.

Much of the use of Big Data in the public sector focuses on effective public management practices, addressing the same type of questions evaluators have wrestled with for years. The expertise evaluators bring to addressing issues of public management is critical. Tricky research questions such as the distinction between causation and correlation, and the appropriate methods to identify causation are not solved by the use of Big Data techniques (Decker, 2013). Some of the tools may be different, but the fundamentals are the same.

Conclusion

A final story highlights both the Big Data and the need to connect evaluation with action. In London in 1854, a key work was established by Dr. John Snow, considered by many in the public health field to be the father of epidemiology. Snow analyzed his version of Big Data using pins on a map of London. Just as the GIS maps plotted the incidents at the Indianapolis Super Bowl, Snow connected the pins showing contaminated drinking water from the Broad Street water pump with the outbreak of cholera. Importantly, he convinced public officials to remove the handle on the pump so people stopped getting sick (Decker, 2013). And just like Gary Coons, he understood that his work was not just evaluation and writing a report. It was about putting evaluation to work to improve policy and well-being—a call to action that is as relevant today as it was 150 years ago.

References

Booker, Carilyn. 2014. *Big Game. Big Data. Bigger Cloud Power*. Accessed October 1, 2014. http://www.peak10.com/blog/post/big-game-big-data-bigger-cloud-power.

Boyle, Philip, and Kevin D. Haggerty. 2009. "Spectacular Security: Mega-Events and the Security Complex." *International Political Sociology* 3: 257–74. Accessed August 28, 2015. http://citeseerx.ist.psu.edu/viewdoc/download?doi=10.1.1.476.8759&rep=rep1&type=pdf.

Brennen, John. 2014. "Super Bowl Will Mean a Weeklong Security Lockdown of Meadowlands Sports Complex." Accessed October 1, 2014. http://www.northjersey.com/news/super-bowl-will-mean-a-weeklong-security-lockdown-of-meadowlands-sports-complex-1.586686.

Celona, Larry, and Jamie Schram. 2014. "NYPD Plans High Security on Super Bowl Boulevard." Accessed October 1, 2014. http://nypost.com/2014/01/27/nypd-plans-high-security-on-super-bowl-boulevard/.

Connors, Edward. 2007. *Planning and Managing Security for Major Special Events: Guidelines for Law Enforcement*. Washington, DC: Office of Community Oriented Policing Service, US Department of Justice. Accessed August 28, 2015. http://www.popcenter.org/problems/spectator_violence/PDFs/Connors.pdf.

Corcoran, Terence. 2014. "De-Fence! Security Force Girds for Myriad Threat." Accessed October 1, 2014. http://archive.lohud.com/article/20140115/SPORTS/301150068/De-fense-Security-force-girds-myriad-threats-Super-Bowl-XLVIII.

Corrin, Amber. 2014. "What Federal Agencies Can Learn from the Super Bowl." Accessed October 1, 2014. http://fcw.com/articles/2014/01/30/super-bowl-security.aspx.

Decker, Paul. 2013. *False Choices, Policy Framing, and the Promise of Big Data*. Accessed October 1, 2014. http://www.appam.org/false-choices-policy-framing-and-the-promise-of-big-data/.

Department of Homeland Security. 2013. *Homeland Security Exercise and Evaluation Program (HSEEP)*. Accessed October 1, 2014. https://www.llis.dhs.gov/hseep.

Farmer, Liz. 2014. "For Super Bowl Security, State and Local Cops Sharing Info at Unprecedented Levels." Accessed October 1, 2014. http://www.governing.com/news/headlines/gov-super-bowl-security.html.

Gehlken, Michael. 2014. "Super Bowl Security Get Extra Practice." Accessed October 1, 2014. http://www.utsandiego.com/news/2014/jan/29/super-bowl-security-terrorism-fbi-sochi-olympics/http://www.utsandiego.com/news/2014/jan/29/super-bowl-security-terrorism-fbi-sochi-olympics/.

Godfrey, Steven. 2014. "Super Bowl Security: Is the NFL Ready for Everything?" Accessed October 1, 2014. http://www.sbnation.com/2014/1/31/5361290/super-bowl-security-nfl-fbi-procedures-practices.

Hays, Tom. 2014. "NY-NJ Security Tight in Super Bowl Run-up." Accessed October 1, 2014. http://bigstory.ap.org/article/ny-nj-security-tight-super-bowl-run.

Joltsik, Jon. 2013. *Big Data Security Analytics FAQ*. Accessed October 1, 2014. http://bigdataanalyticsnews.com/big-data-security-analytics-faq/.

Kouri, Jim. 2014. "Covert Sniper Teams Part of Security for Super Bowl XLVIII." Accessed October 1, 2014. http://www.eurasiareview.com/02022014-covert-sniper-teams-part-security-super-bowl-xlviii/.

Kreft, Elizabeth. 2014. "*Sunday's Super Bowl* Set to Feature Some Intense Layers of Security Most Attendees Will Never See." Accessed October 1, 2014. http://www.theblaze.com/stories/2014/01/30/sundays-super-bowl-set-to-feature-some-intense-layers-of-security-most-attendees-will-never-see/.

McManus, Jane. 2014. "Super Bowl Security Takes Shape." Accessed October 1, 2014. http://espn.go.com/new-york/nfl/story/_/id/10232210/super-bowl-security-starting-take-shape.

Meminger, Dean. 2014. "Law Enforcement Officials Hold Briefing on Super Bowl Security Measures." Accessed October 1, 2014. http://www.ny1.com/content/news/202686/law-enforcement-officials-hold-briefing-on-super-bowl-security-measures.

Nilsson, Frank. 2014. "The Cold Weather Has Been the Strongest Story Line throughout the Entire NFL Season." Sunday's game will be no exception – behind the scene and on the field. Accessed October 1, 2014. http://www.ny1.com/content/news/202686/law-enforcement-officials-hold-briefing-on-super-bowl-security-measures.

Perez, Evan. 2014. "Homeland Security Details Super Bowl Safety Plan." Accessed October 1, 2014. http://security.blogs.cnn.com/2014/01/27/homeland-security-details-super-bowl-safety-plan/.

Police State USA. 2014. "Police State Extravaganza at Super Bowl XLVIII." Accessed October 1, 2014. http://www.policestateusa.com/2014/police-state-at-super-bowl-xlviii/.

Terdiman, Daniel. 2014. "At Super Bowl, Detecting Threats Is Like Finding a Needle in a Haystack." Accessed October 1, 2014. http://www.cnet.com/news/at-super-bowl-detecting-threats-is-like-finding-a-needle-in-a-haystack/.

8

Keeping Traffic and Transit Passengers Moving—The Use of Big Data

Peter Wilkins

Big Data is having big impacts in the transport sector. New uses are emerging for high volumes of real-time information that can underpin active management of the movement of motor vehicles and transit passengers. The same information can be used for planning, better informing users, and potential transport users and evaluation. Much of the aggregated data derives from large numbers of individual events that are integral to the services being provided, and it is this microlevel data that creates many of the new opportunities.

There are significant economic forces pushing governments to improve transportation systems. Traffic congestion is a major challenge for most large cities. Additional time taken for journeys imposes large economic costs and is a significant factor in amenity for residents and visitors. There are practical and cost limitations on the traditional solution of building more roads as a response to increasing traffic congestion so there are particular pressures to get better use out of existing road infrastructure and to grow the use of public transport.

Public transport in cities is seen as an important alternative to use of motor vehicles both to relieve congestion on existing road networks, to reduce adverse environmental impacts, and to reduce the need for new road infrastructure. There is also a priority on improving the efficiency of transit systems and their attractiveness to potential passengers. Providing better information to potential passengers is a significant factor in encouraging use of transit systems.

The McKinsey Global Institute (MGI) highlights transportation and warehousing as a sector positioned for greater gains from the use of Big

Data based on indications it has already shown productivity growth in the United States for the period 2000 to 2008 (Dobbs et al., 2011). It identifies that the sector has advantages in the relative ease of capturing the value potential because IT intensity is in the top quintile (easiest to capture) and data availability is in the second quintile.

The Organisation for Economic Co-operation and Development has given prominence to the need to understand and assess the options involved through the work of its International Transport Forum (2015). It notes that "...Big Data holds much promise for improving the planning and management of transport activity by radically increasing the amount or near-real-time availability of mobility-related data" (10). It points to the benefits of managing infrastructure assets such as roads, bridges, tracks, airports, ports, bus stations, and cycle paths and for operations, planning, and safety.

In addition, transportation has dedicated professions and extensive communication of research and practical experience. In this regard, use of information for planning has a long history, and there is a strong skills base to facilitate the uptake of new opportunities. However, it is also important to recognize that with transportation professions having a dominant role in identifying and applying Big Data solutions that the potential contribution of evaluation as a discipline may not be recognized within the transport industry. Transport professionals may be involved in evaluative activities such as ex ante, ex post, monitoring, strategic projections, and prospective analytics but not identified them as forms of evaluation. This is evident from an assessment of three major reviews of public transport electronic ticketing systems that make no reference to evaluation in a general sense (Mezghani, 2008; Pelletier et al., 2009; AECOM, 2011).

This chapter first overviews the uses of transport data considering traditional forms to enable a better understanding of what is identified here separately as conventional and innovative uses of Big Data. The distinction between conventional and innovative uses of Big Data is based on the extent to which the use is well established or emergent. In each of these following three sections, the uses of data are considered in each case for road traffic and public transport separately, with traffic being across all roads and all vehicle types whereas public transport includes government agencies organizing services along set routes on roads, rail, and water. This chapter then discusses issues and lessons for evaluators, these being the extent and nature of evaluative information regarding the use of Big Data; access to information on

Big Data solutions; identifying whether appropriate Big Data solutions are being adopted; and information privacy.

Traditional Data

Traffic

Traffic count data collected using temporary surface sensor loops has been a traditional data input in determining traffic control rules and signs. Over the last twenty years, real-time data collection through buried loops and similar techniques has enabled real-time control of traffic lights, for instance in nonpeak periods turning a light green on detecting an approaching vehicle when there are no vehicles approaching from other competing directions. Computer systems have been used to coordinate groups of traffic lights to improve traffic flows across road networks. Control rooms with camera monitoring of traffic flows and intersections have enabled manual and computer-assisted overrides of standard settings.

Traffic flows have been modeled for many years having become a sophisticated field with the advent of mainframe computers.

Public Transport

The traditional source of information for transportation planning has been the household travel survey supplemented by on-board surveys (Chapleau et al., 2008). Through this period, public transport had less sophisticated modeling of passenger usage patterns than road traffic.

Traditional approaches to ticketing only provided very limited information, it having been noted that "continual reliance was placed on more labour-intensive fare collection methods such as the employment of conductors on trams and staff at rail stations" (Auditor-General of Victoria, 1998: 37).

Overview of Current Practices in Big Data Use

Conventional Big Data

Over more recent times, there has been a rapid increase in the quantity and quality of data that can be collected and analyzed in real time on road traffic and individual vehicles and transit passengers and vehicles. This can be generated using technologies such as computer processing of camera images and sourcing Global Positioning System data from public transport vehicles. In addition to reducing journey times for the majority of users, these technologies can give priority to public transport buses and taxis and can assist communication about journey options and times to users.

Traffic

The more recent ability to process information in real time and access more sophisticated forms of data capture such as number plate recognition have increased the focus on active management. Lopes and Bento (2010) identified three methods of collecting traffic data: site data where traffic data is measured by sensors located along the roadside, floating car data where vehicles are located and recognized at multiple points in a network, and wide-area data derived from multisensor tracking systems.

In relation to GPS information, MGI identifies journey planning based on real-time traffic information as a major use of personal location data. It can include information about "traffic in real time, including accidents, scheduled roadworks, and congested areas" with some devices not only providing drivers with "recommendations on which routes to take to avoid congestion but also report back information on location and movement to a central server, allowing congestion to be measured even more accurately" (Dobbs et al., 2011: 88).

Government agencies involved in managing road networks have a range of tools available to them, the network management framework for one grouping of on-road management tools including lane use management and arterial road signals along with traffic operations tools for monitoring and provision of travel advice (Vicroads, 2010a). This framework identifies the importance of historical performance monitoring and evaluation, and identifies other tools that include variable speed limits and coordinated freeway ramp signals systems to manage freeway access (Vicroads, 2010b). In a recent planning document, the Western Australian road agency specifically identifies the importance of Big Data as it evolves Intelligent Transport Systems including intelligent infrastructure such as traffic signals messaging signs and freeway ramp signals (Main Roads Western Australia, 2014). It also notes the increased role of the private sector providing services to collecting and disseminating information to road users and observes that this is facilitated by moves of governments across Australia toward an open data approach.

The private sector actively markets Intelligent Transportation Systems that provide centrally controlled traffic signal intersections to improve the efficiency of vehicle movement through a city.

These systems collect information at signals, correlating real-time data and automatically regulating citywide traffic. Features can include detection of approaching transit vehicles to alter signal timings and can include speed limit enforcement, lane management, and accident management (Tropos Networks, 2013).

Big Data can enable provision of real-time information to drivers about traffic congestion and route planning. A user of Google Maps can overlay information on the speed of traffic on the road according to three categories: no traffic delays, medium amount of traffic, and traffic delays, and it can also display typical traffic conditions for the day of week and time of day (Google, 2014). The former relies solely on information about smartphone movements, but in estimating how long a journey will take combines the current information with historical information on journey times that combines its own information with information sourced from road traffic sensors and thereby reducing uncertainties where there are currently low number of phones moving on the route concerned (Palmer, 2014).

The smartphone apps concerned can also allow sharing of information between users in the same locality such as a crash or debris on the road, with these reports being factored into the estimates of journey duration (Palmer, 2014).

Public Transport

It was identified in 1998 that "Internationally, over the last 2 decades, the use of automated techniques for fare collection on public transport systems has become common with the level of automation varying from relatively simple ticket machines and token-activated barrier systems to, in more recent times, the use of smart card technology." (Auditor-General of Victoria, 1998: 37)

While the primary purpose of public transport ticketing has been efficient and effective fare collection, the advent of electronic ticketing systems and in particular smartcard technologies has enabled far more comprehensive and potentially real-time data on passenger movements than is provided through surveys. The information is of potential use to transit operators and planners with potential to compare planned and implemented schedules and adjust schedules systematically (Pelletier et al., 2009).

London's Oyster card is a typical contactless smartcard that requires users to tag on when commencing a journey and tag off when completing the journey. Other forms of electronic ticketing that are also contactless identified by Weinstein (2012) include credit cards (Seoul and New York), key fobs (Seoul), and mobile phone handsets (Tokyo).

Where the system includes tag-on and tag-off requirements, individual journeys can be identified, and where the user device is registered, additional information on the registered residence of the user is also known. This electronic ticketing information can be combined with information on transit vehicle movements to further enhance the quality of information available.

A study of electronic ticketing in public transport identifies improved information for transport planning as one of several factors for the introduction of e-ticketing systems (Mezghani, 2008). It notes that through data mining, it is possible to obtain network performance statistics. In discussing the exploitation of e-ticketing data, it notes that this can provide valuable information on the operators' performance statistics such as bus ridership, service frequencies, and arrival times at bus stops. In addition, data mining can provide information on bus, rail, cards usage, and travel patterns, which can be used for policy, planning, and marketing usages. Card-related information can assist in identifying the travel patterns for different groups of commuters including the mix of modes (bus and/or rail) and consistency of travel patterns. This is supported by the reported demonstration that information about individual passenger movements obtained by the electronic ticketing system in Seoul can be used to identify critical passenger transfer points that need improvement (Jang, 2010).

Information gathered for this chapter indicates that additional uses of the information can include assessing contract compliance where private operators are involved, assessing and improving schedules (for instance by identifying overloaded and underutilized services), identifying take-up of fare concessions, planning of bus routes, and improving connections between services.

Innovative Big Data

More recent and innovative developments in accessing and using Big Data arise in part from the rapid take-up of new technologies and organizations accessing information generated for different purposes such as sourcing GPS data from smartphones or comments on social media.

For example, the MGI report identifies urban planning as a macrolevel use of aggregate location data such as "information about peak and off-peak traffic hotspots, volumes and patterns of transit use, and shopping trends" and that "Singapore's public transportation department is already using 10-year demand forecasts partly based on personal location data to plan transit needs. Traffic agencies in the Netherlands are predicting traffic and pedestrian congestion using personal location data from mobile phones" (Dobbs et al., 2011: 92).

Traffic

There is intensive research into intelligent transportation systems. A particular focus is on connected vehicle technologies that include cars, buses, trucks, trains, traffic signals, smartphones, and other devices. For instance, the US Department of Transportation (2015) identifies that connectivity between and among vehicles, infrastructure, and wireless devices can have benefits to prevent crashes and to enable mobility and environmental benefits.

The use of data from one source can be used to benefit another. For instance, using publicly available data on bus location and velocity in San Francisco, it has been demonstrated that traffic signal phase and timing can be estimated fairly accurately using a few days' worth of aggregated data. It is argued that this ability could

> ... *be valuable in enabling new fuel efficiency and safety functionalities in connected vehicles. Velocity advisory systems can use the estimated timing plan to calculate velocity trajectories that reduce idling time at red signals and therefore improve fuel efficiency and lower emissions. Advanced engine management strategies can shut down the engine in anticipation of a long idling interval at red. Intersection collision avoidance and active safety systems could also benefit from the prediction.* (Fayazi et al., 2015: 19)

The ability to combine data from multiple sources is seen as an area of growing interest. For example, human mobility data derived from the GPS trajectory of vehicles along with analysis of social media postings have been combined to help identify traffic anomalies caused by accidents, sports events, disasters, and other events (Pan et al., 2013).

It appears that use of information about traffic drawn from social media is emerging rapidly as an additional source of Big Data. An example identified is that social media comments about the state of roads could shape advice on routes to avoid (Bleby, 2013).

New technologies also open new opportunities. For example, based on projections that there will be an increasing number of vehicles able to send and receive data. MGI identifies a potential toll collection application with lower overall costs than current electronic toll collections as "a mobile phone could locate the vehicle and tollbooth, pay the toll, and charge it to the user's phone bill, eliminating the need for separate transponder devices and additional bill payment accounts" (Dobbs et al., 2011: 91).

Public Transport

Work is underway to combine multiple sources of information including weather information, real-time information on public transport services, shopping intentions, and historic data to conventional information about roads and road conditions to assist users to plan their route and mode of transport, the project leader stating that "The app will know your train is delayed and that you have to, for example, buy some milk ... It will know from the to-do list in your phone and might suggest you can go to the milk bar five minutes down the road, come back and still get the train" (Bleby, 2013: 1). It is indicated that combining information can assist urban planners understand consumer habits and businesses such as a cafe near a train station that could gain extra sales when a train is running late.

Another example illustrating the power of analysis of a large smartcard database to compare Bus Rapid Transit trips with other bus-based trips identified marked differences between the two and supported the approach for evidence-based Bus Rapid Transit planning, service management, and infrastructure expansion (Tao et al., 2014).

It has been argued that the best candidate for the development of public transit travel data is a combination of smartcards, automatic vehicle location, a geographic information system, and other operational network data (Chapleau et al., 2008). This potential is illustrated by data presentations such as the location of travelers alighting at particular stops classified by fare type and the load profile showing the load between stops on an average weekday for a particular route at different times through the day.

However, it appears from interviews conducted by the author that systematic use of Big Data about public transport drawn from social media is in its infancy.

Innovation is not just coming from technical experts. A weekend program where teams of data enthusiasts are given access to government data sets resulted in a winning entry that sought to address the questions: What are the most interesting trips? How can we make public transport better or help people get more out of it? How can we improve the longest bus trips? What can we learn from looking at bus trips next to other data? The team used the electronic ticket data for the City of Perth for March and April 2014 that covered 16 million journeys made across bus, train, and ferry (BusHack, 2014).

Issues for Evaluators

The brief review above indicates that Big Data is used extensively in the transport sector and that there is considerable potential for this to grow, it is not evident that evaluators have in general been making an active contribution.

Given the central role of data processing to the contribution of Big Data, as secondary users of Big Data evaluators will need to be aware of the capability of current Big Data solutions and emerging trends in data capture and analysis, in particular, understanding nature of the algorithms that shape and determine decisions may be important.

This section looks at the broad issue of the lack of evidence of evaluators being active in the field of transportation Big Data and then considers four specific issues in light of the framework of traditional data and conventional and innovative Big Data uses. The four specific issues are data trustworthiness, access to information on Big Data solutions, identifying whether appropriate Big Data solutions are being adopted, and privacy.

Extent and Nature of Evaluative Information Regarding the Use of Big Data

While transportation sources make no reference to evaluation in a specific way, it is evident from the above that they are evaluating activities including ex ante assessment, planning and critical analysis, monitoring and ex post assessment of worth and value of their interventions. Ex ante assessment is often based on projection of existing data patterns, and the continuity of data flow enables rapid and real-time changes to be implemented. For example, it has been observed from a study that draws observations from individual case studies that while a number of benefits are expected from the implementation of e-ticketing systems, "only a few public transport networks have carried out 'a posteriori' evaluation of their system which makes [it] possible to compare with the situation before the implementation of e-ticketing" (Mezghani, 2008: 49).

It is also evident that Big Data can provide many different types of knowledge. Examples covered include technical knowledge, knowledge about real effects of public interventions, and contextual knowledge on trends and volumes that support better planning. Particularly important are insights into patterns of behavior by road and public transport users.

Exceptions are the work of independent accountability agencies. The work of Auditor-General in relation to the roles of government agencies in managing and delivering transport services provides a useful illustration of secondary use of Big Data. For instance, the Auditor-General of Victoria having undertaken a systemic study of the use of ICT for traffic management (2014a) states the importance of ICT systems in managing traffic flow and found that their deployment "... has not been strategically planned to complement broader statewide integrated transport and land-use initiatives" (2014a: vii).

There were specific findings regarding the availability of key data, including that trams and buses were not able to provide accurate and reliable reference data to traffic signal systems, and the Auditor-General recommended improved performance monitoring of deployed intelligent transport systems and evaluation of the costs and benefits of the further deployment of intelligent transport system approaches such as ramp metering, variable message signs, and reversible traffic lanes.

In a broader study, the Auditor-General reported on the coordination of public transport and found that public transport services were poorly coordinated. The Auditor-General made use of smartcard data on new bus passenger trips for five new bus routes in a case study assessing a service improvement initiative, but observed that the responsible public transit agency did not adequately measure the performance and impact of public transport coordination initiatives (Auditor-General of Victoria, 2014b).

A report by the Western Australian Auditor-General (2015) looked closely at projects by the State's road authority to address traffic congestion and highlighted that "...effective strategic and operational transport decisions require comprehensive, consistent and real time information" and concluded that while the authority "... collects a lot of data, coherent congestion information is limited to a small part of the freeway network, and not reported to [the transport department] or publicly" (6).

Other exceptions are cost-benefit analyses of electronic ticketing systems. For instance, an analysis of the smartcard system introduced by the City of Trondheim identified that authorities benefited from better public transportation statistics would have assisted planning and the scheduling of services but these benefits were not monetized and therefore not included in the analysis beyond the observing their existence (Welde, 2012).

There is not however a wider body of publicly available evaluations that assess the use of Big Data in transport planning and operation. Some performance information is available, an example being Regional Intelligent Transportation Systems Partnership reports for the Phoenix Metropolitan Area quarterly that involve the input of several partner agencies (AZTech, 2014). These measures provide insights into the efficiency of key aspects of the transport system, although not separating out the specific impact of the intelligent transportation initiatives.

A useful holistic framework for the assessment of transit-oriented planning developments includes travel behavior, economic context, the natural and built environment, and the policy context, with a suite of indicators identified for each element. For instance, travel behavior includes kilometers traveled by the vehicle, number of trips per day mode split, frequency of public transit usage, and residents commuting time (Renne, 2007). It is evident that there could be greater monitoring and evaluation related to Big Data in the transport sector and that evaluators could play a significant role in assessing the performance of systems and individual projects. These systems and projects can be of major importance to the community. Their operation is also of considerable interest, and in this regard, the quality of information used to underpin systems and decision making should be subject to particular scrutiny by evaluators.

Data Trustworthiness

In a consideration of traffic data quality and availability, a government road agency provides a reminder that reliable and accurate traffic data from appropriate locations needs to include a dependable traffic detection system (Vicroads, 2010c). More generally, IBM has added a further V "Veracity" to the traditional three V characterization of Big Data, this referring to the quality or trustworthiness of the data, observing that one in three business leaders don't trust the information they use to make decisions and that establishing trust in Big Data presents a huge challenge is the variety and number of sources grows (IBM, 2014).

Considerations of the quality and reliability of data become even more pertinent when Big Data systems combine information from multiple sources. For instance, how would a road management system weight and combine information derived from cameras indicating traffic flows from comments on social media apparently by users of the same roads?

Evaluators need to be alert for the potential for biases and a lack of representativeness of transportation Big Data. An example is the difference between a mobile phone app whose data are marketed to planners and city authorities to help shape urban transport policy that accentuates different bicycle routes than the Copenhagen city's own bicycle traffic survey, reasons given being that the app may have a bias in favor of recreational cyclists' route preferences and the type of bicycle commuter most likely to use the app. They warn that the use of Big Data by policy makers should be assessed according to the specific context and that in some situations

> ... *small, carefully stratified and representatively sampled data may be as, and perhaps even more, effective at finding solutions than the use of Big Data. However, for situations where knowledge is low, Big Data analytics may help elucidate relevant questions to ask and identify potential new directions for policy. (International Transport Forum, 2015: 21)*

Similarly, it has been observed that there is a big difference in geo-tagged tweets between iPhone and Android users that may correlate to income or race (or both) and thus may have real consequences when considering the use of smartphone-sourced location data from apps that only work on one of the two smartphone types. The example given being for an app that provides Washington, DC, authorities with automatic pothole detection reports based on signals from the phone's accelerometer and other sensors that would direct authorities to repair potholes only in those areas with high levels of iPhone ownership which would ignore nearly half of the city's roads (International Transport Forum, 2015: 20).

Evaluators could also be involved in cross-sector analysis of the role and impact of Big Data. For instance, there are differences in the mode and rate of adoption of different Big Data options between the traffic and transit sectors and understanding the reasons for these might assist organizations across a much wider range of functions.

Access to Information on Big Data Solutions

Given the central role of data processing to the contribution of Big Data, as secondary users of Big Data, evaluators will need to be aware of the capability of current Big Data solutions and emerging trends in data capture and analysis. In particular, understanding the nature of the algorithms that shape and determine decisions may be important. It is a significant issue for the public sector to determine whether it should own or at least have access to the algorithms that process the datasets.

Where the public sector is using information provided by the private sector, the private providers may not be willing to disclose the intellectual property in their systems and may prefer to provide a "black box" service. As an example, traffic mapping companies don't disclose publicly the algorithms that process real-time traffic data (Palmer, 2014), but it is unclear how much information is disclosed where a public sector agency is contracting to use the mapping service.

Heavy reliance on the private provider may be warranted if it is possible to closely oversight the performance of the system to ensure that the public sector can be accountable for what is delivered and what is achieved, they would clearly be preferable for the public sector to be able to understand how the system works and thereby potential opportunities and pitfalls. For evaluators, the degree of transparency may determine their ability to compare the capabilities and performance of different options.

Evaluators can usefully consider decisions made by organizations about disclosing or keeping inaccessible or secret various data. Illustrating an innovative approach, New York City reportedly released more than 200 high-value datasets to the public under a 2012 Local Law. It is noted that "Cities across the world, large and small, are utilising Big Data sets – like traffic statistics, energy consumption rates and GPS mapping – to launch projects to help their respective communities" (Larson, 2013: 1).

Identifying Whether Appropriate Big Data Solutions Are Being Adopted

One of the biggest challenges for evaluators will be assessing whether a transport system is adopting appropriate Big Data solutions, and if it is doing so appropriately. With relatively few evaluations undertaken to date, little guidance can be obtained on appropriate methods for undertaking evaluations in this area. Similarly, given the commercial interests in Big Data transport solutions detailed and comparative information is not in general publicly available. It is a rapidly changing area, so up-to-date knowledge and skills will be required to respond effectively to this question.

Evaluations should be able to address most readily performance of traditional transport data systems as these are similar to assignments in other uses of large datasets including human services, justice, and education.

However, where conventional Big Data solutions are available and in use evaluations need to be able to assess the range of options at strategic, tactical, and operational levels. Roles may include evaluating decisions on the solution choice, how it was implemented and the results achieved. In some cases, evaluations may benefit from developing their own analytic tools that harness the value of Big Data.

Recognizing the potential of innovative Big Data solutions poses additional challenges as there is the need to understand emerging technologies for data collection and analysis and identifying how these can be incorporated into an evaluation.

Privacy

Evaluators need to be aware of key constraints on the use of Big Data such as concerns about privacy as well as opportunities and how these are managed. The power of ticketing systems along with public concern about how the information is used is illustrated by an incident in Western Australia in 2009 which aired police use of information from the electronic ticketing system by police to track people's movements across the network (The West Australian, 2009).

Legislation that protects privacy or enables access to government-held information sets minimum requirements, with ethics and community relations being other considerations on the Big Data collected, retained, analyzed, and disclosed.

Legislation in individual countries is seen by some as less likely to have an impact on the type of data collected but that it can be important for the duration for which the data can be held and the extent to which databases can be merged, particularly where merging would provide information about actual itineraries of individual customers (Mezghani, 2008). Privacy concerns in relation to transport smartcards include the types and potential users of the information, who has access to the information and the implications of additional uses being provided through the smartcard have been assessed and legal issues related to the dissemination of smartcard data along with its storage, and encryption have been identified as important considerations in system selection and design (Pelletier et al., 2009).

MGI identifies concerns about privacy and security of information as a barrier to be overcome to realize the full value of personal location data. It identifies lack of clarity in law as to who owns the right to collect, aggregate, disseminate, and use personal location data for commercial purposes and makes the case for a framework that clearly describes permissible and prohibited uses (Dobbs et al., 2011).

Conclusion

Big Data is an integral part of the management of modern transport systems and its role and contribution to improving services and efficiency are likely to increase. There are therefore many challenges and opportunities for evaluators to participate in the transport sector if they are equipped to address the large and growing role of Big Data. They need to be aware of the limited role that evaluators have had in the field of transportation and yet the diversity of evaluation techniques used by transport professionals. They also need to be aware that there are differences that arise between transport sectors, as illustrated here by the differences in Big Data approaches for road traffic and public transport, and also the pressures to coordinate and integrate planning across transport sectors. The analysis in this chapter of the four specific issues of data trustworthiness, access to information on Big Data solutions, and identifying whether appropriate Big Data solutions are being adopted and privacy indicates the commonality of underlying issues across road traffic and public transport, and it is likely that these are relevant to transportation in general.

Lessons learnt by evaluators about the transport sector may usefully inform consideration of Big Data applications in other sectors as there are some common underlying concepts and principles.

Evaluators need to equip themselves with sufficient awareness of current Big Data approaches and emerging trends to be able to identify opportunities and how Big Data analysis might assist their work. From this level of awareness, they can identify the skills and knowledge required if Big Data is to be part of a particular evaluation.

As secondary users of Big Data evaluators working in the transport sector need to be able to communicate effectively with transport professionals who have specialized knowledge and experience. They may also need the skills to contract in specialized analysis and advice. As primary users of Big Data, they will need to have the advanced skills and subject area knowledge themselves.

References

AECOM. 2011. "Study on Public Transport Smartcards Final Report – European Commission." Accessed January 13, 2014. http://ec.europa.eu/transport/themes/urban/studies/doc/2011-smartcards-final-report.pdf.

Auditor-General of Victoria. 1998. "Automating Fare Collection: A Major Initiative in Public Transport." Accessed December 23, 2013. http://www.audit.vic.gov.au/publications/1998/19981111-Special-Report-59-Public-Transport-Fare-Collection.pdf.

———. 2014a. "Using ICT to Improve Traffic Management." Accessed July 14, 2014. http://www.audit.vic.gov.au/publications/20140611-ICT-Improve-Traffic/20140611-ICT-Improve-Traffic.pdf.

———. 2014b. "Coordinating Public Transport." Accessed July 14, 2014. http://www.audit.vic.gov.au/publications/20140806-Public-Transport/20140806-Public-Transport.pdf.

Auditor-General Western Australia. 2015. "Main Roads Projects to Address Traffic Congestion." Accessed March 26, 2015. https://audit.wa.gov.au/wp-content/uploads/2015/03/report2015_02-TrafficCongestion.pdf.

AZTech. 2014. "Performance Measures." Accessed January 14, 2014. http://www.aztech.org/perfmeasure/.

Bleby, M. 2013. "Big Data and the Quantified City: How Data Links Transport Planning with Cafes." *Business Review Weekly*, June 13, 2013.

BusHack. 2014. "BusHack Welcome." Accessed November 27, 2014. http://govhack.itmaze.com.au.

Chapleau, R., M. Trépanier, and K. K. Chu. 2008. "The Ultimate Survey for Transit Planning: Complete Information with Smart Card Data and GIS." *Paper at the 8th International Conference on Survey Methods in Transport: Harmonisation and Data Comparability.* Accessed January 13, 2014. www.isctsc.cl/archivos/2008/13%20B1%20chapleau%20et%20al.doc.

Dobbs, R., J. Manyika, C. Roxburgh, and S. Lund. 2011. *Big Data: The Next Frontier for Innovation, Competition, and Productivity.* McKinsey Global Institute. Accessed December 23, 2013. http://www.mckinsey.com/insights/business_technology/big_data_the_next_frontier_for_innovation.

Fayazi, S. A., A. Vahidi, G. Mahler, and A. Winckler. 2015. "Traffic Signal Phase and Timing Estimation from Low-Frequency Transit Bus Data." IEEE Transactions on Intelligent Transportation Systems 16 (1): 19–28.

Google. 2014. "See Traffic on the Map." Accessed January 22, 2014. https://support.google.com/maps/answer/3093389?hlen&rd1.

IBM. 2014. *Veracity: How Trustworthy Is Your Big Data?* Accessed January 22, 2014. http://www.ibm.com/developerworks/bigdata/karentest/veracity.html.

International Transport Forum. 2015. *Big Data and Transport: Understanding and Assessing Options.* Accessed September 18, 2014. http://www.internationaltransportforum.org/pub/pdf/15CPB_BigData.pdf.

Jang, W. 2010. "Travel Time and Transfer Analysis Using Transit Smart Card Data." *Transport Researcher Record: Journal of the Transportation Research Board* 2144: 142–9.

Larson, E. 2013. *5 Ways Cities Are Using Big Data.* Accessed January 9, 2014. http://mashable.com/2013/09/25/big-data-cities/.

Lopes, J., and J. Bento. 2010. "Traffic and Mobility Data Collection for Real-Time Applications." *13th International IEEE Annual Conference on Intelligent Transportation Systems.* Accessed January 24, 2014. http://ieeexplore.ieee.org/xpl/articleDetails.jsp?arnumber=5625282.

Main Roads Western Australia. 2014. "Intelligent Transport Systems Master Plan." Accessed November 27, 2014. https://www.mainroads.wa.gov.au/AboutMainRoads/Publications/Pages/home.aspx.

Mezghani, M. 2008. *Study on Electronic Ticketing in Public Transport Final Report*. Accessed June 17, 2014. www.emta.com/IMG/pdf/EMTA-Ticketing.pdf.

Palmer, B. 2014. "How Mapping Software Gathers and Uses Traffic Information. The Key Element Is You." Accessed November 25, 2014. http://www.washingtonpost.com/national/health-science/how-mapping-software-gathers-and-uses-traffic-information-the-key-element-is-you/2014/02/14/693606d4-9263-11e3-b46a-5a3d0d2130da_story.html.

Pan, B., Y. Zheng, D. Xilkie, and C. Shahabi. 2013. "Crowd Sensing of Traffic Anomalies based on Human Mobility and Social Media." Accessed January 24, 2014. http://research.microsoft.com/apps/pubs/?id=201131.

Pelletier, M.-P., M. Trepanier, and C. Morency. 2009. *Smarter Card Data in Public Transit Planning: A Review*. Accessed January 15, 2014. https://www.cirrelt.ca/DocumentsTravail/CIRRELT-2009-46.pdf.

Renne, J. L. 2007. "Measuring the Performance of Transit-Oriented Developments in Western Australia." Accessed January 24, 2014. http://www.patrec.org/publication_docs/53_Final%20TOD%20Indicators%20Report.pdf

Tao, S., J. Corcoran, I. Mateo-Babiano, and D. Rohde. 2014. "Exploring Bus Rapid Transit Passenger Travel Behaviour Using Big Data." *Applied Geography* 53: 90–104.

The West Australian. 2009. *Unwitting Commuters*, tracked by Smartrider. November 16, 2009: 9. Perth Western Australia.

Tropos Networks. 2013. "Intelligent Transportation Systems." Accessed June 17, 2013. www.tropos.com/solutions/Intelligent_Transportation_Systems.html.

US Department of Transportation. 2015. "How Connected Vehicles Work." Accessed September 7, 2015. http://www.its.dot.gov/factsheets/pdf/JPO_HowCVWork_v3.pdf.

Vicroads. 2010a. "Freeway Ramp Signal Handbook Chapter 1." Accessed January 13, 2014. http://www.vicroads.vic.gov.au/NR/rdonlyres/60FB9135-C232-47E2-B359-BAD10EBFD33D/0/FreewayRampSignalsHandbook_Ch01_WEB.pdf.

———. 2010b. "Freeway Ramp Signal Handbook Chapter 3." Accessed January 13, 2014. http://www.vicroads.vic.gov.au/NR/rdonlyres/CEDF69F8-6928-462F-B0DB-A050FD76857B/0/FreewayRampSignalsHandbook_Ch03_WEB.pdf.

———. 2010c. "Freeway Ramp Signal Handbook Chapter 5." Accessed June 24, 2013. http://www.vicroads.vic.gov.au/NR/rdonlyres/008F258B-74C5-4860-A630-8715F03AFCD9/0/FreewayRampSignalsHandbook_Ch05_WEB.pdf.

Weinstein, L. 2012. "TfL's Contactless Ticketing: Oyster and Beyond." Accessed November 27, 2014. http://www.bcs.org/upload/pdf/tfl-sep09.pdf.

Welde, M. 2012. "Are Smart Card Ticketing Systems Profitable? Evidence from the City of Trondheim." *Journal of Public Transportation* 15 (1): 133–48.

9

Exploring Big (Data) Opportunities: The Case of the Center for Innovation through Data Intelligence (CIDI), New York City

Steffen Bohni Nielsen, Nicolaj Ejler, and Maryanne Schretzman

Introduction

Recent years have witnessed an exponential growth in globally generated data (Russom, 2013; see also Petersson et al., 2017). The rapid evolution of technologies coupled with dramatically decreasing costs of storage has allowed for a burgeoning of techniques that instantaneously capture, analyze, and exploit these huge data repositories. As a result, investments in analytic solutions are on the rise (Kiron et al., 2014). We are in the era of Big Data.

The vagaries of a definition of Big Data are discussed in the introductory chapter of this volume. Suffice it here to say that Big Data is associated with high volume (amount of data), high velocity (speed of data), high variety (range of data types and sources), veracity (data integrity), and new forms of data processing (Laney, 2012). Most often it is the three to four Vs that are emphasized when talking about Big Data. Yet, it is the analytical techniques (the new forms of processing) that are emphasized when Big Data (using inductive statistics) is distinguished from other forms of data, for example, business intelligence (using descriptive statistics) (Minelli et al., 2013; Russom, 2014).

Breul (2015) has argued that Big Data analytics apply analytical techniques centered around three different inductive statistical approaches:

- *Predication.* Analysts explore relationships and patterns in the historical data, determining which combination of behaviors, attitudes, and characteristics is most likely to result in a specific outcome.
- *Association.* Analysts identify events that occur together and, given a series of events, determine what action is likely to occur next.
- *Clustering.* Analysts find naturally occurring groups in data that exhibit similar characteristics.

As such, a Big Data approach should comprise a collation of data with significant volume, velocity, variety, and veracity and apply inductive statistics such as predication, association, or clustering.

Currently, the notion of Big Data appears to be straddling multiple disciplines and sectors. Business intelligence in turn is a concept more often used in some disciplines (business administration, operations management, and business analytics), largely focusing on the private sector, but in terms of content is very similar to performance measurement and monitoring (Aho, 2010). These terms are frequently used in other disciplines (public administration, performance auditing, and evaluation) largely associated with the public sector.

It is not only in the private sector that investments and explorations into the cyber realm of Big Data take places. In the United States, the Obama Administration has financed an important research project to find ways that Big Data can help alleviate major societal and governmental challenges. In addition, a number of public organizations have explored ways that Big Data can support their operations, including the City of New York, the State of Massachusetts, and the European Commission.

Proponents argue that Big Data holds great potential for enterprises and governments to gain competitive advantage. Others have taken a more critical stance in response to the promises of Big Data (Few, 2012). Critics argue that Big Data has been hyped by technology companies pursuing new market opportunities by installing a sense that "we really need this to survive" in executives all over the globe.

Amidst high expectations, critical voices also ask to what extent Big Data is different from existing constructs in different disciplines such as business intelligence (in business analytics) and performance monitoring and measurement (in the social sciences). Whether the notion of Big Data is here to stay or not is debatable. But it remains certain that the speed and amount of data collected and the computerization of data analysis—and even decision making—are here to stay. It also remains to be seen whether it is only large operations such as Google, Facebook, and Twitter producing their own Big Data that will be able to exploit Big Data's potential, or whether other commercial and public agencies will be able to do the same.

Whether businesses outside the big social media companies and public sector administrations actually possess enough data—or have the ability and the legal possibilities to merge data—sufficiently to actually qualify as "Big Data" remains to be seen. In most countries, it is difficult, and even illegal, to merge personalized data across databases and areas for commercial or governance purposes.

Big Data and its required computational social science approach are likely to challenge the ways and timeliness with which policy analysts and evaluators have worked. According to Peter Daboll, Big Data will outperform evaluations because of these five tendencies (see Breul, 2017):

1. *Scope.* Much of today's evaluation is poorly designed. Either sample sizes are too small or scope is too big for validity of the data analysis being performed.
2. *Timeliness.* Evaluation is often irrelevant and too slow to meet decision makers' needs.
3. *Methodology.* Evaluation methodologies cannot adequately handle the complexities of the real world. Big Data is inherently complex and involves searching for and identifying patterns in large data sets.
4. *Competency.* Evaluators' skill sets are outdated. Many evaluators lack the fundamental quantitative skills needed for data analysis and integration.
5. *Attitudinal.* Evaluators lack the will to change. As with many industries with outdated techniques, the internal resistance to adopting new technologies is great.

These are major challenges for evaluators. As an industry of knowledge producers involving universities, consulting companies, independent contractors, and others, it is incumbent on the evaluators to embrace, explore, adopt, and adapt in this environment of rapidly emerging technologies.

What We Will Do in This Chapter?

While challenges may loom in the abstract it is, perhaps, in the concrete that we will find possible solutions. Therefore, in this chapter, we take a look at the analytical practice of a public sector organization that is at the forefront of research designs, using both evaluation and Big Data approaches. We posit that looking at its Big Data approach and the differences from classic evaluation studies, we will find the ways in which these approaches are either substitutive or complementary forms of knowledge production.

As mentioned, some public sector organizations have pioneered the application of Big Data analytics within the realm of public governance. New York City (NYC) is one of them. Examples of units tasked with such an endeavor are the Office of Strategic Planning (Feuer, 2013) and the Center of Innovation through Data Intelligence (CIDI).

NYC public administration carries a tradition of data-driven management that spans two decades since the introduction of COMPSTAT in the New York Police Department and similar STAT approaches that subsequently spread throughout the NYC departments (Behn, 2014). The tenures of Mayors Giuliani and Bloomberg, and currently Di Blasio, have strongly supported a performance management approach within which frequent data-driven performance reviews formed a centerpiece.

The NYC Department of Health and Human Services established CIDI in 2012 as a way to exploit the new opportunities offered by the emergent technologies of Big Data. While CIDI can currently be seen as a critical instance case study (General Accounting Office, US, 1990), it may potentially form the kind of informational context within which many evaluators will have to operate in the future.

The scope of this chapter is to explore how Big Data techniques can be utilized by government to embrace questions often asked in evaluation studies. The chapter is structured using the following format: first, we describe CIDI and its operations. Second, we describe a concrete application of Big Data and related analytical techniques. Third, we compare and contrast the approaches classically applied by evaluators to those applied by CIDI. As such, this case example of CIDI will be used to compare and contrast this approach to that of a classic evaluation. This approach is similar to Blamey and MacKenzie's comparison of two different theory-based evaluation approaches (2007). Finally, based on the insights derived from the case study, we assess the challenges created for evaluators by computational social science as applied in Big Data analytics and suggest appropriate professional responses.

The Center for Innovation Through Data Intelligence

The CIDI is an interagency analytic and research center in the NYC administration. CIDI is organizationally located at City Hall under the Deputy Mayor of Health and Human Services (DMHHS). The NYC Health and Human Services (HHS) is composed of seven city agencies. The annual budget for HHS is USD 2.4 billion. CIDI has six staff members and a team of interns and consultants. Staff members have experience with Big Data analytics. Their academic backgrounds include computer science, engineering, statistics, economics, public health, and social work.

CIDI's primary goal is building knowledge to improve programs and policies related to human services, including child welfare, public assistance, homeless services, and juvenile justice. The outcome goal for CIDI is to provide actionable research for City agency use to improve services for all of NYC's residents. CIDI reports directly to the DMHHS and works closely with a large range of NYC agencies to perform its work and ensure beneficial and effective results.

To accomplish this, CIDI's methodological approach reflects recent advancements in technology and social science theory. As such, CIDI has spearheaded developments within the NYC administration.

As in many cities, human services in NYC are provided through a number of government channels. Specifically, nine City agencies provide health, juvenile justice, and social services to approximately two million New Yorkers each year. It is no surprise that many clients receiving such services in New York are served by more than one agency. In addition, the most complex and critical social policy issues—such as teen pregnancy, juvenile delinquency, and healthy aging—cut across agency, regulatory, and budgetary boundaries. These agencies generate vast amounts of data on its services, its users, and the outcomes they generate. These data are produced and stored within the different agencies responsible for the services.

Historically, large bureaucracies such as HHS agencies designed outcome measures in a silo, based upon specific agency goals. For example, the child welfare agency measured time to family reunification of youth in foster care by using their own agency's data, but failed to use other agencies' data sets, such as those from the Department of Homeless Services or the Department of Corrections, to determine other relevant outcomes, such as if the youth later entered shelters or jail.

It is to address this issue and to collate large data sets that CIDI undertook to apply Big Data analytics. With Big Data, multiple agency data sets can be collated and used to determine outcomes from a more holistic perspective. It is also now possible to use multi-agency data sets to capture individual and within-group results and variations.

In CIDI, the Big Data analytical approach enabled the NYC administration to identify patterns of behavior that can be seen as early warning symptoms allowing for early interventions aimed at high-risk groups. In example, it led CIDI not only to identify groups of formerly homeless families at risk of returning to shelter and foster care youth at risk of juvenile justice involvement but also to design specific programs to match services with these clients' need.

Such opportunities came about with the ability to match large data sets (volume) with different variables (variety) across agencies, it is now possible to predict and measure outcomes regarding the future of the children, track them over time, and determine as an impact measure the efficacy of the agency over time. Not only are the children tracked and targeted for intervention, but also each agency can itself be monitored for its part in the client outcomes. In addition, proactive measures can be taken to reduce the risks of foster care youth from entering homeless shelters or jail.

Measuring outcomes across agency domains, such as identifying the number of children from foster care entering jail or shelters, allows for a more thorough and speedier understanding of the needs and patterns of vulnerable people. By using large volume sets of data to identify outcomes and make predictions, government agencies can quickly analyze and address emerging problems, breaking a cycle of chronic and multiple agency service use.

In order to collate data (volume) from various agencies (variety), a data agreement protocol was developed across agencies for the use and incorporation of integrated administrative data. The protocol established the legal authority for data use and the procedures for undertaking a research project in accordance with relevant privacy and data protection legislation and protocols. The protocol specified further that the purpose of data sharing was to enhance the efficiency and effectiveness of the delivery of city HHS to individuals, families, and children.

Each research project involves participation of affected agencies at every stage of the process to facilitate learning and subsequent use. Research questions and projects are discussed with the Deputy Mayor and HHS commissioners, where priorities are established and projects are approved. Then, work group teams are established; they are composed of subject matter experts and agency policy staff. Typically, these teams determine the best questions, design and method, thereby creating a collaborative learning process. More specifically, agency representatives provide the context of the shared data, which informs CIDI analysts' research design. In this way, agency representatives join CIDI in helping to maintain the integrity of all data. Staff members are skilled in Big Data analytics and CIDI reaches out to experts in a given field as needed to check on the proposed research methodology.

In the following, we will illustrate the CIDI operation to exemplify its use of both Big Data analytics and the more classical social science quantitative methodologies.

CIDI Case: Coordinated Collective Impact Strategy

Purpose

NYC has an area of 303 square miles, divided into fifty-nine community districts. Within these community districts, there are hundreds of neighborhoods defined by ethnic, racial, cultural composition, and socioeconomic status. In the past ten years, many community districts in NYC have experienced profound changes. This research project sought to answer the following question: *Which areas in the city produce the highest actual numbers of families both entering homeless shelters, children/youth entering foster care and increased number of live teen births?* The clear purpose was to identify high-need communities to execute place-based initiatives and to implement new policies and programs to support families living there. Upon review of various iterations of maps by officials, further questions surfaced about the actual city services designed for preventing family homelessness and entry into foster care in each community.

The work needed to be done quickly to allow the recently appointed Commissioners in the new governmental administration information vital to their placement of services. The data from the three agencies facilitated including neighborhood indicators from a cross-agency perspective. Program evaluations are typically determined by specific outcomes of program users; program impact on the community is not a usual measure or evaluation concern.

Using cross-agency data allowed CIDI to go beyond the simple viewing and evaluating of services from each program. Inclusion of measures on topics as varied as crime rate, educational outcomes, and well-being of children provides essential information for deciding where to locate services in specific neighborhoods.

At the level of government, Big Data allowed the NYC HHS to have an integrated approach to social service provision. Volume data allowed CIDI to measure the impact of initiatives on a wider range of community issues. This expanded focus would not be possible without the use of large data sets from various agencies, each of which addresses different aspects of social well-being.

Structuring and Planning

As an overall approach, CIDI used geomapping, as maps can illustrate with clarity and detail the important issues confronting a geographic area. In addition, maps allow the presentation of a myriad of data points in a way that is easily understood by NYC decision makers.

Knowledge about individual service utilization, as well as the infrastructure and resources that exist in a community, provides the framework to develop a comprehensive and coordinated approach to service delivery and reforms. This translates into a coordinated collective impact strategy that informs individual, structural, and macrolevel changes to strengthen communities.

Data Collection

Data were obtained from a variety of different sources:

- *Department of Homeless Services*: Number of shelter entries for families with children during calendar year 2013 (1/1/13—12/31/13) for each Neighborhood Tabulation Area
- *Administration for Children's Services*: Current addresses for the caretaker prior to removal for children in foster care (including abuse/neglect, voluntary, and PINS cases, as well as juvenile delinquents) with a spell start date during calendar year 2013 (1/1/13—12/31/13) for each Neighborhood Tabulation Area (data pulled March 2014)
- *Department of Health and Mental Hygiene Vital Statistics*: Number of live teen births from 2010 to 2012 (more information can be found here: http://www.nyc.gov/html/doh/html/data/vs-summary.shtml) for each Community District
- *Department of City Planning*: Shape files for mapping, as well as a list of facilities and programs contracted by various NYC agencies
- *New York City Housing Authority*: Building footprints for mapping and list of developments with highest number of incidents
- Google Maps data including photos on blocks and street level

Taken together this data set comprised a large (volume) data set, from a number of sources (variety), which was reasonably timely (velocity) and considered reliable (veracity).

Analysis and Judgment

CIDI currently uses ArcGIS® software by Esri, a mapping software program that presents information based on various geographies. The program also provides the ability to zoom in and look at the details of an area such as block or street. This type of visualization provides CIDI to analyze the information to decide on the top neighborhoods for specific indicator, for example, with the most foster care and homeless family shelter entries. In Figure 9.2, the outlined areas indicate the community districts with the highest number of live teen births. This visualization shows the confluence of foster care entries, homeless family shelter entries, and live teen births as a focal point indicating a community at greatest risk.

Utilization

In addition to using geographical patterns to shed light on the composition of presenting social problems, CIDI wanted to design a pilot program to include all HHS programs (e.g., child welfare, homeless services, and health services) relevant to a collective and coordinated community strategy: Collective Impact. The feasibility of such a pilot was further delineated using the maps to determine the exact locus of the problems within a community district. A drill down procedure further discriminated that in some cases, homeless families were not coming from private residences, but from residential treatment programs for families. This posed an additional impediment requiring that a community pilot include discharge planning for those treatment services that may exacerbate the homeless problem in a given area. In drilling down to the address level of a specific block, CIDI was then able, via Googles maps, to ascertain further information, including the condition of the building in question, adjacent buildings, and street conditions.

As maps were created and discussions held among key stakeholders, more variables were identified, adding richness and complexity to an understanding of the community. CIDI added more variables to the maps and narrowed the focus from citywide to borough level, and finally to community district, detailing all city services in the community, highlighting health-care facilities and transportation services. The selection of these variables emerged from another task force report that focused on immigrants and access to low-cost health-care facilities and city-run hospitals. This information was overlaid with the top five communities in each borough to demonstrate need (Figure 9.1).

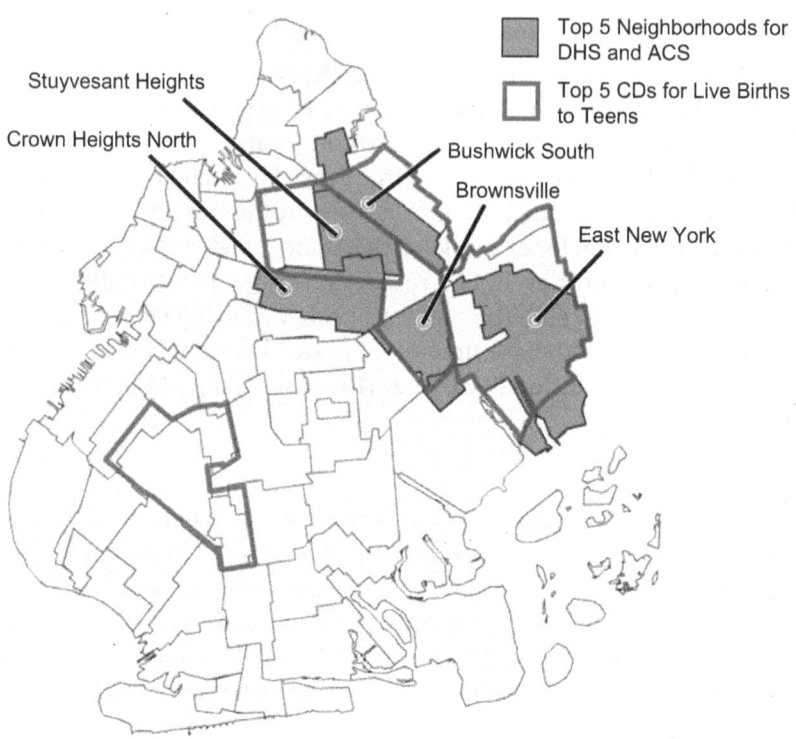

Figure 9.1. Borough Map of Brooklyn and NYC Service (CIDI et al., 2014).

The process for this pilot demonstration embraced both a community approach, which identifies the neighborhood's structural deficits and assets, as well as a targeted approach, which identifies those individuals at greatest risk for poor outcomes within that context, to assess a collective and coordinated impact in specific neighborhoods. The community approach often involves an educational campaign to raise public awareness on issues such as prevention of child abuse/negligence. The community impact approach weighs the structural deficits of neighborhoods, such as poor schools, lack of jobs and poor housing conditions, such as issues that impact residents. With a directed impact on the structural or underlying issues confronting a community, a community pilot can aid those areas at greatest risk, and intervene to change the trajectory of likely poor outcomes for the community residents.

Emerging thinking favors this dual approach, linking a community-based strategy, with a targeted approach, which focuses on the needs of those at highest risk. This two-pronged focus is favored as the most promising. It is probable that further understanding of the intersections of the "community itself" and "individuals within the community's risk pool who may experience a triggering life event" will lead to more specificity and sophistication of interventions utilized. The use of maps in this undertaking has enhanced our ability to understand the complexity of the connections of people to neighborhoods and neighborhoods to people (Figures 9.1–9.3).

An Evaluator's Approach to the CIDI Case

To shed light on the commonalities, differences, and interfaces between the Big Data and evaluation approaches, we present the case under discussion from the point of view of evaluation design and process. The CIDI analysis design in the above-presented case is based on the merging of various administrative databases and geomapping of areas with highest number of families entering homelessness, children and youth entering foster care, and live teenage births, analyzed with advanced statistical analysis techniques.

What would an evaluation design for the CIDI analysis project look like when designed by an evaluator?

Structuring and Planning

First, evaluators would seek to formulate the evaluation question(s). The fundamental determination of whether the question is descriptive, causal, or normative has strong implications for the chosen evaluation, models, design, and methodologies to be applied.

The evaluation questions for a project like the CIDI case commissioned to an external evaluator might well have been:

1. How do social problems such as homelessness, children and youth entering foster care, and live teenage births interact and thereby produce multifaceted challenges for families across generations in NYC? And
2. How can the city administration most effectively decrease the number of families troubled by these multifaceted problems?

Once the evaluation questions are determined with the commissioner, an evaluator would examine the existing accessible data. In this case, we assume that a data protocol could be established (although this may often not be the case) to access all administrative data from within NYC agencies. It is important to note that, without the very existence of CIDI, it may not have been possible to access all agency-wide data?

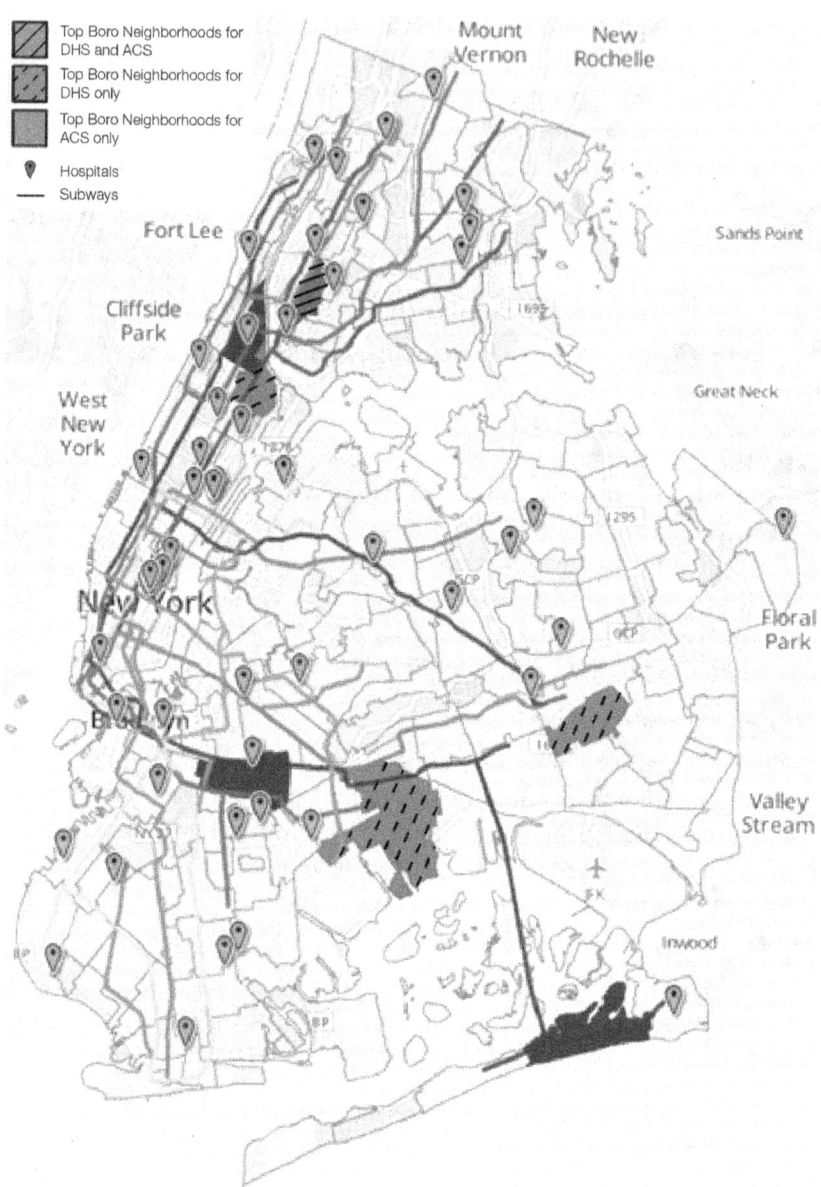

Figure 9.2. Map of NYC with Service Utilization and Hospitals (CIDI et al., 2014).

Exploring Big (Data) Opportunities

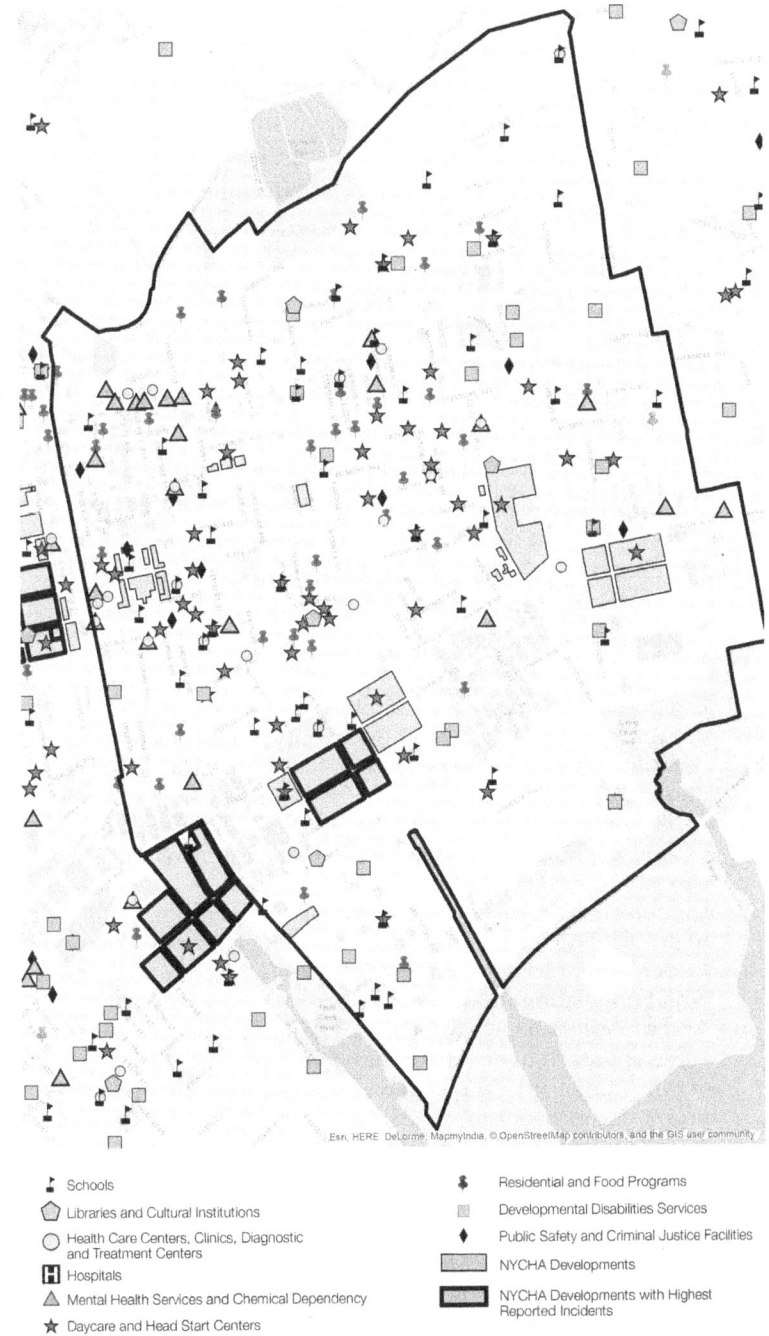

Figure 9.3. Community District Map of East New York City Resources (CIDI et al., 2014).

This data may not have been merged and accessible to evaluators, had it not been for the Big Data agenda? It is a huge task that requires a lot of work in terms of legal foundation, technique in merging various databases probably built in different ways, using various software, etc. It is important to remember that the processing and cleaning of such a high volume of data presents an overwhelming and costly task, and evaluators typically exercise discretion in their choice of variables.

Next, the evaluator develops the evaluation design. In this case, we may well choose a realist evaluation as the methodological approach (Pawson and Tilley, 1997). Realist evaluation stresses the importance of collecting and analyzing data to understand in which context, certain mechanisms lead to specific outcomes that have been triggered by a program. This kind of evaluation will require identifying the mechanisms, context, and outcomes of the program. Additionally, it insists on being theory-driven, placing the program theory at the core, which here implies reviewing the literature on how low social capital drives social problems that are reproduced through generations.

The evaluation design will include a number of sub evaluation questions to be answered, such as:

- Establishing client profiles (numbers of clients and possibly number of families not being served by the city administration, yet facing the same troubles as the clients in focus), number of shelter stays, number of re-entries, etc.
- Identifying characteristics of the families in focus—composition of problems interacting, family composition, history of social problems, education, work, and where the families live
- Defining behavioral patterns, rationales of behavior, factors leading to problems arising, and patterns of acting in response to problems
- Evidence on program effectiveness and efficiency concerning this target population
- And as evaluators, we will ensure taking an operational action-oriented approach to providing the client recommendations on policy, organizational measures, and procedures to strengthen targeted preventive measures to at-risk client segments.

In addition, within the context of realistic evaluation, we could apply a Contribution Analysis (CA) approach additionally identifying, by a theory-driven approach, potential alternative drivers giving rise to the observed outcomes. This would ensure that the analysis design robustly includes assessment of whether these alternative factors constitute a more likely explanation than the variables under consideration in the evaluation (Dybdal et al., 2010). Such potential alternative explanations could be, for example, physiological or individual emotional reactions to certain stimuli and stress. We would search literature for such potential explanations given by the natural sciences, medical and neuro research regarding, for example, health patterns, brain energy, natural reactions of humans under certain stimuli, etc.

Consequently, based on extensive literature review, the evaluation team would, develop a highly elaborated problem tree identifying root causes for the emergent social problems such as homelessness, entering into foster care, etc. Particular attention would be given to preventive and interventional programs that deal with teenage pregnancy and its correlates with the above. An additional particular focus would be the identification of contextual risk factors. These would be analyzed and a set of hypotheses developed leading to testing for the importance of various contextual factors (mediators and moderators) and rival explanations.

Data Collection

Data used in the evaluation might be collected from any number of sources, including the following:

- A literature review, which could be a Rapid Evidence Assessment (REA) (Burton et al., 2007) or a systematic review with the aim of establishing in-depth knowledge on the complex social problems to be evaluated, and potentially natural science (brain and body health) research included in the above-mentioned CA approach.
- Administrative records and more likely records from shelters, foster care organizations, and hospitals.
- Development of a manual for these vendors instructing the method for entering data in a format to ensure that the questions be answered and that data can be comparable.
- Interviews conducted with staff and volunteers in vendor organizations to understand client profiles, composition of problems, behavioral patterns, and services rendered by vendors. The number of interviews would depend on the budget and goals of the evaluation but should not be less than fifty to cover the three main problems in focus and a widespread geography of the city
- Interviews with a client sample to hear the client's voice. This aids in understanding the composition of the problems, behavioral patterns, needs, resources, and capabilities to take action. In addition, we would seek to understand conditions of families in the target group and how they handle their problems in the absence of support from either the public sector or private vendors. Again, depending on budget and the

- goals of evaluation, the number of clients to be interviewed would be established, again not less than fifty families.
- Workshops with selected frontline staff would be held at the end of the evaluation to focus on identifying best practice interventions based on practitioner's reflection.

Analysis and Judgment

This evaluation composed of large data sets of administrative data and a large number of qualitative interviews relies on a triangulation and mixed method approach to data analysis to ensure valid conclusions. Administrative data will require applying advanced quantitative data analysis techniques such as the SPSS program. Qualitative interview data will be recorded and systematically coded for analysis in NVIVO software, for example, allowing us to draw systematic data recordings for the various analyses in the analysis phase.

All evaluation questions that will deal with using a triangulation approach involve the utilization of several data sources to establish robust analyses. Qualitative data will support and guide the interpretation of the quantitative data and its patterns, while quantitative data will establish patterns identified through interviews.

Utilization

As evaluators, we will have a systematic view of utilization from the very beginning of the evaluation as commissioned by a City Administration keen to know more of the composition of problems, as well as how to effectively design interventions to significantly decrease the number of troubled families. Thus, data are collected and analyzed with this operational view in mind. In addition, workshops with frontline staff to identify best practice interventions will be conducted.

Communication strategy of the evaluation will be discussed with the client to ensure that the evaluation optimally serves the client's needs and goals. Different strategies are available to (i) develop one or more specific executive summaries aimed at policy-makers, administrative decision makers, vendors, and frontline staff; (ii) conduct seminars for selected actors; and (iii) design competence development programs for managers or frontline staff.

Table 9.1 provides the structure of elements in evaluation projects. This table is adopted from Nielsen and Ejler (2008), wherein characteristics of a Big Data approach have been inserted. This allows us to

Table 9.1. Comparing evaluation and Big Data approaches

Phase	Item	Evaluation	Big Data Approach	CIDI Case
Structuring and planning	Purpose	Negotiated up front	Agreed in planning cycle + ad hoc ongoing	Negotiated with Deputy Mayor
	Scope	Issue specific	Issue specific or what comes up by trawling data	Issue specific—but new data sets added on the way
	Budget	Separate budget item	Budget for Big Data unit	CIDI funded by NYC + additional funding obtained
	Frequency	Episodic	Ongoing	Decided as part of planning of analyses
	Timing	During or after program[1]	During or after program	During
	Units of measurement	Customized quantitative and qualitative indicators	Quantitative (big) data	Quantitative (big) data + geodata
	Type	Input, output, outcome, impact	Input, output (outcome)	Input, output, some outcome
Obtaining data	Data production	One time	Ongoing	One time—databases can be accessed again and again
	Tools	Desk research, interviews, surveys, information systems	Administrative systems	Administrative systems + geodata
Analyzing	Means	Data triangulation of multiple sources	Merging databases	Merging databases
	Tools	Contribution analyses, time-series, regression analyses, experimental designs	Regression analysis and other advanced techniques	Regression analysis geodata + coupled
	Attribution	Attribution of outcomes to program is mostly a key aim	Correlations ("big is beautiful")	Correlations

(Continued)

Table 9.1. (*Continued*)

Phase	Item	Evaluation	Big Data Approach	CIDI Case
Evaluative judgment	Tools	Benchmarking, cost-effectiveness, cost-efficiency, multi criteria analyses, expert panel, and many other	Big Data rules—correlation, not causality	Correlations
	Performance standard	Descriptive or prescriptive	Descriptive	Descriptive
	Assessor	External or internal program evaluators	Big Data analysts. Could be internal unit or commissioned externally	Internal unit (CIDI, involving departmental experts)
	Format	Evaluation report	Data report	Data report
Utilization	Organizational learning	Low to medium	Medium-high	Medium (learned about correlations that can be used for new and better interventions)
	Budgeting cycle	Occasionally	Ongoing (Big Data unit funded)	Ongoing (CIDI funding in budget)
	Users	Few	Some	Some
	Tactical decision-making application	Low, no current flow of data	High—a lot of data processed, can be accessed and rebuilt again and again	High—concrete data distributed to relevant policy-makers and decision makers
	Strategic decision-making application	Low–medium–high—depending on the quality of evaluation report	Low–medium–high—depending on what data patterns shows	Medium—some clear actions derived out of data

compare the evaluation and the Big Data approaches. The column on the far right provides information from the CIDI case to illustrate the learning from this example.

Conclusions and Discussion

In this case study, we saw the application of a Big Data approach as an alternative to a classic research design that would otherwise have been applied. The CIDI approach, led to an inter-agency accord that allowed the research team to collate and integrate a much *larger data set* from across the NYC administration (volume and variety) and also access data from *other sources* not previously used (variety), that gave in real time, a *more complete* picture of the challenges at hand (velocity and veracity) than normally provided by single city agency analyses. Also, the collection and collation of data not normally applied in evaluation was applied in the CIDI project (geodata). The application of a *GIS software* enabled multi-level analysis and the ability to analyze and report findings at these different levels (data processing). This approach enabled a more responsive reporting process that enabled increased instrumental use of results as decision support by the NYC policy-makers.

As evidenced by Højlund et al. (2017), evaluators rarely apply Big Data analytics. Therefore, we further constructed a hypothetical case of the design of an evaluation of the same case, using evaluation models and methodologies typically used by evaluators. The aim was to consider whether evaluative inquiry had processes, techniques, or overall models and designs to offer that could complement a Big Data approach.

We found that some evaluation tools and approaches such as CA, a focus on testing alternative explanations and stakeholder involvement in the process, potentially could have enriched the Big Data approach taken on behavior, motives, and rationales of clients. In conclusion, the Big Data approach has much to offer evaluators, but evaluators also have something of potential value to offer in return.

In the face of the rapid growth in the global data production (see Petersson et al., 2017), and the corresponding growth in computational advanced analytics, evaluators must come to terms with the increased competition of a rival form of knowledge production that promises insights quicker, cheaper, and more useful than those of evaluators. Whether these promises will be met, the remains an open question. However, in the adjacent discipline of empirical sociology, the challenge is considered profound and very real (Burrows and Savage, 2014).

Therefore, the evaluation community must face and address these issues. Effectively, Big Data challenges the landscape within which evaluators operate in many ways. Below we briefly address these, and how they were handled at CIDI. The challenges are further discussed in the concluding chapter of this volume.

Rival Challenge

As a *rival* with evaluation studies *for scarce resources*—much in the same way that the emergence of performance monitoring has challenged evaluation (Johnsen, 2013; Nielsen and Hunter, 2013). Frequently government agencies instituted performance management structures as part of their routine operations, they moved away from rigorous program evaluation; the data and evaluation staff that once conducted rigorous assessments no longer had the time to do both (Johnsen, 2013; Nielsen and Hunter, 2013). Much of CIDI's work has sought to impress upon the agencies the importance of rigorous, long-term evaluations as a complement to routine performance management and a task that could impose minimal additional burden while providing operational value. CIDI did a lot of work on anchoring the analysis with policy-makers by, in the design phase and subsequently during analysis phases of evaluations, responding to emerging concerns and considerations of the deputy mayor and commissioners as they formulated plans to address emerging issues. The CIDI process established working teams comprising subject matter experts and agency policy staff.

Complementary Challenge

As a *complementary challenge* in exploring how and in *which ways* evaluation and Big Data can cross-fertilize, the CIDI case demonstrates that Big Data analytics are relevant for even smaller data sets and can enrich classic evaluation approach. Meanwhile, this case also demonstrated that evaluation methods can enrich the computational method applied in Big Data analytics by triangulation of sources and methods. Further, the very establishment of CIDI highlights potential synergies between studies and streams of data.

Utilization Challenge

Utilization challenge, as evaluators find ways that evaluative thinking with its tools and processes, become central for learning and decision making. Yet, the evaluation of utilization research and the research into practice research has also shown that the instrumental and conceptual use of evaluation/research findings is possible, if supply and demand side factors are in place (Ouimet et al., 2010). By definition, evaluation exists because of some kind of intended (legitimate or illegitimate) use (Mark et al., 2006). This needs to be the hallmark and key differentiator of evaluators. In the case of CIDI, a close collaboration and process involvement of key stakeholders was integral to delivering actionable insights and reporting to decision makers.

Competence Challenge

As a *competence challenge*, as many evaluators do not possess the requisite quantitative skills. Findings by Højlund et al. (2017) and Forss (this volume) indicate that commissioners and evaluators currently have little experience with and demand for Big Data. Given the exponential growth in data production and its availability, this state of affairs is bound to change dramatically in the years to come. Evaluators must acquire the competences and embrace these new opportunities and insights offered. The CIDI case offers one example of seeking to embrace Big Data analytics and incorporating these techniques with evaluation use at the very core of what CIDI did. This required careful consideration to intended users' needs, careful planning processes, and tailoring reporting to their needs, including providing advice on how to make insights actionable. These insights may be the key factors in securing evaluators a place at the table in the burgeoning era of Big Data.

Note

1. Using Vedung's definition of evaluation, we do not include prospective types of evaluations such as ex ante evaluations.

References

Aho, M. 2010. "The Distinction between Business Intelligence and Corporate Performance Management – A Literature Study Combined with Empirical Findings." *Proceedings from the sixth annual Mini Conference on Scientific Publishing (MCSP)*. Presented at MCSP 2010 in Tampere, Finland, in February 12, 2010.

Blamey, A., and M. Mackenzie. 2007. "Theories of Change and Realistic Evaluation. Peas in a Pod or Apples and Oranges?" *Evaluation* 13 (4): 439–55.

Breul, J. D. 2015. "Using Big Data to Identify Success." In *Success in Evaluation. Why Focusing on What Works Will Increase Learning from Monitoring and Evaluation*, edited by S. B. Nielsen, R. Turksema, and P. Van der Knaap. London: Transaction Publishers.

_____. 2017. "Protecting America's Biggest Sporting Spectacle." In *Cyber Society, Big Data and Evaluation*, edited by G. J. Petersson and J. Breul. London: Transaction Publishers.

Burrows, R., and M. Savage. 2014. "After the Crisis? Big Data and the Methodological Challenges of Empirical Sociology." *Big Data and Society*, April–June: 1–6.

Burton, E., G. Butler, J. Hodgkinson, and S. Marshall. 2007. "Quick but Not Dirty: Rapid Evidence Assessments (REAs) as a Decision Support Tool in Social Policy." In *Community Safety: Innovation and Evaluation*, edited by E. Hogard, R. Ellis, and J. Warren. Chester, UK: Chester Academic Press.

Center for Innovation Through Data Intelligence (CIDI), N. Noyan, L. Pennig, M. Schretzman, J. Raithel, A. Basnandan, and B. Charvat. 2014. "Brooklyn Borough Map", "East New York Community District Map", "New York City Map", "Reentry of Families into the New York City Family Shelter System." *Unpublished*. New York, 1. July 2014.

Dybdal, L., S. B. Nielsen, and S. Lemire. 2010. "Contribution Analysis Applied: Reflections on Scope and Methodology." *Canadian Journal of Program Evaluation* 25 (2): 29–57.

Feuer, A. 2013. "The Mayor's Geek Squad." http://www.nytimes.com/2013/03/24/nyregion/mayor-bloombergs-geek-squad.html?pagewanted=all&_r=2&

Few, S. 2012. "Big Data, Big Ruse." *Visual Business Intelligence Newsletter*, (July/August/September), http://www.perceptualedge.com/articles/visual_business_intelligence/big_...

Gartner. 2014. "Hype Cycle." http://www.gartner.com/technology/research/methodologies/hype-cycle.jsp.

General Accounting Office, US. 1990. *Case Study Evaluations. GAO/PEMD-91-10.1.9*. Washington, DC: United States Government. http://www.gao.gov/special.pubs/10_1_9.pdf.

Højlund, S., K. Olejniczak, G. J. Petersson, and J. Rok. 2017 "The Use of Big Data in Evaluation." In *Cyber Society, Big Data and Evaluation*, edited by G. J. Petersson and J. Breul. London: Transaction Publishers.

Johnsen, Å. 2013. "Performance Management and Evaluation in the Norwegian Local Government: Complementing or Competing Tools of Management." *New Directions for Evaluation* 137: 93–102.

Kiron, D., P. Kirk Prentice, and R. Boucher Ferguson. 2014. *The Analytics Mandate. Findings from the 2014 Data & Analytics Global Executive Study and Research Report*. MITS loan Management Review, Research Report.

Laney, D. 2012. *The Importance of 'Big Data': A Definition*. Gartner. June 2013.

Mark, M., J. Greene, and I. Shaw. 2006. "The Evaluation of Policies, Programs and Practices." In *The SAGE Handbook of Evaluation*, edited by I. Shaw, J. Greene, and M. Mark, 1–30. London: Sage.

Minelli, M., M. Chambers, and A. Dhiraj. 2013. *Big Data, Big Analytics: Emerging Business Intelligence and Analytic Trends*. Hoboken, NJ: John Wiley & Sons.

Nielsen, S. B., and D. E. K. Hunter. 2013. "Challenges to and Forms of Complementarity between Performance Management and Evaluation." *New Directions for Evaluation* 137: 115–24.

Nielsen, S. B., and N. Ejler. 2008. "Improving Performance? Exploring the Complementarities between Evaluation and Performance Management." *Evaluation* 14 (2): 171–92.

Ouimet, M., P. O. Bédard, J. Turgeon, J. N. Lavis, F. Gélineau, F. Gagnon, and C. Dallairen. 2010. "Correlates of Consulting Research Evidence among Policy Analysts in Government Ministries: A Cross-Sectional Survey." *Evidence &Policy* 6 (4): 433–60.

Pawson, R., and N. Tilley. 1997. *Realistic Evaluation.* London: Sage.

Petersson, G. J., J. Breul, F. Leeuw, and H.B.M. Leeuw. 2017. "Cyber Society, Big Data and Evaluation: An Introduction." In *Cyber Society, Big Data and Evaluation,* edited by G. J. Petersson and J. Breul. London: Transaction Publishers.

Picciotto, R. 2011. "*The Logic of Evaluation Professionalism.*" *Evaluation* 17 (2): 165–80.

Stevahn, L, J. A. King, G. Ghere, and J. Minnema. 2005. "Establishing Essential Competencies for Program Evaluators." *American Journal of Evaluation* 26 (1): 43–59.

10

Using "Big Data" for Equity-Focused Evaluation— Understanding and Utilizing the Dynamics of Data Ecosystems

Kim Forss and Jonas Norén

Introduction

Big Data has become a catchy word for many different sources of information on everything from education, health, humanitarian disasters, entrepreneurship, statistics, politics, etc. Policy makers, program managers, journalists, evaluators—the world at large— appear spellbound by the combination of technical excellence (and incomprehensibility) and limitless use. The facts are overwhelming; sources such as online or mobile financial transactions, social media traffic, and GPS coordinates now generate over 2.5 quintillion bytes of so-called "Big Data" every day. And the growth of mobile data traffic from subscribers in emerging markets is expected to exceed hundred percent annually through 2015. This, in turn, is part of a larger phenomenon depicted by Moore's law that suggests an on-going exponential trend where computing power doubles every second year (Letouzé, 2012).

The recent development in this field has generated high expectations on future applications for data driven processes and its utility for a wide range of areas. For example, data collected through mobile devices can be a crucial tool in understanding population health trends or stopping outbreaks of epidemics. When collected in the context of individual electronic health records, this data not only improves continuity of care for the individual, but it can be used to create massive data sets with which treatments and outcomes can be compared in an efficient and cost-effective manner. Likewise, utilizing the data created by mobile phone use can improve our understanding of vulnerable populations and can quicken governments' response to, for example, disasters and natural catastrophes. Actors in the public, private, and development sectors are beginning to recognize the mutual benefits of creating and maintaining a "data commons" in which information benefits society as a whole while protecting individual security and privacy (Vital Wave Consulting, 2014). Such expectations are global and occur in all sectors, but perhaps the expectations are particularly high in the field of development cooperation, where paucity of data often hampers policy analysis and evaluation.

We refer frequently to the UN Global Pulse. This agency is an interesting example of a UN normative body, which develops a vision of a future in which Big Data is harnessed as a public good. The mandate is not primarily about development cooperation. The notion of Big Data as a public good is as relevant in Japan and Denmark as it is in Tanzania and Peru. It applies to all policy fields. UN Global Pulse is not primarily about development aid. The mission is to accelerate discovery, development, and scaled adoption of Big Data innovation for sustainable development and humanitarian action—wherever that takes place.

Purpose

If we are to believe the technocratic guesswork, Big Data has the possibility of revolutionizing the way evaluators gather and analyze data and provide policy recommendations. But will it happen? What is the demand for Big Data from the evaluation community and to what extent is Big Data being used in the evaluation of development cooperation at present? Issues of equity are often focused in evaluation of development cooperation, but to generate data on equity is a constraint and here Big Data implies new opportunities. Does supply meet demand, and if not, what are the problems? Institutional inertia? Lack of competence and capacity among those who commission and undertake evaluations? Or is it possibly so that Big Data is not as easily accessible or as relevant to the questions evaluators struggle with—particularly in respect of equity-focused evaluation. These are the questions addressed in this chapter.

Methods

In order to discuss these questions, the study analyses the demand and supply of Big Data. First, a sample of twenty-five evaluation Terms of References (ToRs) formulated between 2012 and 2014 is selected from international development agencies (UNDP, UNICEF, DFID, Sida, Norad, Danida, and the Millennium Challenge Corporation). We have to analyze the ToRs to find out whether the assignment and in particular the evaluation questions steer or lead the evaluation toward using Big Data, whether the assignment opens up the possibility for the evaluators to creatively use Big Data—or whether they rather close the door, so to say, for Big Data to be used. The result of this analysis of ToRs is presented in the entitled "The Demand for Big Data" section. The twenty-five evaluation reports are presented in Annex A.1.

Second, we look at concepts. What are we actually talking about when we talk about Big Data? Big Data needs to be defined. A mapping of the sources of Big Data describes what is actually there, how it is organized, how it can be retrieved and what costs it might bring for evaluators. This section of the chapter will be a critical examination of how accessible and user friendly Big Data is, and whether the promises outlined in the Background above actually are realistic. In the chapters that follow, we thus use the definition of Big Data that is developed in the "Opening Pandora's Box to Unpack Big Data" section.

Following that, the same sample of twenty-five evaluations is again analyzed, but now looking at the evaluations rather than the ToRs. In this section, we have analyzed what the evaluators actually did (rather than what they were asked to do). One of the questions is what kind of data they have used, and in particular if anything that looks like Big Data could be found. However, the analysis goes one step further and asks the question of whether Big Data could have been used. This is a difficult question that can only get a hypothetical answer, but if we are to understand the opportunities as well as the constraints to use Big Data, some such "evaluability" analysis is necessary. The evaluations we have used both for the study of ToRs and for methods were equity focused and were sound professional studies, considered as examples of good practice.

The analysis in steps 1 and 3 looked at evaluations in development cooperation. Perhaps this policy field is atypical—evaluation in other policy (domestic) domains may have greater opportunities and less constraints to use Big Data. We interviewed a sample of representatives from other agencies in Sweden and present the findings in the concluding discussion.¹ While our purpose is to understand demand and supply of Big Data in equity focused impact evaluation in development cooperation, we are also interested in comparing this sector to others, not the least to see whether there is a learning potential.

Based on these analytical steps, the chapter concludes with a discussion of what the real opportunities are for Big Data in evaluation, and what can be done to facilitate the use of Big Data.

The Demand for Big Data

As mentioned above, we have approached the question of demand by looking at ToRs as that is where demand for data and method is explicitly articulated and easily accessible. We selected a sample of twenty-five ToRs, formulated by major donor agencies. These represent sectors and evaluation topics where the evaluations are meant to pursue impact, and we have chosen projects where you would expect that questions about equity would play a major role in the assessment of worth and merit. The ToRs do indeed also ask the evaluation teams to assess equity—but not with the use of Big Data. We do not think it is likely that our sample is biased, as we have examples from several agencies, different sub-sectors, as well as examples of summative and formative evaluations, policy, program and project evaluations, and midterm reviews. It is a portfolio of evaluations that appear quite typical of how equity focused evaluations that assess impact are commissioned from developing agencies in 2014.

The analysis of ToRs point to some interesting factors that appear to shape whether Big Data will be used in an evaluation or not.

- Seventy-six percent of the ToRs contain rather detailed prescriptions for evaluation design and for the choice of data collection methods.
- Twenty-four percent of the ToRs leave the choice of methods and the design of the evaluation free for the evaluators to either propose in an inception report (to be approved by the commissioning agency) or for the evaluation team to decide.
- In no case did we see that the ToRs expressed any interest in using Big Data, nor did the ToRs steer the evaluation teams to explore such opportunities.
- The most common choice of design,² following from and often explicitly prescribed by the ToRs, is narrative case studies (forty-six percent) followed by theory-based designs (eighteen percent) and experimental designs (sixteen percent).
- None of the twenty-five ToRs make any reference to Big Data as a potential source of information that could be used in the analysis—not even as a supplementary body of evidence within a framework

of triangulation, although the ToRs do express that the evaluations should use mixed methods or triangulation.

The ToRs are prescriptive and leave little leeway for evaluation teams to be innovative. First, the ToRs set very specific questions. Second, the ToRs prescribe the overarching design, even though that may not influence the choice whether to use Big Data or not. Big Data could presumably be used as much in experimental design as in theory-based or narrative case designs. The elaboration of questions could be more confining though. Most of the ToRs refer to the OECD evaluation criteria: efficiency, effectiveness, impact, sustainability, and relevance. However, the detailed questions focus much more on the processes of delivery and management whereas Big Data would primarily feature in the analysis of impact and relevance. Most of the twenty-five evaluations have ToRs that emphasize process aspects and de-emphasize impact analysis and consequently partly close the door for the gathering and utilization of Big Data. The following examples illustrate how the ToRs steer the choice of design and methods:

> *The midterm review will start with review of the available related national, local and UN/UNDP programme policies, strategies, frameworks, programme documents, work plans, manuals, and reports. This will be followed by visits and meetings with the key actors in public, private and CSO sectors at national, regional and local levels. Field visits are to be undertaken to sample no less than six cities.... There will be several interviews and consultations to be conducted with the focused groups and beneficiaries. Data and information to be collected should be evidence-based, as well as qualitative and quantitative in nature.*[3]
>
> *New primary data will be collected mainly through visits to the key Norwegian actors and field studies in the selected countries, limited to the priority issues and a sample of programs or projects. The evaluation will be based also on secondary data in the form of program documents, both collected by the 2006-evaluation team, and by comparing documents and other types of evidence produced during the OfD-period.*[4]
>
> *The purpose of phase II is to collect and analyse field data in order to draw lessons from Sida's support to innovation systems and innovative clusters within its research cooperation, concerning results as well as modalities/work methods used. A total of eight person weeks of work is estimated for this phase. During phase II, the Team-consultants will collect and analyse quantitative and qualitative data in Uganda, Mozambique, Tanzania, Kenya and in Nicaragua and Bolivia.*[5]

Not only do these ToRs give quite specific directives on methods, they provide a detailed workplan for what the evaluators are to do. Under such circumstances it is neither possible nor feasible to explore opportunities to use Big Data.

Two cases have been identified where evaluators made use of some form of Big Data (to be defined in next section). In one case did this follow from specifications in the ToR, and in the other case it was *not* specified in the ToR. The ToRs for the Sida evaluation of support to Public Sector Management Reform[6] specify that; ....*the study will be based on the collection of data from secondary sources such as CPIA, PEFA (6) and HIPC (possibly complemented by other sources such as the Open Budget Index, the Global Integrity Index, etc.) for PFM systems, and on DAC/CRS, PLAID, donor databases and reports, etc. for donor support. Data for control variables will also be collected from existing reputable sources (WDI, PolitylV, etc.)*

In summary, the evidence here indicates that there is no strong demand for Big Data either as a main source of information or as supplementary information in these twenty-five examples of equity-focused evaluations. It is only in two cases that the evaluation teams use Big Data (in the form of public statistics) for their analysis. In these two cases, Big Data account for an important part of the analysis and of the arguments around impact. In one case did the commissioning agency prescribe the data sources, including Big Data, and in the other case, the commissioning agency left no such prescriptions—but in contrast to the majority of ToRs, it did not detail the evaluation process in such a way as to exclude Big Data.

Opening Pandora's Box to Unpack Big Data

In order to approach the questions stated in this paper and unpack the concept of Big Data, it is necessary to understand more about "Big Data," and how the phenomenon has been defined and/or can be analyzed. In the absences of a universal definition, there seems to exist a certain degree of confusion in regard to what Big Data should encapsulate. Despite the described confusion, there is however an emerging consensus on intrinsic drivers of the phenomenon. Besides the exponential growth of computing power, increases in volume, velocity, and variety of data are widely regarded to provide the foundation of the Big Data paradigm.[7] For a more detailed discussion on the definition of Big Data, see the Introduction chapter of this book or Chapter 2.

Another aspect of Big Data relates to how the actual data is being stored. Basically, there is data that is stored in a structured fashion, and then there is data that is stored in an unstructured manner. While structured data usually has undergone some form of a process/analysis, unstructured data relates to untapped data in exhaust sources.[8] The Big Data paradigm can be viewed as an umbrella movement with aim and purpose to make sense and operationalize unstructured data.[9]

Some scholars are, furthermore, of the opinion that the size/volume of data is of secondary importance. Big Data is believed to be of interest not so much due to its vast size, but rather because the introduction of new analytical technics to processes data together with the fact that data is increasingly interconnected to other data sources (Nielsen et al., 2014). According to these scholars, the prime value lies in the patterns that can be extracted from connecting different data sets (Crawford et al., 2011). In other words, the main potential lies in application and utility of data rather than the actual size of the same. As a consequence, the accessibility to data is of the essence. Improved access to public data is therefore another aspect, considered by many as a vital part for Big Data to be/become useful.

It is evident that views and opinions differ in regards to what Big Data is and what it should encapsulate. Most would argue that Big Data usually relates to the fact that new data is produced as a bi-product of digital interaction, rather than data that are made accessible through proliferation policies. However, in this chapter, we have chosen to have an open mind in regard to what should be labeled as Big Data. Based on the understanding from a literature review, we have established an analytical framework with four different categories of Big Data.

The selection criteria for the analytical framework are based on how the data is entered into databases, how it is stored and how it is utilized. The four categories based on the mentioned characteristics for Big Data are as follows.

- *Active driven data*—unstructured data[10] that is *intentionally* stored by users of a specific system. UN Global Pulse metaphorically describes this as "what people say" (Letouzé, 2012). Examples on how evaluations can benefit include: metadata models and discourses on social media (e.g. crowdsourcing/mobile data collection, participatory statistics). Tools such as Radian6, Sensmaker, and Ushaidi can give additional insights to evaluations and value through deductive approaches of social media modalities.

- *Passive driven data*—unstructured data that is *unintentionally* stored by users of a specific system. UN Global Pulse describes this as "what people do." Identified examples for evaluations that fall in this category are methods using, for example, location data and search queries (e.g. estimations on socioeconomic patterns and migration using cell phone records) Soto et al. (2012), Blumenstock (2012) and Talbot (2012). Data exhaust sources such as mobile phone records, financial transactions, and tools such as Google trends and Google search can give evaluations additional insights (Hilbert, 2013).
- *Algorithm driven data (i.e. machine to machine communication)*— unstructured data that is actively and *intentionally* stored by non-human entities. Examples for evaluations include satellite imagery that has been used to estimate economic growth (Henderson et al., 2009). Discussion on intelligent infrastructure and remote sensing is on going (Colville, 2013). Data from surveillance footage, cell-tower triangulation, and different types of survey drones are theoretically available and could be of value for evaluations with specific needs.
- *Public Statistics (or open data)*—usually structured data that is actively entered into databases by specific actors and individuals. Public statistics, which constitute the fourth category, is in many instances not regarded as Big Data per se since it lacks aspects of the mentioned required characteristics. However, we chose to include Public statistics as a category mainly because we share and believe that the possibility for interconnection of data is equally important as Volume, Velocity, and Variety—particular for evaluations within development cooperation. Examples include traditional evaluation data—primary data (collected via reviews, surveys, interviews, focus groups etc.) and secondary data (public statistics, scientific papers etc.). An increased proliferation and transparency of public data in many countries have allowed for data to be interconnected in new ways and on an increasing scale.

Shortcomings Obscuring the Potential of Using Big Data

Big Data, as categorized above, is deemed to be difficult, if not impossible to attain for the general public. This relates particularly to *active-, passive- and algorithm* driven data. The main reason for this difficult/limited accessibility is first and foremost that the lion's share is privately owned. Data is usually regarded as a valuable commodity and important driver of the global information economy. As a result, access to data that could be put to use in public services such as evaluations, is restricted (Bradshaw, 2014). In addition, access to the greater bulk of public data is also restricted and regulated by national polices and laws.

Usage of data submitted via Twitter can shed light on the limited access to the category of *Active driven data*. A limited degree of

Twitter´s accumulated data, in form of user tweets, is made available to the general public. In some cases, researchers can enter agreements with Twitter and get wider access to a so-called "firehose." However, only personnel at the actual company are expected to have full access. *Passive- and algorithm driven data* is believed to be equally or even more difficult to access. Spitz (2012) demonstrated this in his attempt to access his personal data collected and stored by a German telecom company that handled data under the European directive for retention of data (EU, 2006).

A third problematic aspect that is raised in the literature relates to a broad lack of capacity and competence among potential users of Big Data. Manyika et al. (2011) estimate that there will be a shortage of competence necessary to take full advantage of the Big Data paradigm; in particular, expertise for statistics and machine learning, but also talented analysts who can make sense and use of processed data. The gap between demand for talent and supply of the same is expected to be global at scale.

Big Data sources are furthermore considered in some camps to be methodological supreme and less troubled by methodological flaws. Mainly due to its reliance on numbers and "neutral data," which arguably makes scientific methods obsolete (Letouzé, 2013, 2014). This has been rightly criticized and recent research suggests quite the opposite due to the limited insight in the intrinsic infrastructure of Big Data. Twitter can, once more, illustrate this point since there are many uncertainties and unknowns when it comes to the data quality from actors such as Twitter. The data coverage is unclear as well as how the data architecture and algorithms are shaping the data. Crawford et al. (2011) state that:

> *Big Data offers the humanistic disciplines a new way to claim the status of quantitative science and objective method. It makes many more social spaces quantifiable. In reality, working with Big Data is still subjective, and what it quantifies does not necessarily have a closer claim on objective truth—particularly when considering messages from social media sites.*
>
> *Big Data tools and sources are often based on meta data and deductive reasoning, which has proven to be a solid approach to identify correlation. However, lack of insight in a/the specific context has also proven to lead to shortcomings when it comes to ambitions to capture and understand causation. Spurious connections are likely to be neglected. Thus, Big Data needs, as most analytical practices, to be complemented with deeper knowledge and insights of the issues being*

scrutinized (Majewski et al., 2013; Crawford, 2013). By and large, there are good reasons to question and critically assess the reliability and validity when using Big Data sources.

So how easy is it to question and critically assess Big Data? It is not easy at all. In the long run, one of the really important shortcomings of Big Data is the lack of transparency around how it is generated. When an evaluator does not know how data is generated it is not possible to defend reliability and validity. This primarily affects *passive- and algorithm*-driven data, to a lesser extent *active* driven data and even less public data—though this obviously varies from one source to the other. The question is if the large firms owning data are likely to make available information on how data is obtained and stored? In view of commercial interests, it is perhaps not so likely, but as a consequence the use of Big Data for serious research and evaluation will suffer.

The Use of Big Data in Evaluation—A Snapshot 2014

Our review of the demand for Big Data in evaluations showed that clients/commissioning agencies rarely express any such demand. Instead, they request a number of other forms of data collection that close the door for evaluators to pursue and experiment with Big Data.

In our sample of evaluations, no more than two evaluations used what might be called Big Data in accordance with our definitions. However, in both these evaluations did the evaluators use the kind of data labeled as public statistics above—and though this might in one sense be called Big Data, it is not the same as *active-, passive- or algorithm* driven data that often come to mind when people speak of Big Data. The two evaluations that used Big Data were:

- Evaluation of Results-based aid in Education in Rwanda (DFID, not specified in ToR)
- Evaluation of Donor Support to Public Financial Management Reform (Sida, data collection specified in ToR)

Big Data was one of several data sources, in both cases. The evaluations adopted a mixed methods approach and used triangulation from several data sources to analyze the phenomena being evaluated. Big Data was a significant element in the analysis and the conclusions and recommendations would have looked much less "evidence-based" without these sources of information. Furthermore, there is no indication that these evaluations were more costly than others, or that

Big Data took an inordinate share of evaluation expenditures. On the contrary, the most expensive parts of the evaluation are likely to have been preparatory, and the site visits and interviews, and report writing. The actual work on the open data sources such as PEFA would have been a minor share of total costs.

The question is if the other evaluations could have made better use of Big Data? It was, after all, only two out of twenty-five that made use of Big Data. Would the others have been more solid and interesting if they had used Big Data. Could the evaluation process itself have been more efficient?

We have looked at the projects/programs that were evaluated and we have asked ourselves if it is possible to imagine that Big Data could have a role to play in evaluation. This is of course a very hypothetical discussion and we cannot arrive at more than guesstimates. Nonetheless, we would say that in at least twenty of the twenty-three evaluations would it be possible to conceive that one or several of the listed categories of Big Data could play a role in the analysis. For example:

- UNICEF's Final Evaluation of the Millennium Development Goal Achievement Fund: Youth Employability and Retention Programme. The Youth Employability and Retention Program (YERP) aimed to address the problems of high youth unemployment and irregular youth migration in BiH. The program built on close cooperation between government authorities, the private sector and civil society to improve the employability of BiH youth while providing new entry points to the labor market. Furthermore, within the scope of YERP, internal and external migration support was being developed to optimize the potential of migration as an individual employment-seeking strategy that can alleviate local labor market pressures. In theory, it would be possible to consider a number of indicators concerning youth employability and retention, as, for example, analysis of social media, crowdsourcing, participatory surveys as exemplified above. Similarly, in theory, it would be possible to use passive driven data, to find out what people do in terms of job search, relocation, migration, etc.
- Norad's Evaluation of Norway's Bilateral Agricultural Support to Food Security is another example of an evaluation assignment that could have made use of Big Data. In the more "starry-eyed" literature on Big Data and how wonderful it is, the authors often point to the potential use of Big Data to predict food shortages. The logic is that a number of indicators of *passive-* and *algorithm* driven data accurately show the early signs of a looming humanitarian crisis. Hence, if such data exist and would be accessible, it could presumably also be used to assess the effectiveness of interventions to "stem the tide." The projects otherwise had an aim that suggests Big Data would be

available. The final beneficiaries were either smallholders that were reached directly through agriculture, food security, or livelihood programs, or indirectly and in a long-term perspective through research programs with a focus on innovation. But the evaluators conclude that despite the fact that the majority of the selected programs were likely to contribute to enhanced food security, evidence of such a contribution could be established in only a few cases, due to a lack of systematic measuring. That being said, there is no indication that the evaluation team tried to get data (neither big nor small) of any kind to support the conclusions. Hence, the evidence of actual contribution was strongest for food availability and weakest for food utility. With regard to food availability (increased food production), evidence of contribution was found in a considerable number of cases. However, this was not the case with regard to increased food accessibility, despite the fact that, to a large extent, the sampled programs were likely to lead to increased food accessibility. That evidence was based on project documentation and selected interviews with project personnel, and hence quite dubious as evidence. The evaluation team responded to what the ToRs asked for and did not have any choice to look for other data sources, but it does seem likely that an innovative use of Big Data could have supplemented the project data and the selected interviews that the report was based on (as stipulated by the ToR).

- The Millennium Challenge Corporation's Impact Evaluation of Business Service Activities in El Salvador took an experimental approach and gathered data through household surveys in the intervention areas and in a control group of other communities. The survey data appears to be the only source of information. The project aim was to (1) provide technical assistance to farmers and business development services; (2) support capital investment to selected applicants for commercial activities; and (3) provide credit guarantees and technical assistance to financial institutions. Again, this means that a large number of indicators could be gleaned from both *active-* and *passive*-driven data. It would be possible to follow applications for credits, market interventions, data traffic on markets and price developments, etc. It would also be possible to use macro-statistics, and while the evaluation generated its own data from its surveys, such data are often available from open statistics.

It is of course presumptous to pronounce judgments on the evaluations as we do and we would like to emphasize that we are not assessing the quality of the evaluations. On the contrary, we have explicitly chosen evaluations that are of a high professional standard. The fact that the evaluations have not used Big Data where we believe they might have benefitted from so doing does not in any way suggest that they did not serve their purpose. They responded to the evaluation questions without using Big Data. So far, so good. Perhaps—and only perhaps—they could have done so more convincingly and possibly more efficiently by using Big Data.

Comparing Development Cooperation to Other Policy Areas

We are well aware that these conclusions are based on a view of Big Data in evaluation of development cooperation. This policy field is quite special, not least because it spans over international borders and there is often another government involved in project implementation. That sets it apart from all other policy fields. Is it then likely that experiences of Big Data in evaluation look different on other policy fields? Of course it does! Still a number of interviews with a sample of governmental agencies in Sweden do suggest that practical usage of BD is limited. Interviews with personnel directly involved, or responsible for the agencies' evaluations, show that the agencies first and foremost rely on *public statistics* (i.e. interview, survey, and desk studies) as the main sources of data.

Most of the interviewees could nevertheless give valid examples of Big Data, and the common understanding of Big Data was massive amounts of information that is generated electronically with potential to spawn new insights. However, none of the interviewees had or were aware of usage of *active-* or *passive*-driven data within their organizations' evaluation practices. One agency stated that they use satellite data in their evaluation work. This data was however processed through GIS (Geographical Information System) software. The interviewees furthermore stated that several agencies currently assess the potential and possibilities with Big Data for their organizations' work.

Statistics Sweden seems to have taken one step further and started experimental cases where *active- and passive*-driven data is explicitly tested. The ambition is to find models and methods that can use Big Data sources[11] in an effort to supplement traditional statistics. However, and in similarity with the other agencies, these efforts appear to be on an early stage and Statistics Sweden underlined several challenges, such as legislative, technological, and methodological issues, with the usage of Big Data.

By and large, it seems like that the current changes in the data landscape have triggered a broad discussion within (and among) Swedish agencies for how to use and harness electronically generated data. Against this backdrop, an interesting fact is an increasing demand for *passive-* and *algorithm*-driven meta data among Swedish law enforcement agencies. According to Swedish telecom companies the request for the mentioned data is on the rise.[12] So why was Big Data not used in the analyzed evaluations?

Incentives to Use Big Data

Let us first rephrase the title of this concluding section: *There are no incentives to use Big Data*, not even in equity focused impact evaluation in development cooperation. Even if such data is available and could be useful as one part of a data triangulation approach, there are no incentives to use it. It is rather the other way round, there are incentives *not* to use Big Data.

- First and foremost, as long as ToRs in detail regulate evaluation approaches, methods, and data sources—and avoid pointing to utilization of Big Data—evaluation teams are not likely to take another route. Evaluators are obedient, and if they can choose their battles. The most significant battles come when an evaluation team presents inconvenient facts, possibly results the commissioning agents don't want to hear about. Those are battles evaluators are used to and engage in, but to pick an argument whether to use Big Data in an inquiry would seem unnecessary. Evaluations are put on tender and in a proposal the evaluators show how they respond to the ToRs. To do so with a suggestion to use different data sources than the commissioning agency indicates is to invite failure. The job would in all likelihood go to someone else who is more responsive to the ToR.
- Second, planning to use Big Data is to engage with uncertainty. At present, the nature of Big Data is not transparent and basic information on representation, inclusions, origins, possible sources of bias, etc, are unknown. Hence, the scientific credibility, the reliability, and validity of Big Data are open to question. In particular, the validity would be hard to ascertain. Big Data, as we have seen it presented, could be used as indicators in relation to the questions posed by the evaluations. But how valid an indicator would it be? How much other information is needed?
- Third, whether we like it or not, most evaluations have by now become bureaucratic routine exercises in information gathering and processing. Those who commission evaluations and those who undertake them share an aversion to uncertainty. There is an explicit preference for well structured and planned processes that adhere to budgets and timelines. If the competence to locate and use Big Data is not already with the evaluators, it is not so likely that such competence can be generated through "learning by doing."
- Fourth, evaluators are paid to gather data. In the evaluations quoted above, the evaluation team members have been paid to organize, conduct, and use interviews and focus groups, to design, disseminate,

and collect surveys, to observe conditions on project sites, and to meet with stakeholder groups. The typical development evaluation takes the evaluation teams traveling for weeks to do such things. That is what evaluators have learnt to do and perfected, but to engage with Big Data is a different kind of expertise, and one where it is far more uncertain how the evaluator would earn his/her fee. There are strong incentives for evaluators to remain experts on collection and analysis of conventional data.

- Yet another factor that limits the possibilities to utilize Big Data is the restricted accessibility. Access and application of data are of the essence for evaluations. It is probably safe to say that access to information is more valued than scale and scope of the same. As mentioned above, use of Big Data could fill a gap in terms of supplying evidence for impact assessments. The majority of evaluations have a dual focus on implementation processes as well as impacts—but limited resources. Hence, an inventive and uncertain exploration of new data sources is not likely to take place. This is partly due to shortcomings and problems related to attaining relevant and reliable impact data/evidence.

At present, it is thus not surprising that Big Data is not much used; there are good reasons why a status quo reigns in the field of data collection and analysis. The evaluation community focuses on other methodological issues, such as quality standards, utilization, experimental versus other approaches, etc. Institutional inertia, lack of capacity, and competence on how Big Data could be used for impact assessment among those who respond to ToRs as well as those who write them mitigate against any rapid proliferation of Big Data use in current evaluation practice.

Nevertheless, increased innovation, different rules of interaction, and proliferation of digital infrastructure are social changes that will affect the way scholars think about evaluations and force the practice of evaluation to adapt (Preskill, 2013). Big Data could contribute to impact assessments with more refined data, as well as to make evaluation approaches more efficient. For example, usage of passive driven data (what people do) is believed to be more relevant than data from surveys and interviews (what people say) in assessment of relevance and impact. In this light, the heavy reliance, in most evaluations, on stakeholder statements could be partly bridged with utilization of Big Data sources. For this to happen, four dimensions of change can be identified:

- On the demand side, an expression of interest from the agencies commissioning evaluation to be seen in ToRs.

- Capacity development on the use of Big Data, in targeted programs as well as in basic training programs in evaluation and research methodology.
- Institutional development in respect of the access to Big Data, where professional associations can have a role to play in negotiations.
- Transparency in the agencies generating, storing and making Big Data available so that reliability and validity can be verified.

Will the forces of competition make change happen anyway? Perhaps it will, but it is more likely that a relatively quick adaptation of Big Data can be realized if stakeholders have a realistic view of limits as well as opportunities and are prepared to act to realize the benefits that these new technologies might bring.

Appendix

Annex. Evaluation reports.

Evaluation	Agency	Sector
Impact Evaluation of the Farmer Training and Development Activity in Honduras	MCC	Agriculture
Burkina Faso's Threshold Program Evaluation	MCC	Education
Impact Evaluation of Business Service Activities El Salvador	MCC	Agriculture
Mozambique's Rural Water Supply project	MCC	Water/infrastructure
Evaluation of the Sustainable Agriculture Research for International Development Programme	DFID	Agriculture
Evaluation of the Farmer Field School Approach in the Agriculture Sector Programme in Bangladesh	Danida	Agriculture
Evaluation of Results-based aid in Education in Rwanda	DFID	Education
Livelihoods and Food Security Trust Fund—Delta 1 Evaluation	DFID	Emergency aid
Evaluation of the Facility for New Market Development to strengthen the private sector in Occupied Palestinian Territories	DFID	Private sector
Evaluation of Sida financed interventions for increased access to Electricity for poor people	Sida	Infrastructure
Evaluation of Sida's support to innovation systems and clusters		
Evaluation Study of Long Term Development Cooperation between Laos and Sweden	Sida	Country study
Evaluation of Donor Support to Public Financial Management Reform	Sida	Public sector management
IOM Partnership on Health and Mobility in East and Southern Africa	Sida	Health
Evaluation of Results of Support to Land Administration Systems in Belarus and Georgia	Sida	Agriculture

Evaluation	Agency	Sector
Real Time Evaluation of Norway's International Climate and Forest Initiative	Norad	Climate
Facing the Resource Curse—Norway's Oil for Development Programme	Norad	Capacity building public sector management
Evaluation of Norway India Partnership for Maternal and Child Health	Norad	Health
Evaluation of Norway's Bilateral Agricultural Support to Food Security	Norad	Agriculture
Support to Local Economic Development Programme	UNDP	Economic development
Evaluation of the Angolan Enterprise Programme (AEP) and the Growing Sustainable Business Initiative (GSB) Projects	UNDP	Economic development
Evaluation of project on youth participation in local governance	UNDP	Governance
Final Evaluation of the Inclusive Employment and Social Partnership Project	UNDP	Governance
Final Evaluation of the Millennium Development Goal Achievement Fund: Youth Employability and Retention Programme	UNICEF	Employment
External Evaluation of the EU/UNICEF Partnerships on Nutrition Security	UNICEF	Health

Notes

1. The sample includes Swedish Consumer Agency, Swedish National Agency for Education, Swedish Civil Contingency Agency, and Transport Analysis Agency.
2. We use the distinction between evaluation approaches/designs from Stern et al. (2012).
3. TORs for the evaluation of the Support for Local Economic Development Program.
4. Norad evaluation; Facing the Resource Curse—Norway's Oil for Development Program.
5. TORs for the Evaluation of Sida's support to innovation systems and clusters (79).
6. This was the main source of data in the evaluation, and the PEFA Performance Measurement Framework for PFM (PEFA 2005) is the most compre-

hensive attempt thus far at constructing a framework to assess the quality of budget systems and institutions. It comprises twenty-eight indicators that assess institutional arrangements at all stages of the budget cycle, together with cross-cutting dimensions and indicators of budget credibility. It also includes three additional indicators on donor practices. The data set used in the evaluation included the results of national-level assessments for 107 countries and territories.
7. Schmarzo (2013); "Big Ideas" Big Data Business Model Maturity Index. Letouzé (2012), UN Global Pulse, Big Data for Development: Challenges & Opportunities. This is also further elaborated in Chapter 2.
8. Data exhaust sources contain unstructured data that is a bi-product of the online activities of internet users. Other definitions include: Data lake, Data reservoir, Data dump (Schmarzo, 2014; Data lake, Data reservoir, Data dump [...]). Or as Lefebvre-Naré (2014) stated: "As highlighted by Hal Varian (above), 'big data' move away from the (SQL) 'standard relational database' to noSQL and 'data lakes'" 2014.
9. See for example, Bradshaw (2014); Data for Development: One Step Forward, Two Steps Back. Hilbert (2013), Big Data for Development: From Information- to Knowledge Societies. Letouzé (2012), UN Global Pulse, Big Data for Development: Challenges & Opportunities; Manovich (2011) Trending: The Promises and the Challenges of Big Social Data.
10. Unstructured—vast amount of unorganized data that is difficult to handle and decode. Recent estimates suggest that as much as eighty to ninety percent of data generated from credit card and health-care providers is discarded (Hilbert, 2013; Manyika et al., 2011).
11. Data sources mentioned were mobile phone records, credit card registers, and data on electricity consumption (Viveka Palm 2015, Big Data viewed from a Statistics Office).
12. Based on evidence from editorial in Swedish newspaper *Dagens Nyheter* 20150504—http://www.dn.se/debatt/myndigheters-fragor-om-sok-i-vara-register-skenar/; http://www.dn.se/ekonomi/skattefuskare-satts-dit-med-hjalp-av-mobiltrafiken/

References

Blumenstock, J. E. 2012. *Inferring Patterns if Internal Migration from Mobile Phone Records: Evidence from Rwanda.* University of California, Berkeley. Berkeley, CA: Routledge.

Bradshaw, S. 2014. *Data for Development: One Step Forward, Two Steps Back.* CIGI.

Colville, J. 2013. *Discussion Paper – Innovations in Monitoring and Evaluating Results.* United Nations Development Programme (UNDP).

Crawford, K. 2013. *Think Again: Big Data, Why the Rise of Machines Isn't All It's Cracked Up to Be.* Foreign Policy, foreignpolicy.com.

Crawford, K., and D. Boyd. 2011. *Six Provocations for Big Data.* Microsoft Research and University of New South Wales. Paper to be presented at Oxford Internet Institute's "A Decade in Internet Time: Symposium on the Dynamics of the Internet and Society" on September 21, 2011.

European Union (EU). 2006. Directive 2006/24/EC of the European Parliament and of the Council of 15 March 2006 on the Retention of Data Generated or

Processed in Connection with the Provision of Publicly Available Electronic Communications Services or of Public Communications Networks and Amending Directive 2002/58/EC.

Forss, K., and M. Marra. 2014. *Speaking Justice to Power: Ethical and Methodological Challenges for Evaluators.* New Brunswick, NJ: Transaction Publishers.

Henderson, J. V., A. Storeygard, D. N. Weil. 2009. *Measuring Economic Growth from Outer Space.* NBER Working Paper No. 15199.

Hilbert, M. 2013. *Big Data for Development: From Information- to Knowledge Societies.* United Nations Economic Commission for Latin America and the Caribbean (UN ECLAC) Annenberg School of Communication, University of Southern California (USC).

Lefebvre-Naré, F. 2014. *An introduction to Big Data.*

Letouzé, E. 2012. *Big Data for Development: Challenges & Opportunities.* New York: UN Global Pulse.

_____. 2013. *Could Big Data Provide Alternative Measures of Poverty and Welfare.* Development Progress. developmentprogress.org/

_____. 2014. *Big Data for Development: Key Resources.* SciDev.NET

Majewski et al. 2013. *Tracking Anti Vaccination Sentiment in Eastern European Social Media Networks.* New York: UNICEF, Division of Communication, Social and Civic Media Section.

Manovich, L. 2011. *Trending: The Promises and the Challenges of Big Social Data.* Debates in the Digital Humanities, edited by Matthew K. Gold. The University of Minnesota Press, 2012.

Manyika, J., M. Chui, B. Brown, J. Bughin, R. Dobbs, C. Roxburgh, and A. Hung Byers. 2011. *Big Data: The Next Frontier for Innovation, Competition and Productivity.* McKinsey and Company.

Nielsen et al. 2014. *Exploring Big (data) Opportunities: The Case of the Center for Innovation through Data Intelligence (CIDI).*

Preskill, H. 2013. *Introducing Next Generation Evaluation.* FSG. fsg.org.

Schmarzo, B. 2014*"Data Lake, Data Reservoir, Data Dump...Blah, blah, blah...* Hopkinton: InFocus, EMC Corporation.

Schmarzo, B. 2013. *"Big Ideas" Big Data Business Model Maturity Index.* Hopkinton: InFocus, EMC Corporation.

Soto, V., E. Frias-Martinez, and J. Virseda. 2011. *Prediction of Socioeconomic Levels Using Cell Phone Records.* Telefonica Research.

Spitz, M. 2012. *Your Phone Company Is Watching.* TED Talks. ted.com.

Stern, E., N. Stame, J. Mayne, K. Forss, R. Davies, and B. Befani. 2012. *Broadening the Range of Designs and Methods for Impact Evaluation: Report of a Study Commissioned by the Department for International Development.* London: DFID Working Paper.

Talbot, D. 2012. *How Cell-Phone Data Could Slow the Spread of Malaria.* MIT Technology Review.

Vital Wave Consulting. 2014. "Big Data, Big Impact: New Possibilities for International Development." Paper presented at the World Economic Forum, Davos.

11

Real-Time Monitoring and Evaluation—Emerging News as Predictive Process Using Big Data-Based Approach

Francesco Mazzeo Rinaldi, Giovanni Giuffrida, and Tom Negrete

Introduction

Imagine the following situation: a policy maker comes to you (as an evaluator) asking a couple of "simple" questions: I need to know the impact of my planned program/reform has on jobs, economy, citizens, firms, etc.? However, I also need to estimate reaction to the intended reform? I need to know to what extent my reform will be socially and politically acceptable. Whether or not the new measures will be judged well enough by public opinion? In other words, I really need to estimate the likelihood of success of my program/reform.

After posing his/her questions, the policy maker looks at you intensely and says: but of course what I need more than anything else is to get the answers as soon as possible and, lastly, please consider we have a very limited amount of resources available to carry out such evaluation.

We know that the situation we just described is rather rough, but we also know that, after all, it is not that far from reality. Now, the evaluator might soon realize that he/she has to deal with predictive evaluation methodologies and will start thinking what type and kind of data he/she needs to answer (some of) those questions. At the same time, he/she has to decide on the best macroeconomic, statistical models, input–output matrix, etc., to estimate the causal effect on jobs, gross domestic product, firm productivity, and consumptions as well as on the best approaches and techniques for evaluating the program reform social acceptance. Would a probability sampling be the best possible option to carry on public opinion polls? Would the telephone polls be the best option available to measure public opinion? Would a better approach be face-to-face interviews? And so on and so forth.

At the heart of our evaluator's reasoning, while knowing the risk of oversimplifying, lies the data collection task. For many evaluators, data collection is the most significant part of their work. Of course, he/she needs to understand the theory or logic behind the reform and about its inputs and outputs. Also about the key indicators to define the right logic model to adopt in search of causality or evidence (if this is the case) to understand the reasons of a possible success or failure.

But our evaluator knows that:

1. Decisions are urgent—as in our example and as often happens in reality, decision makers ask for quick answers. Numerous public decisions need to be made before the evaluation project can be planned, proposed, approved, fielded, processed, reported, and interpreted (Daboll, 2013).
2. Resources are limited—in a time when the public demand for policy or program evaluation increases, the public resources for carrying out applied research, monitoring, and evaluation drop significantly. Most of the time, data collection is the most expensive activities in evaluation research field; thus, new approaches are now competing for scarce resources.
3. Risk of inappropriateness—quite frequently evaluation research deals with very large issues with inadequate and poor sample sizes to be sensitive enough to be measured correctly. Evaluation has a tendency to oversimplify complexity not only due to the "boundaries" of the measurement tools in large data sets (Daboll, 2013) but also due to the "need" for searching for causal effects, even when alternatives would exist, especially in large scale problem.

In this context, a new trend is taking place, at the cost of losing in accuracy at the micro level, but gaining substantial at the macro level, moving from the search for causality in favor of predictions and correlations—a movement away from the "why" toward the "how likely" (Mayer-Schonberger and Cukier, 2013: 14). This is the era of Big Data (see also Chapter 12 by Lemire and Petersson). As pointed out, several decades ago by the British philosopher and mathematician Alfred North Whitehead, modern science began when men stopped asking "why?" and starting asking "how?"

Even if we strongly believe that the "why" question is still central in the evaluation field, we are just as confident that the new availability of huge and large amounts of data, together with pioneering data mining and predictive analytics techniques, represents an effective and competitive opportunity, particularly in supporting decision making in answering different evaluation questions, such as the ones used in our example. In fact, there is a general agreement that more complete social data and, more specifically, large social trace data collections provide more discovery opportunities and significant contribution to research (Murthy and Bowman, 2014). The extensive use of social media sites together with the increasing of online access to any kind of news has generated great amounts of a new type of data, known as social media data (Kumar et al., 2013; Zafarani et al., 2014, among others), and strongly modified the relationship between news producers and (active) readers. The data are big in scale with rapid updates and spreads far and wide in an increasingly flat, or digital, world (Liu, 2014). Although it is mainly user generated, incomplete, and informal, this form of data is an exceptionally rich resource that can help researchers to study social behavior in new ways (Gold, 2012). The emerging computational social science (Nigel, 2010; Cioffi Revilla, 2014; among others) and social media mining approach (Zafarani et al., 2014; Moens et al., 2014, among others) is expected to challenge the ways that analysts and evaluators have worked so far.

Moreover, the new evolving technology is rapidly changing how people receive news and how journalists deliver it. Hence, every year online spaces become progressively used by people to engage in public discussion (Vitak et al., 2011), and one of these most prominent spaces is the reader comment sections on a typical news website. More than ninety percent of the most important 150 US newspapers have implemented commenting systems (Santana, 2011). "Indeed, it is in the reader commenting sections that a great deal of collective meaning making occurs about current, newsworthy affairs, making them important, yet remarkably understudied, spaces" (Trice, 2011, cited in Zamith and Lewis [2014: 2]). This is why journalists and technologists are now reconceiving the creation of dynamic spaces for online news discussion in the era of Big Data. The combination of large amount of digital data logs produced in real time and the technology to collect and process those is definitely pushing social sciences, in general, and evaluators in particular, into a strong revision of their role and practice.

In this context, this chapter focuses on the implications of the Big Data phenomenon for evaluation research, attempting to address two main questions. Which Big Data tools should be developed or oriented in supporting decision making in the emerging news context? What evaluators can learn from how journalists are dealing with Big Data?

We address these issues by exploring the opportunity of using Big Data as real-time monitoring and evaluation approach in online news context to support policy making. To do this, we developed a novel Big Data tool that collects information from user interactions with published news and comments to measure people's sentiment. We apply this to a real-case study related to a recent reform strongly supported by the California Governor Jerry Brown who signed legislation on September 30, 2014, that makes California the first in the country to ban single-use plastic bags. The ban will go into effect in July 2015, prohibiting large grocery stores from using the bags. The issue has significant political implications. It has been widely reported online and generated a lot of interest from online readers. The Sacramento Bee newspaper (www.sacbee.com), one of the most important online newspapers in California, will be our main source of data for this analysis.

Before describing the empirical part of our research—*the analytical framework, the case study and the data analysis*—the chapter illustrates the main implications and challenges faced by journalism in the Big Data era.

Journalism and Its Evolving Role in the Big Data Era

Declines in print readership and advertising revenues between 2003 and 2012, according to the American Society of Newspaper Editors, resulted in the loss of 16,200 newsroom jobs, more than a third of newsroom staffs in the United States. Digital revenues were growing too slowly. How could newspapers turn things around? Was it even possible? Were newspapers' core problems internal (something publishers could fix themselves by making changes) or external (something beyond the control of publishers)? Up until 2012, the general answer from publishers was to grow more monthly digital visitors from within the local market to attract local advertisers. More eyeballs would lead to more ad dollars. Publishers would soon realize that their biggest advertisers cared less about the quantity of the audience. Advertisers were finding ways to use customer data to send targeted messaging to key audience segments, which was made clear to publishers by an article by The New York Times' Charles Duhigg in 2012.

Duhigg wrote about how the retailer target tracked its customers' digital, social media, and purchasing behavioral patterns. Through tracking and structuring of customers' data, target developed the ability to predict which customers were most likely expecting a child; thus, target could tailor messages to these customers to increase sales and brand loyalty among new families. As more stories like Duhigg's were published in various newspapers across the United States, it became clearer that focusing on total monthly digital visitors was a path to nowhere in the era of Big Data.

Journalists have long understood the importance of collecting, organizing, and analyzing data for meaningful insights and relationships. "The more points, then, at which any happening can be fixed, objectified, measured, named, the more points there are at which news can occur," legendary American journalist Walter Lippman wrote in 1922. In Lippman's day, newspapers could become watchdogs of the rich and powerful in their communities by assigning reporters to courthouses, police stations, city hall, regulatory agencies, and union halls, where data could be collected and mined for stories. Reporter Philip Meyer was practicing and preaching the importance of combining journalism, the research methods of social scientists and computer data work in the late 1960s.

Following the 1967 Detroit riots, sparked by a police raid of an unlicensed bar that led to one of the biggest and most violent riots in US history in which forty-three people were killed, 1,189 injured, 7,000 arrested, and more than 2,000 buildings were destroyed, many American journalists and politicians, most of them white, struggled to understand why the rioters, most of them black, had looted, and burned buildings in their own city. Many speculated that the rioters were mostly poor and uneducated or new arrivals from the rural South who had a hard time fitting into modern society and wrongly took their frustrations out on Detroit businesses. Meyer proposed that the Detroit Free Press partner with academics to design a survey that would reveal the identities and attitudes of the rioters, as well as residents of where the riots took place. Interviews were turned into punched computer cards. What Meyers found ended up winning a Pulitzer Prize for the Free Press:

> *There was no correlation between economic status and participation in the disturbance. College-educated residents were as likely as high school dropouts to have taken part. Recent immigrants from the South had not played a major role; in fact, Northerners were three times as*

likely to have rioted. The top grievances of those surveyed were police brutality, overcrowded living conditions, poor housing, and lack of jobs. Finally, the rioters were a distinct subgroup and did not reflect the overall attitudes of area residents. "The survey helped defuse the situation by showing how much good will there was in the Black community," Meyer said. (Rosegrant, 2011)

Meyer's work inspired other investigative reporters to embrace and follow his example. Today, data journalism is increasingly something everyone in the newsroom must able to do—not just investigative reporters. Stanford University, for instance, now asks its graduate journalism students to take courses in computer coding, entrepreneurship, and design thinking and to use data-driven reporting to produce their stories and multimedia work. Stanford professors in computer science now collaborate with journalism instructors to expose their students to the power and insights that come from interdisciplinary research and collaboration.

Publishers are just starting to realize the potential data that they can collect on readers. How might that data be leveraged to increase reader loyalty and improve the work journalists do to serve readers? How might news be personalized? What's the best format, time of day, platform to reach readers interested in political news about California government? Might still other academics be interested in researching if it is possible to measure how political news coverage changes readers' opinions about certain public policy? If so, could a newspaper tell in near real time if its coverage is causing readers to embrace or reject new public policy? What implications might that have for an editor, publisher, and columnist in how they adjust or keep up their coverage? What implications might it have for policy makers in understanding how they work with journalists? What implication might that have for advocacy groups or political advertisers?

The tools and knowledge of Big Data will not always lead to better journalism or smarter businesses decisions and strategies by newspapers. However, the tools most likely will get cheaper and more accessible. How will the tools be used to help journalists play a stronger watchdog role, grow their business, help society? Do data scientists have an interest in helping journalists? What are the commercial and beneficial societal intersections where smart collaboration can occur between newspapers, academics, and other private or public industries? The opportunities seem as enormous as the data itself.

Method—Overall Analytical Framework

Here, we describe the audience analysis system we developed for extracting valuable information from the user traffic on the online newspaper Sacramento Bee. This is a generic data model that we can easily apply to many other papers as well.

The main concepts defined by the model are that of **user** and **content**. A user browses the website and performs actions on specific contents. A content is an html document published on the paper website. An action is a pageview generated by a user on a given content.

Given the set of users, the set of contents, and the actions performed by users on contents, important information can be extracted and analyzed. This information helps in understanding the features and characteristics of the users and can be used for different purposes. For instance, it is possible to understand the main users' interests and leverage such information for advertising purposes. This is typically a two-step process. In the first step, contents are classified into categories such as "Business" and "Automotive" using advanced text mining techniques. These categories can be interpreted as interests. Then, users are associated to the different categories based upon the stream of contents they read.

In general, every single action a reader performs against a content is stored, together with an appropriate timestamp, in the database. By storing every single action, a user performs, even moderate size websites tend to generate very large amount of data. The main challenge, from a technical standpoint, is to cope with such large amount of data. Tools need to be properly devised to make sure such data are promptly available for real-time analysis, which are often needed. In the appendix, we describe, in more technical detail, the model we developed to store all such data.

Case Study

Originally introduced in the 1970s, plastic bags now account for four out of every five bags handed out at the grocery store. Most grocery store baggers do not bother to ask anymore—"plastic or paper?"—they simply drop single item in plastic bag. The plastic bags are so cheap that in the stores, no one treats them as worth anything. Customers choose plastic bags far more frequently than reusable bags to carry their purchases. People like the fact that compared to reusable bags, plastic bags are strong, flexible, and moisture resistant. Despite their "attractiveness," a growing number of states and some municipalities are enacting laws aimed at reducing the use of plastic grocery bags (Burnett, 2013). The success of the plastic bag has meant an intense increase in the amount of sacks floating in the oceans where they choke and starve wildlife around the world (Roach, 2003). Nearly ninety percent of the debris in our oceans is plastic, and plastic bags are among the twelve items of debris most often found in coastal cleanups. Proponents of plastic grocery bag bans argue that banning plastic bags saves cities money by reducing litter, solid waste disposal, and recycling costs. And when municipal budgets are strained or reduced, the argument is rather persuasive (Burnett, 2013).

California became the first state in the United States to ban plastic bags that grocery stores use to package products at the checkout line. On September 30, 2014, Gov. Jerry Brown of California signed legislation that bans the use of plastic bags starting on July 1, 2015. "This bill is a step in the right direction—it reduces the torrent of plastic polluting our beaches, parks and even the vast ocean itself," Brown wrote in a signing message. "We're the first (state) to ban these bags, and we won't be the last." This bill seeks to cut those costs by prohibiting single-use plastic grocery bags in supermarkets and drugstores starting July 1, 2015. By July 1, 2016, smaller grocery stores and convenience stores must also comply with the requirements. Other bags (paper, reusable, and in some jurisdictions, compostable) are allowed only with a ten cent minimum charge.

California indeed has set many legislative precedents that other states follow. Given the possibility that other states would follow California and adopt their own bans should the policy succeed, soon after Gov. Brown signed Senate Bill 270, an industry-backed organization (American Progressive Bag Alliance) announced a referendum drive to allow voters to have the final say on whether to ban plastic bags in California. Plastic bags distributed in California carry a wholesale value of about $195 million annually, and bag makers' profits would suffer if that market ceased to exist. Opponents of the ban dispute the argument that plastic bags pile up huge volumes of waste. A provision in the law allowing grocery stores to charge customers ten cents or more for paper or reusable plastic bags, they say, is a giveaway to a grocery industry that pushed for SB 270.

The Alliance has mounted a campaign to collect 500,000 signatures to qualify an initiative that would go before California voters in 2016.

So far, opponents of the ban have raised $3 million to launch an advertising and social media campaign against the ban. Given that the low threshold to qualify an initiative in California and the money plastic manufactures such as Hilex Poly are expected to pump into to qualify the initiative, California voters are expected to have the final say on whether to ban plastic bags statewide. Indeed, referendum backers said that they had accumulated more than 800,000 signatures, many more than 504,760 needed to qualify (the referendum closed on December 29, 2014). If enough signatures are deemed valid and the referendum does go to the 2016 ballot, the law will be suspended until the electorate weighs in (White, 2014).

About a third of California's municipalities already have some prohibitions on the use of plastic bags. In the Sacramento region, one city—Davis—has a ban. The ban will become real for most Sacramento residents on July 1, 2015, when the ban goes into effect. The mayor of Sacramento has been urging the City Council to pass a citywide ban so that regardless what happens statewide, Sacramento would have a ban in place.

The issue has been widely reported on and is expected to get increased coverage this summer and into the 2016 election. In general, Democrats support the ban, and Republicans oppose the ban. The Sacramento Bee's readership includes areas and readers that are heavily Republican and other areas that are heavily Democrat.

Data Analysis

We first identified twenty-eight articles published from "The Sacramento Bee" online newspaper talking about the California plastic bags ban initiative. Most of the articles on this topic appeared within the "Politics and Government" section. Thus, we focus on this section and compare those articles with the other articles published within this section. Our twenty-eight articles were published in the period October 15, 2014, through January 1, 2015; therefore, we restricted our analysis to that time range.

We want to assess how readers' engagement with the plastic bag ban initiative issue compares with the average engagement to the rest of the articles appearing in the same section within the same time period.

Let's first start with same basic distribution to get an initial sense. For plastic bag ban-related articles, as shown in Figure 11.1, about one-third of the articles attracted most of the readers, the most read articles peak

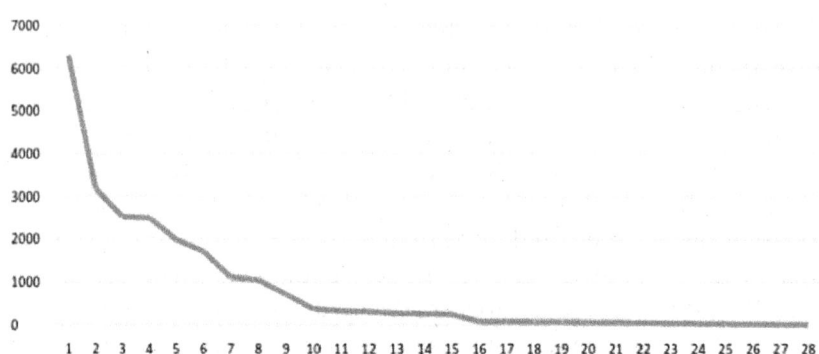

Figure 11.1. Plastic Bag Ban-Related Articles' Number of Reads (Sorted by Most-to-Least Popular).

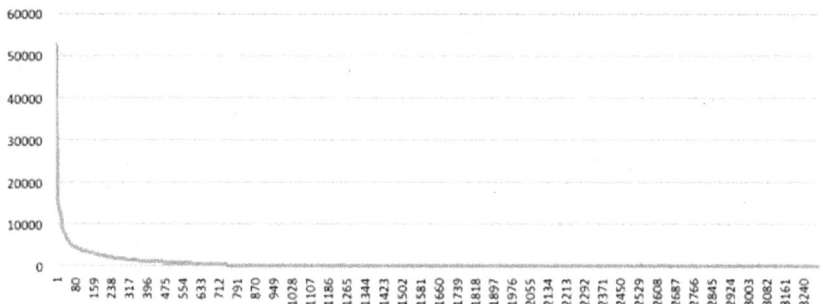

Figure 11.2. Articles' Number of Reads in the Considered Section (Sorted by Most-to-Least Popular).

at 6,200 reads. Figure 11.2 shows the same chart computed across the 3,305 benchmark articles appearing in the Political and Government section. The trend looks different with a much higher concentration toward a smaller percentage of article, attracting many reads. This does not seem to be the case also for the target articles, as the trends go down in a much smoother way.

The average number of reads computed across all twenty-eight target articles is 832, which is more than forty percent (567) higher than the average reads, computed across the 3,305 benchmark articles in the same time period. To emphasize the interest aroused about the plastic bags ban, it is worth noting that the article on plastic bag ban with the most views (6,282) is among the top two percent of the most read articles in the section.

Real-Time Monitoring and Evaluation

Getting into more details, for our study, we identified the following three quantitative indicators:

1. Average reads per article.
2. Average number of comments per article.
3. Probability of commenting.

As already said, for fair comparison, we measured all metrics during the same time span.

To compute these metrics, we basically need the number of reads and the number of comments for each of the twenty-eight target articles and the same for all other articles appeared on that section in that time range. Basically, we want to compare the readers "engagement" toward the plastic bag ban issue compared to the average engagement toward other issues appearing in the same section of the newspaper. In order to do so, we collected some quantitative measure about the overall section (i.e., "General Politics and Government") and about the twenty-eight articles within the same section discussing our topic of interests.

Follows the aggregate values:

	Articles	Reads	Comments
Plastic bag ban-related articles	28	23,303	17
General Politics and Government articles	3,305	1,876,056	344

Based on these numbers, we measured the readers' engagement by detailing three metrics discussed in the following sections.

Average reads per article—The average number of reads per article for the plastic bag ban topic is given by: 23,303/28 which is 832.25. The same for the other category is: 1,876,056/3,305=567.64. Thus, we notice how the average number of reads per article is much higher (about forty-six percent) for the plastic bag ban articles, denoting a greater interest in the topic compared to the average value. See Figure 11.3 for a graphical representation.

This is a very interesting results as it measures a greater readers' interest for the issue analyzed compared to the average interest for an article in that section. This is a quantitative measure to denote an increased interest in getting knowledge about the "plastic bag ban" proposal by our readers.

Average number of comments per article—This is computed as 17/28=0.6 for plastic bag ban versus 344/3,305=0.1 for general interest

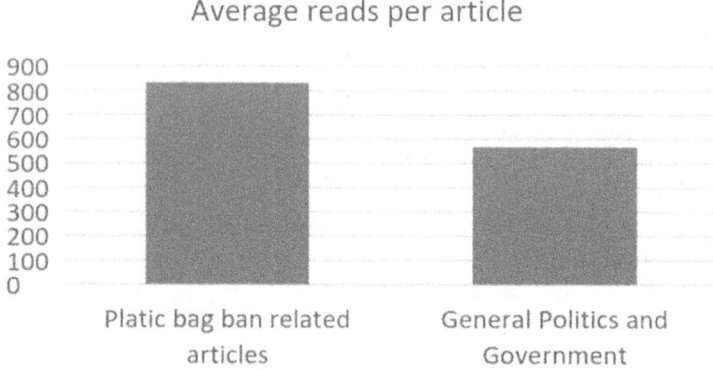

Figure 11.3. Comparison of the Average Reads Per Article.

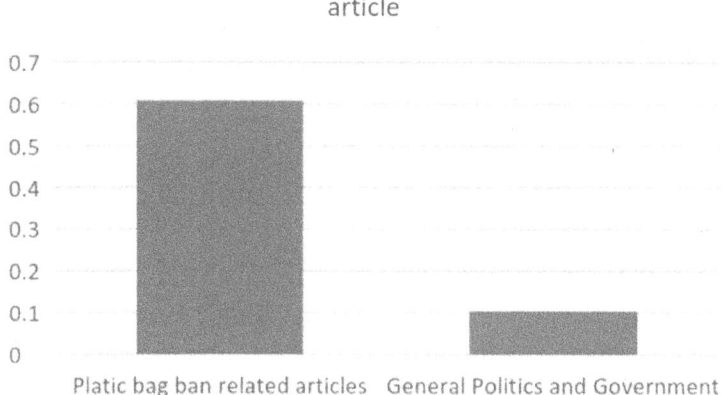

Figure 11.4. Average Number of Comments for a Given Articles Between the Two Groups.

articles. Again we can see as a much number of comments are generated, on average, for each article. We believe this is a very meaningful metrics and it really shows, in this particular case, how interesting the topic is for the paper's readers (see Figure 11.4).

This is another meaningful result as it shows how readers are willing to discuss this issue. Basically, this is telling us that readers are 600 percent more likely to discuss this issue compared to the average. We believe that this is a great indicator for how sensitive people are to the issue and this should represent great feedback to politicians.

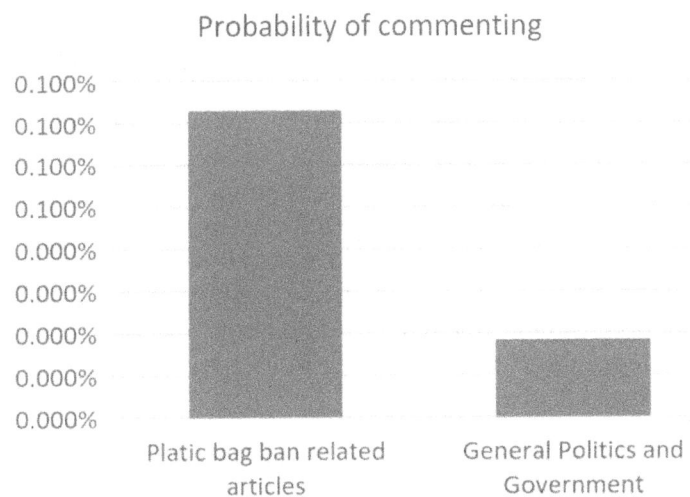

Figure 11.5. Probability That a User Comments on a Given Article Read.

Probability of commenting—We define this metric as the probability that a user comments on a given article as soon as he/she reads the article. It is somewhat similar to the above measures, but this one takes into account the number of reads of each article. Thus, for plastic bag ban we get 17/23,303 = 0.07 percent versus 344/1,876,056 = 0.018 percent (see Figure 11.5). Again, even this metrics denotes a greater interest for the plastic bag ban-related articles compared to the benchmark.

Even in this case, as in the above metric, we noticed a much greater willingness of the readers to engage in discussions about the issue at hand. Basically, the probability that a user writes a comment on the issue analyzed is about 380 percent (i.e. 0.07/0.018) more likely compared to the average article.

Sentiment Analysis

After having measured quantitatively people's interest for the target articles, we switch now to measure readers' opinion, analyzing positive or negative sentiments. Sentiment analysis, also known as opinion mining, allows one to analyze people's opinions, sentiments, emotions, etc., toward entities such as products, people, issues, and events and their attributes (Liu, 2012 among others). In this case, the goal was to determine the polarity of the contextual content of comments posted (positive, neutral, and negative). The indicator defined in our example is the "opinion polarity." To do this, we selected all the comments posted on the twenty-eight articles and applied a novel model dedicated to sentiment analysis. While most sentiment systems work by looking at words in isolation, giving positive scores for positive words and negative scores for negative words and then summing up the scores, the Recursive Deep Models for Semantic Compositionality Over a Sentiment Treebank (Socher et al., 2013) works by computing the sentiment based on how words compose the meaning of longer phrases. Thus, the model builds up a representation of whole sentences based on the sentence structure, attributing to each sentence a sentiment score as follows:

- 0, very negative,
- 1, negative,
- 2, neutral,
- 3, positive,
- 4, very positive.

In the following examples, we apply the algorithm to a real comment that appeared on the paper's website:

> Comment: "I would vote NO on any kind of a government-imposed bag ban, or bag requirements/standards simply for the sake of telling the government to shove it. Not one more intrusion into our lives, no way, no how. BTW, I see hardly a spec of trash along the highways in my neck of northern California."

The algorithm proceeds by splitting it into sentences and measuring sentiment for each sentence. Thus, we have

- "I would vote NO on any kind of a government-imposed bag ban, or bag requirements/standards simply for the sake of telling the government to shove it." (Sentiment score = 1)
- "Not one more intrusion into our lives, no way, no how." (Sentiment score = 2)
- "BTW, I see hardly a spec of trash along the highways in my neck of northern California." (Sentiment score = 1)

We can then simply compute the overall sentiment of the entire comment as the average sentiment of the three sentences, and we get 1.3 as the overall comment sentiment. The example above clearly shows how the model works, and more, it seems that it is able to properly capture the single sentence sentiment detection for a positive/negative sentence classification.

Considering that sentiment analysis models suffer from different application problems and the complexity of the issue addressed here (e.g. analyzing comments of articles talking about Senate Bill 270 and others about the referendum to repeal the plastic bag ban), we decided to read and manually compare every single comment with the sentiment model outputs. The results are quite interesting and raise some issues especially for those who intend to use these tools in social and evaluation research. Consider the following example:

> *Comment: I won't be signing this petition. Keep the plastic bag ban in effect.*

> "I won't be signing this petition."(Sentiment score = 1)

> "Keep the plastic bag ban in effect." (Sentiment score = 2)

> Average sentiment = 1.5

In this case, the model attributes a negative opinion to a comment that, actually, expresses a positive sentiment to the plastic bag ban. We found several other examples as this one. Though this aspect shows that the use of automatic sentiment modeling in this field cannot (yet?) replace that of the analyst, and that a qualitative analysis is certainly essential, the overall result (total average comment sentiment) obtained by the model is not too far from the one manually attributed by the analyst. In fact, the latter is 1.70, while the average sentiment calculated by the software was 1.446.

Another important aspect, worth noting, is that the analyst discovers that one of the common roots of the negative comments from readers is dealing with the "intrusive" character of the proposal. There are several comments that criticize the proposed ban because it is considered a new intrusion into the private sphere of citizens: "...not one more intrusion into our lives" and "...stay the hell out of our private lives." Considering also the way in which these opinions are formulated. It would be very difficult for any text- or opinion-mining system to highlight this aspect.

Concluding Remarks

Today, the never-ending development of social media allows us to share and create online content, developing new forms and patterns of social participation in public life. The new abundance of data, the ways in which these data are available today, along with the increased computational power, allows data scientists to analyze the levels of reality simply unimaginable yesterday. The main goal of this chapter was to stimulate interests in public policy evaluators to adopt Big Data technologies to better support policy makers. In particular, we explored the opportunity of using Big Data as predictive evaluation approach in emerging news context.

We started this chapter by asking ourselves a couple of questions: Which Big Data tools should be developed or oriented in supporting decision making in emerging news context? What evaluators can learn from how journalists are dealing with Big Data? And we progressed through the chapter trying to show how the novel and fluid Big Data wave of technology can provide insight into complex problems.

We developed some novel audience analysis methods used for extracting and analyzing information from the online newspaper Sacramento Bee. The techniques here described represent a general data model framework that can be easily applied to any online newspaper.

The model has been tested in a case study, involving a recent reform that makes California the first in the country to ban plastic grocery bags. The case is interesting because it exhibits all the main ingredients needed: high level of political interest, high stakes in play, widely reported online, lots of interest from online readers, and *variable* social acceptance. We showed the potentiality of these systems in handling and analyzing in real time very large amounts of data. We made some comparisons between a target set of articles covering a specific topic versus all articles in the section (benchmark). We made some quantitative comparisons to measure general readers' engagement with the topic and some qualitative comparison to measure more people's opinion and sentiment. And consequently the ability to predict possible conflict risk, social acceptability level, political cost, etc., of adopting a particular reform, as in our plastic bag ban case. All valuable information is for policy and decision makers. The target used in our case is limited to SacBee readers, but the Big Data tool can be implemented in order to integrate the newspaper readers' interest and opinion with those of major social networks, thus widening the information base.

As we write, the field of Big Data processing techniques is quickly evolving. Even for computer scientists, it is hard to keep pace with the ultrafast innovation speed in this field. We have also seen that the analytical tools in this complex field still need the analyst's work, for a better interpretation of people's opinion and sentiment. As already mentioned, we firmly believe that today the main value is not in the tools but on the ability to choose the right mix of tools for the project at hand.

In the changing journalism environment, Big Data is coming to mean more than just the science of how to structure and leverage data. The term has come to represent an attitude of constant innovation, intellectual curiosity, and valuing and embracing research opportunities with scientists. Various news organizations around the world have made great strides in data-driven journalism and personalization. Some have made greater progress than others. Having a huge amount of resources does not appear to be a key factor in predicting progress. And even if costs/resources are a factor today, the technology cost to move into Big Data becomes more accessible and affordable every day. Based on anecdotal observation alone, we would bet that those news publishers with the "Big Data" attitude will do best at leveraging Big Data tools.

The evaluator today cannot afford not to be a part of this process so he/she needs to understand better trends and technologies in, at least:

(1) Which data to use? Which data are available and which to acquire from third parties?
(2) How to acquire, process, and structure data into data models?
(3) Tools and techniques to manage and query Big Data.
(4) Algorithms to infer knowledge and user sentiment from data.
(5) How to communicate derived insight from data to the right audience (e.g. journalists)?

Of course, he/she doesn't need to know all technical nuances of those, but he needs to understand the underlying principles.

We firmly believe that today "modern" evaluators need to fully understand and appreciate the great value of Big Data tools and strategies being adopted by modern news organizations. This allows the real-time measurement of readers' opinions about certain public policy, and this is invaluable to support the policy-making process. The modern approach to online news is definitively a challenge that an evaluator needs to master. Such an evaluator needs to work jointly with a team of experts from various disciplines, such as data mining, computational sociology and social simulation, data journalism, and storytelling. Again, we believe that under such conditions evaluation research can create a tremendous value. Integrating traditional evaluation techniques and expertise with the opportunities provided by the Big Data today represents a significant turning point for the evaluation research. Indeed, our idea in this chapter was not to prove that Big Data is an alternative to "classical" evaluation methods, but, rather, that in some contexts, in particular where predictive decision making is needed, where answers are urgent, almost in real time, and where resources are scarce, the use of Big Data can strongly contribute to the evaluation field, as well as to the professional enrichment of the community of evaluators.

In a time where sources go digital, evaluators have to be closer to those sources. When data and information are scarce or insufficient, most evaluators' energies are devoted to searching and collecting. In the era of Big Data, where information is abundant, structuring and processing seems to get more and more importance. Evaluators have to learn how to use, analyze, understand, and structure out the never-ending flow of Big Data, and at the same time, opening up their techniques, they have to be able to present findings grounded in a sound scientific basis.

Appendix: The Model at a Glance

The following picture shows an entity-relationship diagram depicting the model. The diagram shows all tables in the model. Tables are the collections of rows, where each row contains several fields arranged in columns. Each table is updated with a given frequency, such as daily, weekly, and monthly. Lines connecting tables indicate the kind of relationship linking them, which can be one to many, many to many, or one to one. A one to many relationship happens when one row in one table corresponds to many rows in the second table. For instance, a user performs many actions, giving rise to a one to many relationships (Figure A.1).

A many-to-many relationship happens when many rows from one table correspond to many rows in the second table. As an example of a many-to-many relationship, consider a table relating users to banks. A user can have an account in more than one bank, and a bank holds many accounts. Finally, there is the case of a one-to-one relationship, for instance, the example in our model of the tables aa_content_metadata and aa_content_attribute, which have all one row for each unique content.

The following sections describe in detail each table with their fields and how derived fields are computed.

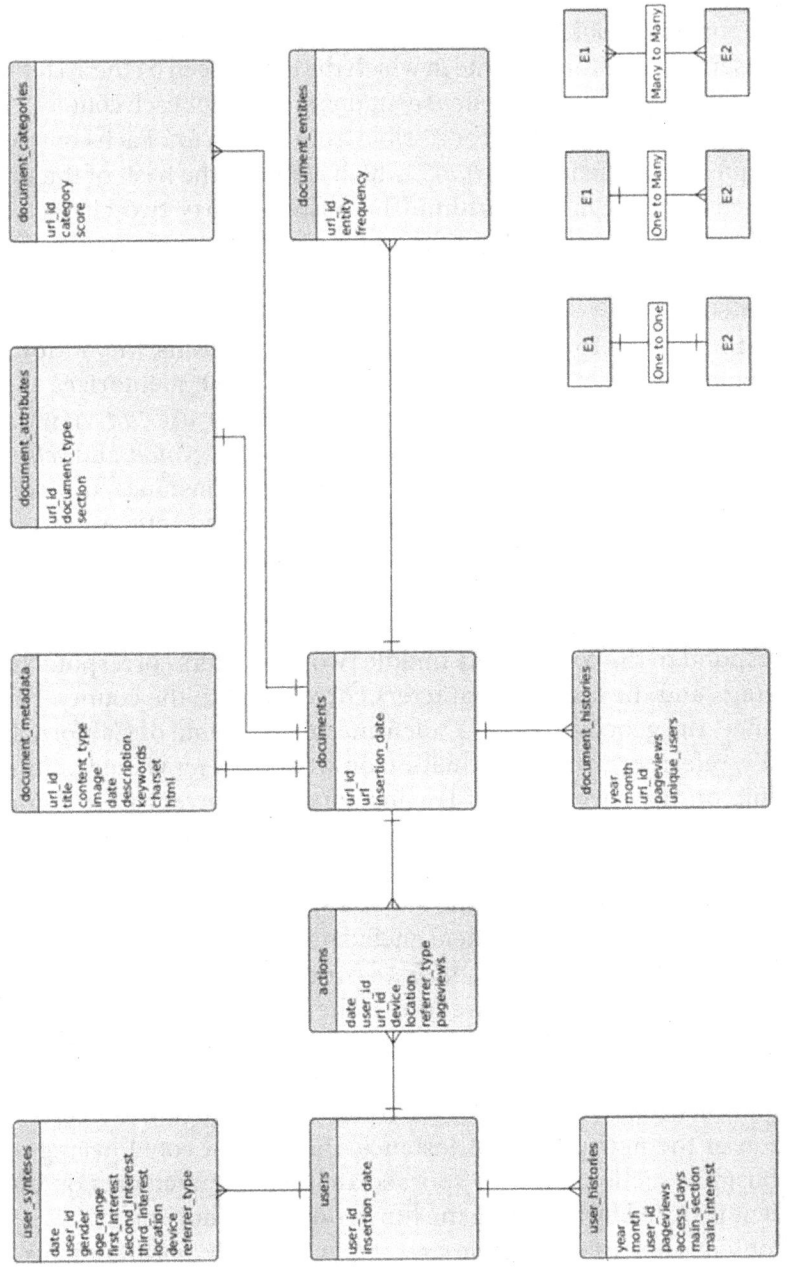

Figure A.1. Entity Relationship Diagram.

User—The table *aa_user* contains one row for each user. Each user is identified by a *user_id*, which is a thirty-three-character hexadecimal string stored in a cookie maintained by the browser of the user. Then, for each user, we store the first date in which the user is seen by the system.

Content—The table *aa_content* contains one row for each content. A content is an html document accessible from a given *url*. Each content is uniquely identified by a *urlmd5*, which contains the hash of the *url* obtained using the md5 algorithm. This hash is a thirty-two-character hexadecimal string and is used throughout our system to identify the content. As for users, we store the first date that a content is seen by the system.

Action view—The table *aa_action_view* contains the actions performed by users. For each given day, this table memorizes the number of *pageviews* that a user identified by a *user_id* views a content identified by a *urlmd5* from a given *device, geoloc*, and *referrer*. A device gives us information on whether, for instance, the user connected from a desktop, a laptop, a mobile phone, etc. A geoloc, which is derived from the ip address of the user, gives us information on the geographic location from which the user connected from. Geocodes are six-character strings where the first two characters correspond to the country, the middle two characters correspond to the state, and the last two characters correspond to the county. For instance, the geocode "us05—" identifies the US state of California. Finally, referrers give us information on what the user visited before landing on the current page. For instance, the current page could have been found because linked by the home page of the online newspaper, or because it was linked from a social network site, or it could have been found with the aid of a search engine.

Content attribute and content metadata—The tables *aa_content_attribute* and *aa_content_metadata* contain information that are related to the content. What we store is the type of the content, which tells us whether the content was a homepage, a section page, an article, a gallery, or a video. Moreover, each content is classified using an algorithm, which analyzes the url of the content, as belonging to a certain section of the newspaper. For instance, the content could belong to the business section or to the sport section. Finally, metadata on the content is stored by analyzing the html code of the document.

Content category—The table *aa_content_category_norm* contains a textual classification for each content in the database. For each content, we use a text classifier that analyzes the text extracted from the html of the content and associates it to one or more categories. Thus, each content may generate more than one row in the *aa_content_category_norm* table. The classifier assigns to each category of the content a score, which indicates the level of confidence to which the category belongs to the content. The categories which we use are those set forth by the International Advertising Bureaux and are the following. There are twenty-three categories, ranging from Arts and Entertainment, Automotive, Business, and others.

Content entity—The table *aa_content_dbpentity_lemma* contains semantic entities extracted by analyzing the html document of each content. For each content, we use a text annotator that analyzes the text extracted from the html of the content and annotates this text with one or more entities. Thus, each content may generate more than one row in the *aa_content_dbpentity_lemma* table.

The text annotator which we used is Tagme (http://tagme.di.unipi.it/), a tool that is able to identify meaningful short phrases in an unstructured text and link them to a pertinent Wikipedia page. An entity is, therefore, a Wikipedia page associated to a short phrase included in the text extracted from the html document.

As an example, consider the following short text: *Congress has approved the law proposed by the President.*

This text is annotated by Tagme as follows: **Congress** *has approved the* **law** *proposed by the* **President**.

Three entities were extracted. In particular, the word congress is associated to the Wikipedia page **United States Congress**. The word law is associated to the Wikipedia page **Law**. The word President is associated to the Wikipedia page **President of the United States**.

Content history—The table *aa_content_history* contains statistics relative to the fruition of each content by the users in a given month. We store the *pageviews* generated by the content in the given month and the number of *unique visitors* that have generated at least one pageview for the content in the given month. Moreover, we count the number of unique loyal visitors, where a visitor is loyal if it has accessed the site at least ten days in the given month. We also count the number of unique consuming visitors, where a visitor is consuming if it has visited at least eighty contents in the given month. We also count the number of unique article visitors, where a visitor is counted if it has visited at least eighty contents of type article in the given month. Finally, we count the number of unique video visitors, where a visitor is counted if it has visited at least twenty contents of type video in the given month.

User history—The table *aa_user_history* contains statistics for each user relative to their consumption of content, computed for a given month of navigation. We compute the number of pageview generated by the user, the number of days that the user has accessed the site, the number of content of type article visited by the user, and the number of content of type video visited by the user. We also compute the section most visited by the user, and the geocode from which the user has generated the highest number of pageviews. Finally, we compute the three International Advertising Bureaux categories most visited by the user. They are computed by summing, for each visited content, the scores in the *aa_content_category_norm* table and then taking the three categories with the highest sums. The highest sums are memorized as appropriate scores. For instance, suppose that a user has visited three contents. The first content is categorized as "Automotive" with score 1.0, the second document is categorized as "Pets" with score 0.7 and "Careers" with score 0.3, and the third content is categorized as "Pets" with score 1.0. Then the main categories of the user are "Pets" with score 1.7, "Automotive" with score 1.0, and "Careers" with score 0.3.

User profile—The table *aa_user_profile* contains statistics computed for each user, on the basis of their history in a given month. We compute *loyalty, consumption level, consumption depth*, and *video level*, which are numerical codes whose values can be decoded as "high," "medium," and "low" and are established according to predefined ranges over a relative measure. The *loyalty* refers to the number of days that the user has accessed the site. The *consumption level* refers to the number of pageviews generated by the user. The *consumption depth* refers to the number of pageviews of content of type article generated by the user. The *video level* refers to the number of pageviews of content of type video generated by the user. Finally, we compute the *main interest*, the *main section*, and the *main geoloc*, which are the most visited category, the most visited section, and the most used geocode of the user, respectively.

References

Burnett, S. 2013. "Do Bans on Plastic Grocery Bags Save Cities Money?" National Center for Policy Analysis, Policy Report No. 353. Accessed December 2013. http://www.ncpa.org/pdfs/st353.pdf.

Cioffi Revilla, C. 2014. *Introduction to Computational Social Science*. London: Springer.

Daboll, P. 2013. "5 Reasons Why Big Data Will Crush Big Research." Accessed February 11, 2005. http://www.forbes.com/sites/onmarketing/2013/12/03/5-reasons-why-big-data-will-crush-big-research/.
Gold, M. K. 2012. *Debates in the Digital Humanities*. Minneapolis, MN: University of Minnesota Press.
Kumar, S., F. Morstatter, and H. Liu. 2013. *Twitter Data Analytics*. New York, NY: Springer.
Liu, B. 2012. *Sentiment Analysis and Opinion Mining*. San Rafael, CA: Morgan & Claypool Publishers.
Liu, H. 2014. *How to Mine Social Media – Big Data Derived from Online Platforms Produce Bigger Challenges*. Accessed November 25, 2014. http://theinstitute.ieee.org/ieee-roundup/opinions/ieee-roundup/how-to-mine-social-media.
Mayer-Schonberger, V., and K. Cukier. 2013. *Big Data: A Revolution that Will Transform How We Live, Work, and Think*. New York, NY: Houghton Mifflin Harcourt.
Moens, M. F., J. Li, and T. S. Chua, eds. 2014. *Mining User Generated Content*. Boca Raton, FL: Chapman and Hall/CRC.
Murthy, D., and S. A. Bowman. 2014. "Big Data Solutions on a Small Scale: Evaluating Accessible High-Performance Computing for Social Research." *Big Data & Society* 1: 1–12.
Nigel, G. G., ed. 2010. *Computational Social Science*. Thousand Oaks, CA: Sage Publications Ltd.
Roach, J. 2003. "Are Plastic Grocery Bags Sacking the Environment?" *National Geographic News*. http://news.nationalgeographic.com/news/2003/09/0902_030902_plasticbags.html.
Rosegrant, S. 2011. "Revealing the Roots of a Riot." Institute for Social Research, University of Michigan. http://home.isr.umich.edu/sampler/revealing-the-roots-of-a-riot/.
Santana, A. D. 2011. "Online Readers' Comments Represent New Opinion Pipeline." *Newspaper Research Journal* 32 (3): 66–81.
Socher, R., A. Perelygin, J. Y. Wu, J. Chuang, C. D. Manning, A. Y. Ng, and C. Potts. 2013. "Recursive Deep Models for Semantic Compositionality over a Sentiment Treebank." In *Proceedings of the Conference on Empirical Methods in Natural Language Processing (EMNLP)*, Vol. 1631, 1642.
Vitak, J., P. Zube, A. Smock, C. T. Carr, N. Ellison, and C. Lampe. 2011. "It's Complicated: Facebook Users' Political Participation in the 2008 Election." *Cyber-Psychology, Behavior, and Social Networking* 14 (3): 107–114.
White, J. B. 2014. "California Plastic Bag Ban Referendum Has Enough Signatures, Backers Say." By Jeremy B. White. http://www.sacbee.com/news/politics-government/capitol-alert/article5122236.html.
Zafarani, R., M. A. Abbasi, and H. Liu. 2014. *Social Media Mining. An Introduction*. New York, NY: Cambridge University Press.
Zamith, R., and S. C. Lewis. 2014. "From Public Spaces to Public Sphere: Rethinking Systems for Reader Comments on Online News Sites." *Digital Journalism* 2 (4): 558–74. doi: 10.1080/21670811.2014.882066.

12

Big Bang or Big Bust? The Role and Implications of Big Data in Evaluation

Sebastian Lemire and Gustav Jakob Petersson

Introduction

This may be the exact right time or the exact wrong time to write a chapter about Big Data in evaluation. On one hand, it may be the right time because we seem to be teethering on the cusp of a data analytic revolution, or perhaps a "data analytic arms race," as the more dramatically inclined may chose to frame it (Welles, 2014). Collecting our thoughts on what this all means is perhaps called for. On the other hand, it may be the exact wrong time because we have little grounding on which to predict what that data analytic revolution will look like, even less grounding on which to predict where it might take us, and close to no grounding on which to predict where it might leave us. Perhaps caution is called for, too.

To be sure, the conversation on Big Data and social science has already begun. In current debates about the implications of Big Data for the social sciences, the assumption is sometimes evident, or even explicit, that Big Data analytics may replace the scientific method of formulating and testing hypotheses to explain society (Graham, 2012). Big Data is in these debates characterized as "paradigmatic" and "revolutionary" in power (Kitchin, 2014), motivating changes in the very "constitution of knowledge," "how we think about research," and even how we think about "the nature and categorization of reality" (Boyd & Crawford, 2012). Big Data, in other words, will render all but obsolete our traditional ways of doing research. Strong stuff.

The promises and perils of the Big Data revolution have not been lost on evaluators. With equal parts excitement and anxiety evaluators are debating themselves back and forth between eureka and doomsday, between utopia and dystopia. Conspicuous by their absence in these waging exchanges are concrete, real-world examples of Big Data applications in evaluation. As such, the contributions on Big Data and evaluation are as of writing resoundingly hypothetical—present chapter included. Big Data, it seems, as in the context of evaluation becomes almost mythological, something yet to be seen, yet something dearly desired, something to be both feared and befriended. In perusing the burgeoning literature on Big Data, the image of the three proverbial blind men arguing over the description of an elephant sometimes come to mind, at least for the authors of the present chapter.

So what, then, are we as evaluators to make of the Big Data revolution? Which, then, are the promises and perils of Big Data? And what is the potential role and implications of Big Data in the context of evaluation? These are the questions that will be entertained in this chapter.

The starting point for the chapter is the promise by proponents of Big Data that new data analytics will fundamentally transform how we produce—or ought to produce—knowledge about society. If there is such potential, Big Data may challenge—perhaps even undermine—the traditional ways in which we think about data (analysis) and theory in evaluation. In the view of the authors, this promise may be formulated in the form of four fundamental shifts:

1. A shift from *theory* to *data-driven* knowledge production.
2. A shift from *causation* to *correlation*.
3. A shift from *samples* to *total populations* (n = all).
4. A shift from *clean* to *messy* data (Cukier & Mayer-Schoenberger, 2013, among others).

All of these shifts are purportedly integral to the Big Data revolution in the social sciences generally speaking and the field of evaluation more specifically. As such, they merit our critical attention. Toward this aim, we will in what follows consider both how fundamental these shifts may be in the context of evaluation and whether pushing them as far as possible would meet our informational needs as evaluators. With the risk of spoiling the plot, the position of the authors on these proposed shifts is perhaps best described as critical optimism, whereby Big Data is viewed as posing both opportunities and challenges for the field of evaluation. A point we will return to at the end of the chapter. For now, let us first consider the four proposed shifts in turn.

Shift One: From Theory to Data-Driven Knowledge Production

Touring the small but rapidly growing literature on Big Data analytics reveals a pervasive move toward what might be termed a data-driven empiricism. Robert Kitchin captures the core idea of this new empiricism when writing: "Big Data ushers in a new empiricism, wherein the volume of data, accompanied by techniques that can reveal their inherent truth, enables data to speak for themselves free of theory" (2014).

The underlying assumption of this new empiricism is "that the patterns and relationships contained within Big Data inherently produce meaningful and insightful knowledge about complex phenomena" (Anderson, 2008). Indeed, it is this unique quality of Big Data that allows for insights to be "borne from the data," and even for researchers and others to "finally learn the answers to questions that they didn't know to ask in the first place" (Clark, 2013, cited in Kitchin [2014]). From this perspective, Big Data is prescient, inherently anticipating the informational needs among social scientists, evaluators, program funders, and policy makers. More than that the application of preconceived theories, models, and hypotheses only serve to unduly restrict the analyses and the knowledge produced. Or at least so it appears.

To be sure, the proposal that Big Data analytics can replace theory has potentially severe implications for evaluation. For instance, following this proposal, evaluators ought to skip all reasoning about program theory, including any and all deliberations about hypothesized mechanisms and mediators, confounding factors, and anticipated outcomes. After all, these theoretical structures would simply serve to constrain the potential insights emerging from the data. We should let the data speak for themselves. We should also discard social scientific theories borrowed from various disciplinary fields (e.g. social psychology, economics, and sociology) to describe and understand the evaluated program, the participants, and its context. Instead, we should ground our evaluations on predictions "borne from the data," relying on Big Data to release meaningful patterns about the social program to be evaluated. By having Big Data in our corner, we would need no theory in our practice (Anderson, 2008).

The end-of-theory scenario is perhaps compelling to some, especially in a practical and pragmatic-oriented field such as evaluation.

Allowing our critical minds a moment of rest, the idea of findings emerging from data pure and untainted by theoretical persuasions does have an air of authenticity. However, there are at least two arguments why Big Data cannot replace theory in evaluation (and even the social sciences more broadly speaking).

First and foremost, the end-of-theory proposition relies on the idea that data actually speak for themselves. Data never speak for themselves. Data are inanimate, silent. Data have no (evaluative) value without active analysis, interpretation, sensemaking, and human engagement. Tweets, clicks, bits, and bytes are not inherently meaningful—they require interpretation. They are dots, and they do not connect themselves.

To illustrate, consider the widely referenced Google Flu Trends that relies on aggregated Google search terms to provide near real-time predictions of the spread of flu epidemics (Kirkpatrick, 2012). To make these predictions, Google relies on specified query models containing search terms relevant to influenza infection, symptoms, and complications. The design of these queries, the specification of which search terms to be aggregated, is grounded on anticipated internet search behavior, that is, a theory of how someone with flu symptoms might behave on Google. Even the algorithms connecting and aggregating the specified search terms involve theory. This is because algorithms are themselves the product of theory; algorithms, too, reflect rationales and decisions. In this way, any knowledge "borne from Big Data" is at a fundamental level theory-laden. As noted by Leonelli, "the ways in which [Big Data] datasets are arranged, selected, visualized, and analyzed become crucial to which trends and patterns emerge" (2014). Returning to the example of predicting flu epidemics, the specification of a nomenclature for flu-related search terms in combination with the equation determining how to aggregate these queries influences the patterns produced. In this way, the very creation of Big Data presupposes theory, implying that Big Data even in its own creation cannot avoid—much less replace—theory.

What makes theory unavoidable is the simple fact that any inquiry—evaluative or not—relies on a specification of scope, that is, a specification of what to award attention to and what to leave ignored. There is nothing novel about this idea. Popper (1957) emphasized that there is a subjective bias in the definition of variables—and even data points—which makes it possible to come up with an infinite number of variables: "If we wish to study a thing, we are bound to select certain aspects of it. It is not possible for us to observe or to describe a whole piece of the world, or a whole piece of nature; in fact, not even the smallest whole piece may be so described, since all description is necessarily selective" (section 23: 77).

In other words, we always use more or less elaborate theories to decide what do describe and what to leave out. What Google Flu Trends serves to remind us, then, is that the connections made between data points will in fundamental ways (and without fail) be influenced, shaped, and informed by some kind of theory—whether implicitly or explicitly stated. "Raw data," Bowker observes, "is both an oxymoron and a bad idea; to the contrary, data should be cooked with care" (cited in Boyd and Crawford [2012]). Big Data is no exception.

Another argument against the end-of-theory proposition is that theory comprises a cornerstone for making predictions—one of the oft-cited aims of Big Data analytics. To understand why this is we first need to consider the nature of predictions. In broad strokes, the premise for making a prediction is that information about past and current events with some degree of accuracy allows us to say something about future events. The proposition that Big Data—without any element of theory—is all we need to make sound predictions only holds if the past mirrors the future, that is, if the past and the future are symmetrical. However, this raises a big question: Is the assumption of symmetry between past and future events sound in the context of real-world evaluation?

We find this assumption dubious, not the least since the society in which evaluated programs are embedded changes over time. Various background conditions—in the evaluation literature sometimes referred to as moderators—such as values, beliefs, and the knowledge base of stakeholders—are constantly transformed. In effect, knowledge of the past is not always sufficient to predict the future—not even with the support of Big Data. We should not presume that past correlations will be perfectly mirrored in the future without having an explicit theory that accounts for how changes in background conditions might influence the accuracy of our predictions. As Cartwright and Hardie states, "There are two further kinds of facts you will have to nail down, or nail down as best as you can, to build a road from 'it works somewhere' to 'it will work here.' These are [...] facts about the causal role the policy plays and facts about the support factors that must be in place if the policy is to work" (2012: 6).

The "support factors" mentioned by Cartwright and Hardie may encompass, for instance, the target populations' experiences from previous interventions. Such experiences are of importance since decision making is based on the (presumed) knowledge at hand. As we gain experience and knowledge, we may value our choices for action differently. Also values change over time, influencing our choices of action.

Interventions may therefore not always produce the same outcomes when repeated over time. A training course may receive a positive or a poor reputation, influencing enrollment and drop-outs. And it would probably be difficult for teachers to draw on the didactical strategies that were used hundred years ago; pupils have a different knowledge base than previously, and the general attitudes to teachers and the values surrounding knowledge have been transformed. The introduction of a new tax may be rendered ineffective by widespread allegations of corruption among politicians since such allegations may make tax evasion seem morally less unacceptable than previously. Society changes—perhaps progresses—continuously and along numerous dimensions.

Popper (1957) emphasized in particular that the accumulation of new knowledge affects human agency. To Popper, human agency was something that could not be foretold; we always *choose* to respond in a certain way to new knowledge.[1] We can therefore, according to Popper, never know for sure by looking at the past how people will respond to new knowledge. In effect, we can never obtain certain knowledge about the future of society, only theories about what *would* happen *if* humans were to choose a certain action.[2] To Popper, this was an essential argument against the position that the development of society is governed by eternal laws of change that may be discovered by social scientists (by Popper referred to as the "historicist" position).

Even the very act of making predictions may, for some, provide new knowledge, and therefore affect human agency. An extreme case in point is when the act of making a prediction serves to confirm or defeat same said prediction. This point may be illustrated with Robert Merton's ideas of self-defeating and self-fulfilling prophecies (1936). Consider the case of a bank failure; a bank is believed to be about to fail, and this view is diffused over media, which is then reason enough for the bank to fail. Why? Because (presumed) knowledge about the bank's failure (stakeholders hearing about the potential bankruptcy) will affect choices of actions (great numbers of stakeholders withdrawing their funds), which in effect may promote the predicted outcome (the bank collapses due to lack of funds). The important point to be noted is that the bank may have to file for bankruptcy even if it originally rested on sound reserves. Predictions may thereby influence the future and thereby the symmetry or asymmetry between the past and the future.

Where does this take us? Are we arguing that predictions should be avoided? No. Rather, we hold the position that purposeful predictions are made with care—that is, not without sound theories about the subjects under study. Theory allows us to anticipate certain aspects of the future—on a sound level of abstraction—which we may expect to behave symmetrically to the past. This role of theory in accounting for asymmetry is also evidenced in the example of Google Flu Trends, in which information about flu-related search terms allows us to make close to real-time predictions about the future spread of flu epidemics. As noted by Google, "past performance is no guarantee of future results." Accordingly, and to ensure the accuracy of their predictions, Google reiteratively adjusts their predictive models to reflect anticipated changes in internet search behavior. These adjustments are deeply grounded in anticipated behavioral patterns among people experiencing flu symptoms, for instance, which search terms they might use, how search terms might be combined, and so forth. As Google users, perhaps during a media hype, learn more about how to protect themselves against a flu, the knowledge base of a typical person starting to feel ill may change and, therefore, also the typical search behavior. Again, some degree of theory, whether in the form of implicit or explicit hypotheses, is an inevitable ingredient when anticipating these search behaviors. Without theory, we therefore could not choose which search queries to code and aggregate.

There are other reasons, too, why it might not even be desirable to give up theory in evaluation—even when bringing in Big Data. As Kitchin reminds us:

> *Whilst Big Data analytics might provide some insights, it needs to be recognized that they are limited in scope, produce particular kinds of knowledge, and still need contextualization with respect to other information, whether that be existing theory, policy documents, small data studies, or historical records, that can help to make sense of the patterns evident. (Kitchin citing Crampton, 2012)*

We agree with Kitchin on this point. Theory plays a central role in our current practice and can certainly be envisioned to continue to play an equally central role in evaluations involving Big Data. To understand why this might be, let us first consider two kinds of theory that many an evaluator tends to rely on and which sustain relevance in the context of Big Data:

1. program theory detailing the way in which the program to be evaluated (i.e., the evaluand) is expected to bring about change (which for our purpose may be treated as synonymous with intervention theory and theory of change) and
2. social scientific theories about the kinds of objects studied (typically borrowed from economics, sociology, cultural geography, etc.).

To be sure, this is not the place for a more comprehensive discussion of the different roles, nature, and types of theory in evaluation (see Pawson [2003] for an exemplary contribution on this topic). It should be noted, however, that our distinction is far from novel, but rather conventional in the evaluation literature. Similarly, Leeuw and Donaldson (2015) make a distinction between, first, the theories of policy makers, stakeholders, and evaluators underlying their professional work, and, second, social scientific theories that are capable of explaining the consequences of policies, programs, and evaluative actions with other factors than the intentions as such.

The case for using program theories in the context of Big Data is easily made. As philosopher Nancy Cartwright argues, the concept of causal structure is essential if we take interest in formulating rational strategies for action (1979). In the language of evaluators, this translates into as saying that we need to understand mechanisms—the how(s) and why(s) in a causal chain—if we are to gain external validity and formulate evidence-based policies—that is, strategies for action. And, as also pointed out by Cartwright and Hardie, evidenced-based policies are no more evidence based than the weakest link in the evidence chain (2012). As such, specifying each link in the causal structure is important. This holds also if we are to make good use of Big Data. And therefore, Big Data or not: We cannot evaluate programs without the notion of causal structure. From this perspective, program theory cannot—and should not—be discarded on account of Big Data. Social scientific theories have value too. In this wide category of theories, Leeuw and Donaldson (2015) place, among others, social, behavioral, and institutional theories, which provide possible explanations of what happens—intended or not—when policies and programs are implemented. Only a few widely adopted theories in this category are social learning theory, attachment theory, cognitive dissonance theory, social capital theory, public choice theory, and transaction costs theory.

Let us illustrate how one such theory may be utilized drawing on work done in economics. Note first that interventions to mitigate economic crises are frequently intended to be preemptive. It may therefore be helpful to start with a theory that could give us a picture of how, for instance, a particular sector, market segment, or group of firms is likely to develop in the future in the lack of an intervention. See, for instance, Rogoff and Reinhart (2009), entitled *This Time Is Different: Eight Centuries of Financial Folly*. The authors look into the anatomy of a number of crises during the last 800 years and report on recurring patterns regarding cycles in housing and equity prices, capital flows, unemployment, and government revenues around these crises. Unfortunately, the authors conclude, the similarities between ongoing and previous crises are seldom recognized in time. Various theories about the anatomy of economic crises are nonetheless potentially valuable to evaluation since they may be utilized to explicate a counterfactual—a picture of how, for instance, a market or government revenues would have developed in the lack of an intervention, for instance, during the American sub-prime crisis. Theory would assist us in selecting the data points relevant for tracing meaningful correlations and then construct a counterfactual. Note that this may be done even before an intervention is implemented; using Big Data, it is potentially possible to compare a predicted future with an intervention to a predicted future without an intervention. But the point is that Big Data do not do this work on their own. We must do the work ourselves—drawing on theory—to select the data points of relevance. Again, raw data have no meaning, because they are silent.

The end message is clear. First and foremost, we should be cautious of the claim that Big Data is a-theoretical. Any sensemaking—with or without Big Data—necessarily requires some element of theory. More than that, theory constitutes an important and unavoidable component of making predictions—a central aim for Big Data analytics. For these reasons, Big Data cannot reasonably be expected to replace theory in evaluation. Second, even if we were to accept the idea of the possibility of a-theoretical Big Data analytics, there are still reasons why we would want and need theory in evaluation. Indeed, we may benefit greatly from bringing together Big Data, evaluation-specific theory, such as program theory, and social scientific theory. Big Data analytics may pose a promising new avenue for analysis and knowledge production, but it cannot (and should not!) be a replacement of theory. Our evaluator hackles should never fail to rise when faced with attempts at reducing our practice to mere dustbowl empiricism, a completely a-theoretical foraging of correlations. Big Data is no exception.

Shift Two: From Causation to Correlation

Closely related to the first claim proclaiming the end of theory, some Big Data advocates have been quick to rejoice the shift from causation to correlation. The strongest—or at least boldest—manifestation of this claim is perhaps provided by Chris Anderson, former Editor-in-Chief of Wired, who in a widely cited opinion piece suggests "correlation supersedes causation, and science can advance even without coherent models, unified theories, or really any mechanistic explanation at all. There's no reason to cling to our old ways" (2008).

Anderson is professing to what is perhaps the most oft-predicted implication of Big Data in the social sciences. Underlying the view that there is an ongoing shift from causation to correlation is typically two different arguments, namely

(1) the claim that causation may be defined in terms of correlation; that is, correlation is both sufficient and necessary to infer causation and
(2) the claim that correlation is sufficient to satisfy our informational needs.

Let us consider these two claims in turn. The first claim posits that correlations grounded on Big Data suffice to infer causation. From this perspective, correlation is both (1) a sufficient and (2) a necessary condition for causal inference. In assessing the validity of this claim, it is helpful to briefly revisit the debates of the 1970s and 1980s on the nature of correlation and causality.

Prominently in these debates, Wesley Salmon and Patrick Suppes argued that causality can be defined in terms of time order and probability—a proposition that to this day perseveres. According to Suppes (1970), at the core of what we mean by causality is that one factor (A) raises the probability of another subsequently occurring factor (B), while this correlation is not accounted for by any other preceding factor. What Suppes wanted to get at was that there must be no other preceding factor that is correlated with both A and B, which is the actual cause of both of them and which, therefore, give rise to the correlation between them. If there is such a factor, we have a case of a so-called spurious relationship between A and B.[3] To avoid confusing these spurious relationships with causation, we must trace the preceding factors, which

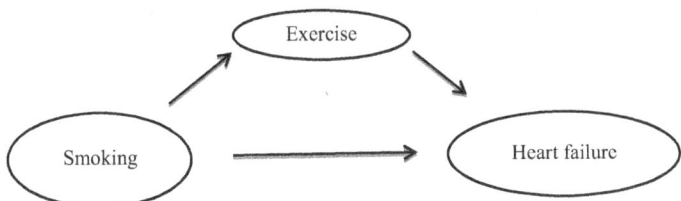

Figure 12.1. Causal Model for Smoking and Heart Failure.

may give rise to the correlation between A and B, critically scrutinizing the relationship among these. So far, so good.

In practice, difficulty often arises in relation to identifying and controlling for all other possible (even plausible) factors, which may give rise to a correlation between A and B. This challenge persists—even if we have access to Big Data. To illustrate, let us consider an optimal scenario: If we had *all* the data and the necessary capacity to process that data, would that not bridge the gap between correlation and causation?

Not necessarily, as mentioned earlier, a central element in delineating between correlation and causation is that of a causal structure (Cartwright, 1979). By bringing in the concept of causal structure, Cartwright brings attention to the fact that A may cause B via several different mechanisms, why understanding these is central when establishing causal claims about A and B. Consider Cartwright's classic example of the effects of smoking (1979). In this hypothetical example, smoking increases the probability of heart failure. However, since smokers are aware of this increased risk, they tend to exercise more than nonsmokers, which in turn reduce the probability of heart failure. The situation is illustrated in Figure 12.1.

In this example, the correlation between smoking and heart failure may be positive or negative or zero. Let's assume that the aggregated correlation between smoking and heart disease is zero. To conclude that there is no causal connection between smoking and heart failure would then be wrong. In fact, there is more than one causal connection between smoking and heart failure. This illustrates that correlation is not necessary for causation.

The example can also be used to illustrate why we basically need to take *all* other factors into account when determining causal relations only by correlation and time order. Let's turn back to the above figure and instead assume that the aggregated correlation between smoking and heart disease is negative. Is it then a reasonable conclusion that smoking causes good health? After all, if we compare exercising smokers to exercising nonsmokers, smokers will be the ones to face the greatest risk of heart failure. We will come to the same conclusion, if we were to compare non-exercising smokers to non-exercising nonsmokers. So perhaps it is a reasonable conclusion that smoking is a cause of heart failure after all? But also this conclusion runs into difficulties since if we divide our sub-groups by bringing in one more factor—for instance, gender or socio-economic status—the correlation may again be reversed. Since we must basically control for *all* other factors that may affect both smoking and heart failure, the conclusion must be that correlations under real-world conditions are insufficient to infer causation. In Cartwrights terminology, this example shows that a definition of causality should include the concept of causal structure. Correlations between data points are not enough.

But given the proposed revolutionary nature of *Big* Data, is it least possible that causation can be a property of a specific type of data? The answer must be no. There is nothing about the size of the data, or its comprehensiveness, which allows for the evaluator to bridge the gap between correlation and causation. This is because the credibility or validity of a causal claim is not a property of a specific type or amount of data. Making causal claims, bridging the gap between correlation and causation, typically involves a carefully thought-out combination of design, theory, and analytical strategy. In evaluation (and the social sciences more broadly), we employ specific designs to prove causal relationships, social and program level theories to understand these, and a broad range of analytical strategies to explain them. Indeed, it is the combination of these designs, theories, and analytical strategies that allows us to strengthen and sharpen the credibility of our causal claims, to filter out spurious correlations, and to bridge the gap between correlation and causation. There is nothing about the volume, veracity, or variety of Big Data that suffice to bridge the gap between correlation and causation.

In sum, the idea that correlation is causation in the era of Big Data appears to have less bite when partnered with the end of theory proposition, to have few teeth left when considering the often spurious nature of correlations, and to be all but ready for new dentures when accepting the demanding nature of supporting causal claims. No wonder the arguments for the correlation–causation shift often appear mumbled.

Moving past, then, this idea that correlation is causation is there anything to the second proposition; that correlation may still be sufficient for our informational needs? Perhaps this proposition will have more bite to the bone in the context of evaluation. After all, and in the words of Cukier and Mayer-Schoengberger, "If we know that certain correlations are robust, we do not need to know how and why that is. All we need is to predict what will happen" (2013).

The argument here is admittedly compelling: If we often don't need information or confirmation beyond correlation, is the extra burden required to infer causation even called for? In the view of such writers, there is simply no need to reason in terms of causality if we know enough about statistical correlations. In other words, if we know very much about how the world actually is, we do not need to speculate (i.e. formulate theories) or try to understand how and why the world is the way it is. This may hold some truth in marketing and retail, where the name of the game is to accurately predict shopping habits for the purpose of product placement. Similarly, making predictions about economic, cultural, social, and technological phenomena and trends surely has and continues to be of central importance in the social sciences.

Difficulties are likely to arise, however. Even with Big Data—perhaps particularly with Big Data—we will always run the risk of ending up with correlations between factors that have a common cause of which we remain unaware—perhaps a cause far back in time or a cause of which no human is aware. Such correlations may seem random and be of little use. We must remain open to this idea.

The consequences of the all too common forgetfulness of the spurious nature of many correlations are potentially severe. Casual consideration of a couple of empirically derived, real-world spurious correlations may serve to refresh our minds. Simply consider the following examples, which are not easily made sense of:

 a. The negative correlation between number of pirates and global average temperature.
 b. The positive correlation between the divorce rate in Maine and per capita consumption of margarine.
 c. The correlation between per capita consumption of chicken and total US crude oil imports (retrieved from http://tylervigen.com/).

Big Data or not: the authors would like to think that most evaluators would remain skeptical—hopefully dismissive—of any intervention offering to increase the number of pirates as remedy for global warming. This is an important point because the wonderful, messy world we do evaluation in and on is packed full of these entertaining—yet nonsensical—correlations. As noted by Boyd and Crawford, "too often, Big Data enables apophenia: seeing patterns where none actually exist, simply because enormous quantities of data can offer connections that radiate in all directions" (2012). This is an important point because casually capturing these correlations by casting out the big old net (while mildly entertaining) is potentially misguiding and harmful, especially if the correlational catch is misinterpreted as causally relevant and sufficient. Big Data or not, we should continue to heed the textbook warning: correlation is never causation. Pirates, of course, may disagree.

Another important point is that making accurate predictions is not likely to be the end-all, that is, the only aim of evaluation. Despite the many merits of these, is it likely that predictions will satisfy all of our informational needs, or even most? Is it reasonable to assume that our interest in how and why the world works would simply vanish? We think not. In the context of evaluation (and most other social sciences), the confinement inherent in this methodological singularism is analytically suffocating. This is because we typically entertain a broad range of questions in evaluation. To illustrate, consider the fictive evaluation of the widely implemented Scared Straight Programs—a juvenile impact program in which first time offenders are confronted by ex-convicts in an attempt to scare the participants straight, that is, deterring them away from criminal activities. In evaluating the impact of a Scared Straight Program, some or more of the following causal questions might be relevant:

1. Are the program participants scared straight? Just how scared are they?
2. Are the participants scared because of the program?
3. How and in what way are the participants scared straight?
4. Are specific components of the program particularly scary?
5. Would the participants be equally scared by an alternative program?

Leaving the fictional aspect of these questions aside, what each questions serves to exemplify is a different informational need. One question asks for causal proof (i.e., is the participants' fear caused by the program?), another question begs for explanation (i.e., how and in what way are the participants scared straight?), and yet another question—the policy-makers favorite—demands a comparative judgment (i.e., would the participants be equally scared by an alternative program?). Each question surely has a place in evaluation. And each question calls for much more than simple correlations and predictions.

With this example as our backdrop, reducing our informational needs to mere predictions seems oddly conservative—especially for a data analytic revolution! Would we really aspire to such a narrow field of practice? The correlation-is-all scenario suddenly appears intellectualy lazy, even undesirable and farfetched. As Kitchin (2014) opines "It is one thing to identify patterns; it is another to explain them, This requires social theory and deep contextual knowledge. As such, the pattern is not the end-point but rather a starting point for additional analysis, which almost certainly is going to require other datasets."

In summary, the purported shift from causation to correlation seems questionable for several reasons. The credibility, validity, of a causal claim/interpretation is not a property of a specific type of data but rather an argument relying on different configurations of theory, analytical strategies, and designs. More than that, the idea reducing valuable knowledge to predictive relationships and patterns seem strangely limiting and orthodox—counter-revolutionary even. Why should the promising avenue of Big Data limit the types of question we seek to answer? Why would expect Big Data to reduce rather than broaden the types of questions we would want to entertain? Big Data should expand and not limit our practice.

Shift Three: From Small Samples to Total Populations

The third purported shift in the Big Data analytic revolution is from small samples to total populations. The n = all is a compelling feature of Big Data. The potential benefits of conducting total population studies are obvious. If possible, the Big Data revolution would swiftly undermine traditional sample-based statistical methods and concerns. Gone would be the F statistics, the Student's t-tests, the chi-squares, the P values, and their coveted asterisks too. The power of n = all is simply beyond significance. Or is it?

Before rolling out the revolution, let us briefly consider what it is we mean by a "sample" in statistics. In its most basic formulation, "a sample is the subset of the population on which the study collects data" (Agresti and Finlay, 1997). The purpose of the sample then is to tell us something about the total set of subjects in our study (i.e. the population). This generalization from the sample may target a larger set of subjects, subjects in different settings or—perhaps most importantly—subjects in future populations (Redelings et al., 2012). However, this latter sampling in a temporal sense is where it gets a little philosophical: A sample is not just a subset of a population here, and now, it is also a subset of future populations to come.

The implication is that Big Data in many situations is still to be viewed as samples. And this is important if we are to utilize Big Data the way many proponents argue, namely to make predictions. Only if we view Big Data as a sample of a population including also future subjects, does it make sense to make predictions. More than that, and as previously discussed, the possibility of asymmetry between past and future conditions must be considered, at least theoretically. This is observed by Karpf, when stating: "Online behavior at Time X only predicts online behavior at Time X + 1 if (1) the underlying population from which we are sampling remains the same and (2) the medium itself remains the same" (2012).

These are two important yet dicey assumptions, especially in the rapidly changing world of technosocial phenomena, such as Twitter, Snapchat, and Facebook (what Karpf refers to as medium in the above quotation). In evaluation, we are rarely interested in what happened last year, or the year before; we would want to know about what will happen this year or next year. In this way, we gather data retrospectively to inform and generalize our findings to future events, situations, populations, and settings. Stated differently, we like to examine the past to learn about the future. As such, and probably more often than not, the sample we rely on is not only intended to provide insights about a current population but also rather intended to say something about how programs will work in future settings, for future populations, and so forth. From this perspective, we will still need to treat Big Data as a sample—at least in the temporal sense. And if circumstances are likely to change, even Big Data may be seen as a poor representation of the total population.

In light of these observations, how does Big Data (n = all) then fare as a statistical fortune teller? Well, it depends. First and foremost, statistical significance tests will be rendered useless because of the sheer size of the data set. Significant tests based on n = extremely high samples will result in even minor, practically insignificant, differences to be identified as statistically significant. In this way, many oft-relied statistical tests in the social sciences will have little if any role to play in Big Data analytics. The abandonment of statistical significance tests will probably be mourned by some and celebrated by others. However, other statistical techniques for measuring and visualizing dispersion around central tendency measures—confidence intervals, as just one example—would still be relevant and of interest, especially when making generalizations about future populations, which is arguably a common aim in evaluation. The motivation to explore—rather than to control—the variation in our data would likely persist, perhaps even be strengthened by the abolishment of significance tests.

There are other reasons too why we might not want to risk throwing out sampling considerations with the Big Data bathwater. Both Harford (2014) and Karpf (2012) remind us that the n = all is often a mirage, a rarely realized state when doing Big Data research. The importance of this point is illustrated in the following example offered by Boyd and Crawford (2012) on the use of Twitter for research purposes. As neatly illustrated by Boyd and Crawford (2012), research on Twitter traffic should be cautious—or at least cognizant—of the fact that Twitter does not represent all people—as such, even a complete sample of Tweets, Twitter users, or Twitter accounts is already skewed, if the researcher aspires to make claims about people more generally.

This is first and foremost because certain segments of society Tweet. The idea that these Twitter users are the representatives of the population more generally is likely to be flawed. What is more, as Boyd and Crawford point out, researchers should be mindful of the sample being skewed by "fake accounts" (simply consider Senator Newt Gingrich's infamous purchase of more than one million fake followers as part of his campaign for the 2012 Republican Party presidential nomination), users having multiple accounts, accounts being used by multiple users, or even accounts in which the content is produced by "bots" (2012).[4] More than that, the content of Tweets might be protected or private or even censored, again leading to systematic bias in subsequent analyses. Differential access to Tweets may also introduce bias. This is because subsets of Tweets are made publicly available for researchers through application programming interfaces; however, the sampling strategy for extracting these Tweets is unclear (Boyd and Crawford, 2012). Boyd and Crawford's example illustrates that many sampling issues might still persist—even with Big Data.

To make matters worse, there is nothing about the sheer size of the data set that remedies these problems. In fact, and as pointed out by Leonelli, the size of the data set may worsen the situation: "If all data sources share more or less the same biases (for instance, they all rely on microarrays produced with the same machines), there is also the chance that bias will be amplified, rather than reduced, through such Big Data" (2014).

This is because the bias stemming from a microarray will continue to grow relative to the size of the data. While massive amounts of data may remedy the threats of random error—nonrandom error continues to be a big concern. These nonrandom errors can be broadly divided into two types:

(1) Internal errors (also known as biases) such as misdiagnosis, underreporting, refusal bias, and confounding, which lead to errors in our estimates even if they are applied only to the population in our study; and
(2) Extrapolation (generalization) errors, which arise when the populations or times of interest differ in relevant ways from the population we actually studied (Redelings et al., 2012).

Both of these types of systematic errors will be relevant to consider as we sample our subsets of "tweets," "searches," mobile pings to the nearest phone mast, clicks on a website, "likes," or other types of digital traces. Big Data or not, we still run the risk of "construct underrepresentation"—systematically under-mining a subset of all the relevant "tweets" representing a concept. From this perspective, sampling error is still relevant to consider in relation to Big Data, not only in order to correctly mirror the past and the present but also since we will often aspire to make inferences on future populations.

Shift Four: From Clean Data to Messy Data

The fourth and final purported shift of the Big Data revolution is that of moving from clean to messy data. To broach the implications of this messiness, let us begin by considering what the nature of this messiness amounts to—what is messy about Big Data? Big Data is messy in at least two different ways. First, and in the words of Cukier and Mayer-Schoenberger, Big Data is messy in the sense that they are "data in the wild" (2013). What we think Cukier and Mayer-Schoenberger is getting at is that Big Data is generated without a specific research purpose—Big Data is authentic, unprompted by the researcher. Big Data comes out of the growing "datafication" of our everyday lives. The digital traces that emerge from this datafication are the building blocks of Big Data analytics. One implication of this "data in the wild" is that it is sometimes difficult to know how the data were produced (Boyd and Crawford, 2012). In this way, Big Data is at time "black box" data.

Second, Big Data is messy in the sense that they are fluid and fleeting. Simply consider how digital traces from social media are in constant flux, dynamic, and ever changing. The data set rapidly changes and expands. Big Data is also fleeting in the sense that they are not archived and available over time. Counter to common perception, only some—but by no means all—data are forever stored and available on the internet.

So what are the implications of this messiness? For some, the sheer size of the data is expected to compensate for the messiness. For example, as suggested by Cukier and Mayer-Schoenberger, we need to:

> "... shed our preference for highly curated and pristine data and instead accept messiness: in an increasing number of situations, a bit of inaccuracy can be tolerated, because the benefits of using vastly more data of variable quality outweigh the costs of using smaller amounts of very exact data" (2013).

The truth of this claim is of course to be verified over time. Unfortunately, the advocates of this position often leave unstated the way in which the sheer size should compensate for systematic errors (recall the Twitter example above). Perhaps the position assumes analyses at a very general level (relying on high aggregations of data). Perhaps the analyses are conducted at a much higher level than what many/most evaluations are conducted at. Perhaps we can accept a high error margin at local levels, if our goal is to make claims at a national level. Perhaps the position is simply grounded on revolutionary optimism. We don't know. However, for the purpose of many an evaluation, we often wish to make claims at the local level, which requires both acceptable margin of errors and some story to tell about how the data were generated. Our modest hope, then, as methodologically aware evaluators, is that there is still some room in the revolution for a more nuanced and balanced position on how to deal with the messiness.

Big Bang or Big Bust ... or Maybe Just a Big Beast to be Tamed? Concluding Thoughts on Big Data in Evaluation

The "datafication" of our everyday lives is a reality. Big Data offers us the opportunity to analyze human behavior at an unprecedented scale. Expectations have been high, and proponents of Big Data tend to argue that it will fundamentally transform how we produce—or ought to produce—knowledge about society. The present chapter has critically assessed the promises of Big Data in order to formulate a view on the role of Big Data in evaluation.

The starting points of this chapter were four fundamental shifts, which advocates of Big Data predict will result from the application of Big Data in the social sciences. The shift from theory to data-driven appears unfavorable for several reasons. First and foremost, data never speaks for themselves and are inherently reliant on theory, even in their creation. Secondly, the application of program and social scientific theory in evaluation allows us to make the most of Big Data. This is because the potent combination of theory and Big Data allows us to better understand how and why programs work.

The purported shift from causation to correlation also appears dubious upon closer examination. As noted earlier, there is nothing about the properties of Big Data that bridges the gap between correlation and causation. More than that, there is no reason to believe that our informational needs will be reduced to a-theoretical correlations.

The third proposed shift from samples to total populations appears to rely on fundamental assumptions about the populations and settings remaining stable over time—assumptions that in the context of many real-world evaluations appear questionable. More than that, attention should be awarded whether the n = all is realized even with Big Data, especially given the messy nature of tweets, likes and clicks.

This brings us to the fourth and final shift: the proposed shift from clean to messy data (Cukier & Mayer-Schoenberger, 2013, among others), which to be sure demands more attention. Big Data is messy in the sense of originating from non-evaluation prompted behaviors and from being inherently fluid and fleeting. The implications of this messiness are as of writing unknown.

Critically examining the promises of Big Data is not intended to dismiss the great potential of Big Data in evaluation. Instead, the authors hold the position that Big Data should be treated as a most valuable new tool in the evaluator's toolbox, rather than a replacement for theories, causal reasoning, or "small" data. The position of the authors is that the opportunities inherent to Big Data should be pursued to the fullest and that one of the great challenges to take on is to consider how Big Data is best combined with other existing data sources and analytical tools available to evaluators.

The authors, therefore, find that there is something ill-advised about the faddish and dismissive nature of the current debate on Big

Data in evaluation, especially the swift and unfounded dismissal of other equally important aspects of evaluation (e.g. the end-of-theory position falls in this category). Why is the conversation about Big Data one of the replacement rather than betterment of evaluation? Why is Big Data presented as a counter rather than a complementary avenue for evaluation? Why should Big Data crowd-out existing rather than crowd-in new and innovative methodologies? Does Big Data have to be reductionist?

We think not. In fact, we strongly believe that Big Data—when partnered with critical and methodological thinking—offers an unprecedented opportunity for evaluation.

Notes

1. Whether free will be predicted or not is, however, a debate going back at least to David Hume. The issue is far from settled. The important point for our purpose is, however, that nobody has been able to predict human agency at a grand scale—and Big Data does not seem to make a difference.
2. This follows from Popper's view that a theory is nothing but a hypothesis, which has not yet been falsified. An existing theory may always be falsified in the future. Therefore, no matter how much data we have, we will never have a verified theory.
3. According to "Reichenbach's principle", a so-called genuine correlation between two factors A and B is due to A causing B, B causing A (reverse causation), or A and B having the same cause C (spurious causation). There are, according to Reichenbach, no further options.
4. A "bot" can be defined as "a software application that runs automated tasks over the Internet" (Wikipedia).

References

Agresti, A., and B. Finlay. 1997. *Statistical Methods for the Social Sciences*. Third edition. Prentice-Hall, Inc.

Anderson, C. 2008. "The End of Theory: The Data Deluge Makes the Scientific Method Obsolete." *Wired*. Accessed July 21, 2014. http://archive.wired.com/science/discoveries/magazine/16-07/pb_theory.

Boyd, D., and K. Crawford. 2012. "Critical Questions for Big Data." *Information, Communication & Society* 15: 662–79.

Cartwright, N. 1979. "Causal Laws and Effective Strategies." *Noûs* 13 (4): 419–437.

Cartwright, N., and J. Hardie. 2012. *Evidence-Based Policy: A Practical Guide to Doing It Better*. New York, NY: Oxford University Press.

Crampton J., M. Graham, A. Poorthuis. 2012. "Beyond the Geotag? Deconstructing 'Big Data' and Leveraging the Potential of the Geoweb." http://www.uky.edu/~tmute2/geography_methods/readingPDFs/2012-Beyond-the-Geotag-2012.10.01.pdf.

Cukier, K. N., and V. Mayer-Schoenberger. 2013. "The Rise of Big Data – How It's Changing the Way We Think about the World." *Foreign Affairs*. Accessed July

21, 2014. http://www.foreignaffairs.com/articles/139104/kenneth-neil-cukier-and-viktor-mayer-schoenberger/the-rise-of-big-data.
Dupré, J., and N. Cartwright. 1988. "Probability and Causality: Why Hume and Indeterminism Don't Mix." *Noûs* 22 (4): 521–36.
Graham, M. 2012. "Big Data and the End of Theory." *The Guardian*. Accessed July 21, 2014. http://www.guardian.co.uk/news/datablog/2012/mar/09/big-data-theory.
Harford, T. 2014. "Big data: A big mistake?". *Significance, 11*(5): 14-19.
Karpf, D. 2012. "Social Science Research Methods in Internet Time." *Information, Communication & Society* 15: 639–61.
Kirkpatrick, R. 2012. "Harnessing the Power of Real Time Data: A 21st Century Approach to Monitoring and Evaluation." Keynote awarded at the 10th European Evaluation Society Biennial Conference, Helsinki.
Kitchin, R. 2014. "Big Data, New Epistemologies and Paradigm Shifts." *Big Data & Society* 1: 1–12.
Leeuw, F. L., and S. Donaldson. 2015. "Theory in Evaluation: Reducing Confusion and Encouraging Debate." *Evaluation* 21 (4): 467–80.
Leonelli, S. 2014. "What Difference Does Quantity Make? On the Epistemology of Big Data in Biology." *Big Data & Society* 1: 1–11.
Merton, R. K. 1936. "The Unanticipated Consequences of Purposive Social Action." *American Sociological Review* 1 (6): 894–904.
Pawson, R. 2003. "Nothing as Practical as Good Theory." *Evaluation* 9 (4): 471–90.
Pawson, R., and N. Tilley. 1997. *Realistic Evaluation*. Thousand Oaks, CA: Sage.
Popper, K. 1957. *The Poverty of Historicism*. London: Routledge.
Shirky, C. 2009. "Newspapers and Thinking the Unthinkable." Accessed July 21, 2014. http://www.shirky.com/weblog/2009/03/newspapers-and-thinking-the-unthinkable/.
Raghaven, P. 2014. "It's Time to Scale the Science in the Social Sciences." *Big Data & Society* 1: 1–4.
Redelings, M. D., F. Sorvillo, L.V. Smith, and S. Greenland. 2012. "Why Confidence Intervals Should Be Used in Reporting Studies of Complete Populations." *The Open Public Health Journal* 5: 52–4.
Reichenbach, H. 1956. *The Direction of Time*. Berkeley: University of Los Angeles Press.
Rogoff, C. M., and K. S. Reinhart. 2009. *This Time Is Different: Eight Centuries of Financial Folly*. Princeton University Press.
Suppes, P. 1970. *A Probabilistic Theory of Causality*. Amsterdam: North-Holland Publishing Company.
United Nations. 2012. "Big Data for Development: Opportunities & Challenges: A Global Pulse White Paper." Accessed July 21, 2014. http://unglobalpulse.org/BigDataforDevWhitePaper.
Welles, B. F. 2014. "On Minorities and Outliers: The Case for Making Big Data Small." *Big Data & Society* 1: 1–2.
White, H. 2010. "A Contribution to Current Debates in Impact Evaluation." *Evaluation* 16 (2): 153–164.

13

Cyber Society, Big Data, and Evaluation: A Future Perspective

Gustav Jakob Petersson, Frans Leeuw, and Karol Olejniczak

Data mirroring various aspects of our lives are today being recorded automatically—and in real time—for instance, as we take our lives online and as we are recorded by sensors in the physical world. Such data can be combined with data generated in more traditional ways, and databases grow to the extent that it gets difficult to analyze them by traditional methods. Data grow big and bigger, mirroring more and more aspects of human behavior and interaction.

Perhaps the most striking example illustrating how much data are being recorded on the most intimate aspects of our lives is the Quantified Self (QS) movement, which is devoted to incorporate technology into data acquisition on aspects of a person's daily life in terms of inputs (e.g. food consumed and quality of surrounding air), states (e.g. mood, arousal, and blood oxygen levels), and performance (mental and physical). Data are generated through self-monitoring and self-sensing with wearables (=wearable sensors, such as electroencephalography, electrocardiography, and video) and wearable computing.[1] There are also websites where information about oneself can be uploaded and compared with others, and according to Swan (2013: 86), this movement "is starting to be a mainstream phenomenon."[2] When QS is merged with "Quantified Communities," which include sensorized ("smart") streets, buildings, houses, and the Internet of [other] things, also contexts in which behavior is taking place will be monitored (in real time).

Big Data is important for a community, which seeks to understand changes in human behavior and what causes them. This is exactly what evaluators do when asking questions about programs, interventions, regulation, and other activities aimed to influence the physical or the digital world. We ask questions such as

- Did the intervention X have the intended effect on the target group's behavior?
- Which factors and mechanisms were responsible for the observed change?
- Were there any unintended side effects of the intervention?
- How could the design and delivery of the intervention be improved to increase its effectiveness and utility?

We may, for instance, investigate whether web-based information campaigns to influence the consumption of alcohol are effective. We may estimate the potential consequences of an intervention to influence traffic flows in a certain district with certain characteristics by comparing to similar previous cases. We may investigate whether an intervention to reduce digital piracy affects the norms surrounding illegal downloading. We could in all these and many more cases draw on Big Data.

And yet the current book strongly indicates that evaluators so far have been reluctant or ignorant to recognize and utilize Big Data. Algorithms are being produced, data are being automatically stored and are therefore potentially cheap to use, but evaluators working in this "tradition" are hardly to be found. Chapter 3, by Højlund, Olejniczak, Petersson, and Rok, tells the story of a survey on the use of Big Data in evaluation, which was sent to all members of the American Evaluation Association and European Evaluation Society *LinkedIn* groups. A strikingly low response rate of less than one percent, combined with almost no trace of evaluative work with Big Data in the current literature, arises suspicion and worries: have evaluators got nothing to say about Big Data? Have we—as a profession—failed in recognizing the new opportunities?

At least as worrying, commissioners seem to create few incentives for evaluators to tap into Big Data. And, as shown in chapter 10, sometimes they not only neglect the opportunities associated with Big Data but even close the evaluators' door to Big Data by regulating that evaluations should be performed with more traditional methods.

We therefore conclude that although there are links between evaluation and Big Data, they have by far not been explored or used as deep and wide as possible. This not only entails a challenge and the perspective of a bright Big Data Evaluation Future, but also a risk. The risk is that other professionals may take over (parts of the) roles that evaluators have been performing the last decades. These are communities like data scientists (with a training in working with (small/big T) theories and capable of—at the least—understanding and addressing evaluative questions) and cyber and biospecialists (like infodemiologists) and also "citizen scientists" (through crowd sourcing and apps that make data collection and analysis an "easy piece of cake").

Recent research by Professor Erik Brynjolfsson from MIT (see White Paper "Big Data for Development: Challenges & Opportunities," Global Pulse, 2012)[3] clearly indicates a significant difference in the data payoff between companies relying on "data-driven decision-making processes" and companies relying primarily on "experience and intuition." It is not very far fetched to transfer this insight to the contributions that *could* be made by evaluators working with and using Big Data to enhance (public) policy making and implementation compared to those that do *not*.

We therefore imagine that evaluators must either accept to play a small role or embrace Big Data, while at the same time proactively showing how their traditional skills and methods can enrich decision makers' understandings of problems and their potential solutions. The bright sight of the future is evaluators that either do Big Data work themselves or collaborate with "these folks" and add insights coming from theory-driven evaluations, knowledge repositories, expertise in stimulating utilization of findings, and much more.

Four Challenges

To enhance "the bright side of things," we have demonstrated that evaluators could engage with Big Data in several different ways. Also others have demonstrated that it may prove rewarding for evaluators to engage with Big Data.[4] Big Data may help us perform tasks at the heart of the evaluator profession, such as providing timely and accurate evidence for the design of new interventions. But at present, it is also clear that to be able to use Big Data at its full potential, we will need to learn more about the new data sources, designs, and tools at hand. We should also seek collaboration with and learn from other communities currently working with Big Data to provide timely results. And we must make clear that we have important insights to deliver in return.

We see the following four main challenges for evaluators to work with Big Data:

(1) to seek a new role in the policy process,
(2) to learn about new designs and tools used by others for evaluative purposes,
(3) to obtain new competencies to manage data, and
(4) to obtain cocreation with communities with great insights into Big Data.

We will consider these challenges in turn.

Challenge 1: Seeking a New Role in the Policy Process

Big Data create new opportunities to do ex ante work—that is, to assess the results of interventions already before they are implemented. Such work encompasses modeling, drawing on previous similar situations, as well as testing interventions in small-scale pilots, perhaps in the form of an RCT. In our opinion, this may be a game changer because it is a highly pragmatic and user-oriented way to work—and yet firmly grounded in data and research. Contrary to evaluation results that are postponed in time (especially ex post assessments) it offers just-in-time knowledge. As evaluators, we may therefore need to rethink our role in public policy from noninvolved assessors of worth and merit to codesigners and testers of policy.

We will need to draw inspiration from other policy fields, such as the work done by *behavioral insights teams* (aka *nudging*; Haynes et al., 2012; Olejniczak and Śliwowski, 2015; Shafir, 2012; World Bank, 2015). Such areas of research blur the lines between design, monitoring, and evaluation. Researchers and analysts assist policy decision makers in theory building (often by searching for mechanisms through pattern recognition in data or in the psychological literature), then testing policy prototypes with data (Big Data) or with pilot experiments, and then adapting those prototypes and scaling them up to full-size interventions. In short, they design, test, evaluate (predict), and adapt as they go![5]

Similarly, in economics, Big Data is being used to predict future economic trends (as predicted with and without interventions) as well as to predict the influence of marketing. Big Data is being used both as a mean to capture difficult-to-map features of society and as a cheaper or more accurate substitute for more conventional data sources, such as census data and labor market data (Taylor et al., 2014).

Another example is Chapter 5 of the present volume, by Frank Willemsen and Frans Leeuw, which demonstrated the use of Google Correlate. This tool was used to trace search queries closely correlated with the frequency of bankruptcies in the Netherlands. The important lesson was that search queries associated, for instance, with unemployment support seem to precede rises in the actual number of bankruptcies. Such correlations highlight new opportunities for predictive work: starting in a situation where certain search queries become more common, it would be possible to model different future scenarios depending on which interventions are implemented.

We conclude that the new real-time data sources disrupt the traditional policy cycle and create new opportunities for impact evaluations, no matter if the evaluations are performed before or after an intervention has been implemented, remembering that we previously pointed out that the affluence of Big Data allows for the creation of baselines backwards in time. So far, this potential seems to have been realized to a greater extent in ex ante than in ex post work.

Also with a focus on prediction, the United Nations Global Pulse—an important advocate of Big Data in policy making—suggests the use of Big Data to protect communities from multiple slow-onset crises. The working hypothesis is that when people begin to be impacted by slow-onset crises, such as a descent into poverty, they change how they use services and participate in programs. For instance, changes may occur in how people use mobile phone services. Suggesting a hypothetical model for changes, which may occur at different stages of a descent into poverty, it is suggested that the digital trails created by mobile phone usage potentially could be used to take the pulse of communities in real time and secure that interventions are implemented before it is too late: "We think of these changing patterns of usage as potential 'digital smoke signals' that could alert policy makers that vulnerable populations are in trouble."[6]

We previously also touched upon the ongoing digitization of registers of administrative data. The resulting data sets create new opportunities for data mining and information retrieval, helping developing legal analytics. One form of legal analytics uses fact patterns and precedents to *predict* a case's outcome, thereby better equipping lawyers to assess the likely result of litigation (McGinnis and Pearce, 2014). Computational legal studies constitute another example. Thousands of documents are being analyzed to predict decisions of the US Supreme Court—with seventy percent validity (Katz et al., 2014)[7]—and to make the legal world more transparent for civilians and organizations (Katz and Bommarito II, 2014: 3–4).

It is, however, important to remember what should and what should not be expected from relying to a greater extent on modeling. Contrary to what has been emphasized by some observers, Chapter 14 of the present volume by Sebastian Lemire and Gustav Jakob Petersson, argued that data-driven knowledge production appears unfavorable unless combined with sound theories to explain observed correlations. Data never speak for themselves and are inherently reliant on theory, even in their creation. To understand correlations, the authors argue that we need theory about the generative causal mechanisms. Otherwise interventions may be severely misled.

In some cases, however, using Big Data to guide interventions in a sound way will require neither modeling nor *explicit* theory. The velocity of the data may be more important. Global Pulse[3] highlights the example of an administrator of the United States' Federal Emergency Management Agency advocating the use of Twitter messages to decide where to use resources during a series of devastating tornadoes in the American mid-west in 2011. Federal Emergency Management Agency began monitoring Twitter and noticed an unusual number of different geographical locations being mentioned for tornado damage. These Twitter messages may have not been very accurate estimates of the level of damage, but they did provide an opportunity to dispatch resources in time—that is, before it turned impossible to reach damaged communities. Therefore, it proved better to rely on the Twitter messages—delivered in real time—than to await more thorough analyses.

Challenge 2: Learning About New Designs and Tools Used by Others for Evaluative Purposes

In the era of Big Data, evaluators will have to redefine their toolbox, as Big Data and its related technologies provide new opportunities to perform tasks at the very heart of the evaluator profession. Let's exemplify by looking into how others create new possibilities to trace the results of interventions—a task discussed thoroughly, for instance, in relation to realist evaluations and experimental designs (Astbury and Leeuw, 2010; Pawson, 2013; Shadish et al., 2002). In the following, we discuss new possibilities to conduct pilots, to trace mechanisms, to conduct randomized experiments, to create baselines backwards in time, and to measure behavior traditionally held to be difficult to observe.

A recently emerging family of research designs, which may be used already as a pilot, is simulations, serious games, and gamification. This kind of design does not create the ethical problems associated with laboratory experiments, and it provides good insight into both the effects of interventions and mechanisms which generate the effects (Gillert, 2008). Such designs can be positioned in the broader group of quasiexperiments.

Serious games are used to test solutions in a safe environment. They can test behavioral reaction to interventions, but they also allow to explore possible dynamics of very complex policy interventions (like reform of the health-care sector financing) (Duke and Geurts, 2004; Harteveld, 2011). One example of such a promising new design is *VRET: Virtual Reality Impact Assessments*. One of the foundations of this development dealt with assessing the impact of interventions and therapies on certain phobias. The idea behind VRET is that one need not be in "real (classic) reality" to experience phobia-inducing situations and the (beneficial) impact of behavioral interventions reducing these feelings. These interventions and the realities in which they are tested ("evaluated") can be virtual.

According to te Velde et al. (2015) the literature shows that video games seem to have a lot of potential to be used for educational and training purposes. They hold that the main distinction with entertainment (video) games from the earlier years is that in serious games, there is always a higher goal beyond the game itself—it teaches the user something that he or she can apply in everyday life. The premise remains that the game should be able to immerse the player into the gameplay in order to achieve the learning objectives.

Gamification is to apply game principles to processes in the "real world" (such as work processes in an organization), using game mechanics (e.g. fun, competition, curiosity, and feedback) to drive people toward more engagement in certain behaviors and habit building (namely buying products and working or studying harder). It is used by business and education (Burke, 2014; Kapp, 2012). Cyber therapies, sometimes in the form of serious games, are available and evaluated in virtual reality settings, which stimulate people to refrain from smoking, influence their level of depression, and prevent them from drinking too much alcohol—in the real world. Many other examples are available in the world of health, safety, and aggression, resilience of first responders (when there are disasters), and corrections (in prisons), for example, the 2013 issue of the *Annual Review of Cybertherapy and Telemedicine*. Section 4 details about the evaluation studies and includes the following papers:

- Clinical Experiment to Assess Effectiveness of Virtual Reality Teen Smoking Cessation Program.
- The German VR Simulation Realism Scale—Psychometric Construction for Virtual Reality Applications with Virtual Humans.
- Virtual Multiple Errands Test: Reliability, Usability, and Possible Applications.
- Virtual Reality as a Method for Evaluation and Therapy After Traumatic Hand Surgery.

Would it not be possible—we ask—to adopt the principles of serious games also in relation to real-world interventions—perhaps to construct cost-effective pilots? Think again of the cyber therapies, which draw on virtual reality settings intended to reduce smoking, alcohol consumption, or the level of depression. Could the physical world in some cases be modeled upon the virtual realities that seem the most promising?

Of a different nature are studies that develop new instruments to increase the depth of interactions in cyber space (while at the same time collect data). An example is Huisman et al.'s (2013) study of the TaSST: the *Tactile Sleeve for Social Touch*. The "basic idea of the TaSST is that when two persons both wear a sleeve, a touch to the sleeve of one person is felt as a vibration on the sleeve of the other person. This way, the TaSST enables two people to touch each other over a distance."[8] These devices may help reduce the distance between people when they are acting in the cyber (or augmented) reality and can be of use in detecting how cyber actions influence emotions and behavior, as if they were acting in the "real, i.e. classic reality." As more and more policies and programs focus on triggering behavioral responses *in digitalis*, tools to measure reactions to these stimuli and their underlying mechanisms are becoming important (Leeuw and Leeuw, 2012).

Others already use real-time Big Data to conduct full-scale randomized experiments. Let's have a look at how organizations like Google and Microsoft do "their" online experiments. Web-facing companies, including Amazon, eBay, Facebook, Google, Groupon, LinkedIn, Microsoft, Netflix, StumbleUpon, and Yahoo, use online controlled experiments to guide product development and accelerate innovation. They are often referred to as A/B experiments. This allows organizations to test different [e]solutions (or web design approaches

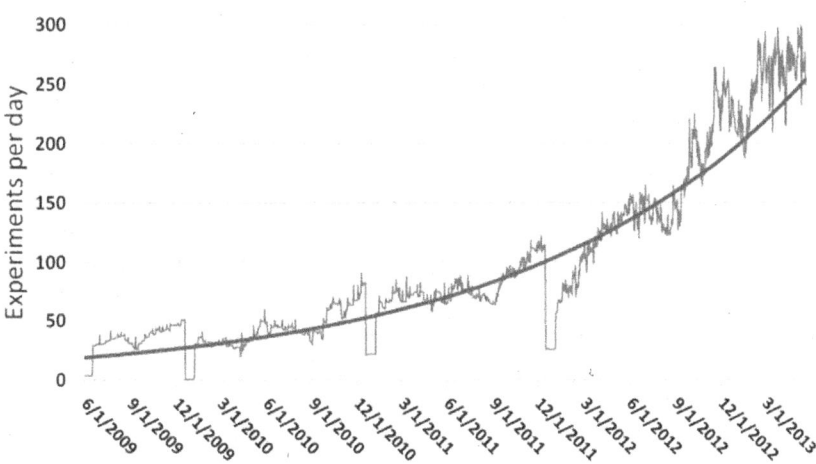

Figure 13.1. Exponential Growth in Experimentation Over Time (Kohavi et al., 2013).

and layouts) by randomly displaying either a "control" page or a "treatment" page containing the change to users. The focus is often on metrics like click-through rates. At Microsoft's Bing, the use of controlled experiments has grown exponentially over time, with over 200 concurrent experiments now running on any given day. Kohavi et al. (2013) for Microsoft and Tang et al. (2010) for Google describe the way in which these Big Data organizations carry out their numerous experiments. Figure 13.1 shows the growth of experimentation at Microsoft Bing's.

These experiments are organized in the so-called *Bing Experimentation System*. This system is "one of the largest systems in the world for running online controlled experiments, with over 200 experiments running concurrently, exposing about 100 million active monthly customers to billions of Bing variants that include implementations of new ideas and variations of existing ones." Kohavi et al. (2013: 4 ff) also discuss "negative experiments," where in principle the treatment group gets a lower speed or other negative experiences when on the Internet.

The affluence of real time-generated Big Data also provides opportunities for *creating baselines backwards in time*. For instance, consider the digitization of registers of administrative data. An example may be drawn from legal Big Data. Lawyers, legislators, and regulators have been producing documents, notes, memoranda, rules, and regulations for decades, if not centuries, which are now being digitized. Ravellaw.com[9] illustrates what working with and visualizing legal Big Data is about. In Ravel Law, you may plug in a term—let's say: climate change. You will then receive a list of cases relating to your search term and also an interactive graphic representation of the citation network of all cases using the search term. The visual representation allows the user to identify cases citing cases, the strength of each case as a citation source for others, and the timeline of cases in the network. Ravel Law may therefore be used to identify the "big case" in a topic or to trace the growth of the topic in case law—that is, to create a baseline backwards, perhaps reaching further back in time than the introduction of the latest regulation in that field.

Another challenging development is to do *digital evaluations* of *digital policies*. As many evaluators are fully aware, sometimes it is difficult not only to estimate the counterfactual development on a target variable but also to estimate the real-world development. This may be so, for instance, if the target variable mirrors morally questionable, or even illegal, behavior. Changes in such behavior due to an intervention would be difficult to capture through, for instance, a survey. Focusing on one such intervention, Chapter 6, by H.B.M. Leeuw, tapped into real-time Big Data to estimate impacts. The evaluated intervention was intended to reduce the frequency of digital piracy, that is, of illegal downloading. Since it is difficult to directly measure the frequency of digital piracy, the development of this phenomenon was indirectly measured through the frequency of search queries associated with downloading. Big Data proved valuable and easily accessible. The important lesson is that Big Data enhances the possibilities to observe how people act and, therefore, reduces the need to ask.

Challenge 3: Obtaining New Competencies to Manage Data

Evaluators have a lot to learn on the technical level, including how to work with Big Data sources, highly complex analytical procedures, algorithm development, etc. Not the least importantly, evaluators will have to learn more about how to combine different sources of (big and "small") data to provide timely, valid, and reliable results and recommendations. As will be elaborated further on, carefully selected primary data may be important to secure the validity of results when working with Big Data. Being able to combine them may therefore be important. Apart from this, evaluators have a lot to learn on the conceptual level, including such issues as the logic of theory building from pattern recognition and dealing with hidden biases of apparently immense data.

Consider, for instance, the example provided by US president Obama through the introduction of the Precision Medicine Initiative, which we touched upon earlier. Basically, Precision Medicine Initiative means combining different sources of data to enhance more individualized treatment. Since the announcement, the National Institutes of Health has been convening a working group to build a foundation of rules, standards, and principles. As a part of this project, the largest portion of funding is being dedicated to the development of a voluntary national research cohort of a million or more volunteers to propel our understanding of health and disease. As a part of engaging this cohort, the National Institutes of Health is considering the role of patient-generated data from mobile phones and sensors.

What are the options for evaluations? The generation of more data on social interaction, for instance, from the Internet, on individual states and movements, for instance, through self-tracking, and the option to combine different data sets, potentially allows for similar developments in social interventions. If you change Precision Medicine Initiative into *Precision Evaluation Initiative*, you will have this first future perspective. Precision Evaluation Initiative will be able to use QS data (anonymized unless somebody wants to share her/his own data), link it with other data sources, and therefore go for a new level of mixing mixed methods.

The beginning of such an approach, which is crucial for fact finding and understanding how things work (or don't) for evaluators, is described by Blok and Pedersen (2014). The work of these authors highlights both the value and the challenging nature of combining different kinds of data. They give an example of how Big Data on social networks may rewardingly be combined with ethnographic fieldwork data. They describe how their Copenhagen Social Networks Study seeks to make continuous recordings of social interactions at all communication channels in a freshman class of the Danish Technical University ($N > 1,000$). Smart phones were distributed to students as measurement devices ("sociometers") and then used to capture face-to-face encounters via Bluetooth, geolocation proximities via GPS, social network data via apps, and telecommunication data via call logs. Parallel to this data collection, an ethnographer collected "thick" ethnographic fieldwork data on friendship and other social relations among the same group of students. Additionally, researchers tracked different components of the social fabric via the application of established survey methods. Blok and Pedersen term their approach "remixing mixed methods."

Do we as evaluators have the necessary skills to perform such work? Some of us undoubtedly have, others don't. However, getting started with Big Data is not only about acquiring technical expertise. The evaluator must also adopt a new mindset. We must be able to address the following questions: what should we seek to manage on our own when working with Big Data (analytics), what should we perform in cooperation with other communities and persons, and what should be outsourced? What relevant data may be out there already, how can it be accessed, and what primary data should it be supplemented with? Evaluators will need to assess their own skills and the skills of their teams to determine what needs to be supplemented and how.

This is not to say that all analyses including Big Data must be technically advanced. Several of our chapters have shown that it is possible for evaluators to work with Big Data without including the heavy artillery of Big Data analytics. This has been demonstrated, for instance, in the chapters of the present volume, which draw on Google Correlate to find correlations of value for predictive work. Also, the tools to analyze new sources of data are frequently plenty and for free, such as Google Correlate. As pointed out in Chapter 11, by Francesco Mazzeo Rinaldi, Giovanni Giuffrida, and Tom Negrete, the main value that makes a difference is not in the tools as such but in the ability to choose the right mix of tools for the project at hand. But as pointed out in Chapter 4, by Maria Barrados and Jonathan Mitchell, evaluators are often reluctant to turn to secondary data sources. Innovative approaches to searching through the data to identify reasonable and appropriate measures will surely need to be developed.

To answer some questions more advanced technical skills will be needed, but the question may be raised if it is really wise for evaluators to seek to acquire the competencies needed to conduct the Big Data analytics today performed by data and computer scientists. Another option would be to seek cooperation with Big Data analysts, forming teams for evaluative inquiry. Cocreation may be a key concept for the future.

Challenge 4: Obtaining Cocreation

We believe that the advent of Big Data analytics will mean an increased need for evaluators to collaborate with Big Data analysts and other innovative communities. It is not reasonable to expect evaluators to acquire the key competencies of, for instance, data scientists. For evaluators, collaboration may also be a way to secure access to data. This is important, since the existence of enormous amounts of data does not imply that data are accessible to evaluators, although sometimes they are.

But let us also consider another pertinent issue. Is there a risk that Big Data will render the competencies of evaluators obsolete, meaning small incentives for others to collaborate with evaluators? Indeed, the expectations on Big Data have been high, and proponents tend to argue that it will fundamentally transform how we produce—or ought to produce—knowledge about society.

We believe or not. As emphasized previously, a shift from theory to data-driven knowledge production appears unfavorable for several reasons. Rather, the application of program and social scientific theories in evaluation allows us to make the most of Big Data. This is because the potent combination of theory and Big Data allows us to understand how and why programs work. This is particularly so since a shift from samples to total populations—which is sometimes proposed by Big Data proponents—is not a realistic idea since it should be doubted that the n = All proposition is realized even with Big Data. The messiness of the data, the "cyber exclusion" of communities without smart phones and Internet access, and the doubtful stability of the populations and settings contribute to this problem. "Blind" Big Data predictions, therefore, seem ill-advised for policymaking.

We will instead argue that it is important to realize complementarities between traditional evaluator skills and skills associated with Big Data. Big Data analytics has demonstrated its ability to analyze large sets of both structured and unstructured data. Evaluators, on the other hand, have demonstrated important abilities, for instance, in designing studies, obtaining primary data, analyzing and inferring judgment, and converting data into actionable information, thereby securing good opportunities for intended uses of findings.

It is important to emphasize evaluators' experience in working with program theory, theory of change, and social scientific theory. This experience will remain valuable since a data-driven approach cannot replace the need for theory. It will allow us to formulate hypotheses about the causal mechanisms at play. As pointed out by Pawson (2013), understanding these mechanisms greatly enhances the improvement of the evaluated programs. These hypotheses may be tested by applying Big Data. Also the other way around, the experience of working with theory will help us understand the correlations that we find in Big Data when adopting a data-driven approach. Evaluators' experience of working with theory will also remain central to find and reject alternative explanations, which is a central element, for instance, in the General Elimination Method and in Contribution analysis. Chapter 6 by H.B.M. Leeuw discussed how we can move from finding correlations between interventions and changes on target variables to estimate impacts and discuss quasiexperimental designs and the General Elimination Method. This study is an example of how evaluators' skills can be used to answer questions generated by monitoring performed with Big Data. Similarly, Big Data analytics may show patterns but cannot always explain the underlying motivations and rationales, calling for evaluators' skilled reasoning. Combining big and small data will therefore elevate the validity of evaluators' conclusions and recommendations. This has been emphasized in several chapters of the present volume. Chapter 9, by Steffen Bohni Nielsen, Nicolaj Ejler and Maryanne Schretzman, demonstrated that evaluation methods can enrich the computational method applied in Big Data analytics. Another way to conceive the complementarity between big and small data is that Big Data because of its messiness has its greatest value on the aggregated, perhaps national, level and should therefore be utilized as comparative or benchmark data for evaluation purposes at the local level. Others have argued that evaluation by definition exists because of some kind of intended (legitimate or illegitimate) use made of it (Shaw et al., 2006). If Big Data analytics and data visualization promise new ways to produce results relevant for decision making, then evaluators are well equipped to design relevant analyses and to transform results into actionable recommendations. Also, Nielsen et al. (2015) discussed the identification of evaluator skills. These include the ability to identify informational needs of intended users in the entire chain of decision makers. The involvement of intended users throughout the process, tailored reporting, and nuanced interpretations are critical for the findings to matter. Identifying users' needs and planning how to best meet them may have to be done in new ways to incorporate opportunities associated with Big Data. And indeed evaluators have great experience in stakeholder involvement, which may enhance the value of the recommendations.

And finally: just as evaluators are capable and well positioned to analyze "new" developments like nudging and the works of "behavioral insights teams" in government,[10] evaluators can also shed light on what the contributions are of working with Big Data to increase efficiency and effectiveness of public policies. Thinking that evaluation and Big Data analytics should be considered as valuable supplements—not as alternatives—we find it important to avoid a revival of the dichotomized qualitative versus quantitative debate. We find such debates ill-advised since social science, and evaluation, will always benefit from the existence of a plurality of methods and perspectives. To achieve meaningful coproduction is, however, not a challenge that can be met by evaluators alone. It is also a challenge for commissioners of evaluations, since it may require new management competence practices. In Chapter 10, by Kim Forss and Jonas Norén, it is found that commissioners seem to create few incentives for evaluators to tap into Big Data. Commissioners sometimes not only neglect the opportunities associated with Big Data but also close the evaluators' door to Big Data by regulating that evaluations should be performed with more traditional methods.

Concluding Remarks

As evaluators, we must embrace and learn more about what Big Data and its analytics have to offer. We must learn more about how other communities work with Big Data, not the least to be able to elaborate on and update our own methods to analyze results. We must also adopt a new mindset to data and seek to fill new roles in the policy process, not the least to contribute in new ways to predictive work when designing new interventions. To enhance our work, we must spread the message to other key players, such as commissioners of evaluations. Otherwise it may be rendered difficult to adopt innovative approaches. Also professional development on emergent quantitative techniques may be a crucial factor.

We should also seek to pitch what evaluation has to offer when collaborating with Big Data experts. We believe that the ability to combine different theories, methods, and perspectives as well as the ability to enhance use will be keys for evaluators to stay relevant in the Big Data era. We have a lot to learn from and about emerging communities, such as the community of Big Data analysts, and also have valuable insights to deliver in return.

Notes

1. Standard contemporary QS devices include Fitbit pedometers, myZeo sleep trackers, and Nike+ and Jawbone UP fitness trackers. The Quantified Self web site lists hundreds of these tools. http://quantifiedself.com/guide/) (accessed March 15, 2016).
2. Swan (2013: 86): QS "is starting to be a mainstream phenomenon as 60% of U.S. internet using adults are currently tracking their weight, diet, or exercise routine, and 33% are monitoring other factors such as blood sugar, blood

pressure, headaches, or sleep patterns. Further, 27% of U.S. Internet users track health data online, 9% have signed up for text message health alerts, and there are 40,000 smartphone health applications available."

3. "Big Data for Development: Opportunities & Challenges," http://www.unglobalpulse.org/projects/BigDataforDevelopment (accessed March 15, 2016).
4. See also http://betterevaluation.org/blog/big_data_in_evaluation (accessed March 15, 2016).
5. However, see Kosters and van der Heijden (2015) for a critical analysis of nudging.
6. "United Nations Global Pulse." http://www.unglobalpulse.org/blog/digital-smoke-signals (accessed March 15, 2016).
7. "Computational Legal Studies." http://www.computationallegalstudies.com/ (accessed March 15, 2016).
8. See also http://gijshuisman.com/?p=215 (accessed March 15, 2016).
9. "Ravellaw." https://www.ravellaw.com/ (accessed March 15, 2016). This is based on J. B. Ruhl's "Law 2050" post on http://law2050.com/tag/ravel-law/ (accessed March 15, 2016). Also see Leeuw and Schmeets (2016) for more examples.
10. See Kosters and van der Heijden (2015: 276) paper on "evaluating Nudge theory," in which they address questions like these: "Is nudging evaluable as a theory and a practice, and if so how? Is there solid evidence available of nudge success over other governance interventions? What is to be considered a nudge success? What data and evaluative techniques may assist in evaluating nudging beyond individual cases?"

References

Astbury, B., and F. Leeuw. 2010. "Unpacking Black Boxes: Mechanisms and Theory Building in Evaluation." *American Journal of Evaluation* 31 (3): 363–81.

Blok, A., and M. Pedersen. 2014. "Complementary Social Science? Quali-Quantitative Experiments in a Big Data World." *Big Data & Society* 1 (2): 1–6.

Burke, B. 2014. *Gamify: How Gamification Motivates People to Do Extraordinary Things*. Brookline, MA: Bibliomotion, Inc.

Duke, R., and J. L. A. Geurts. 2004. *Policy Games for Strategic Management. Pathways into the Unknown*. Amsterdam: Dutch University Press.

Gillert, A. 2008. "Simulations as Learning from the Future – An Interview with Ivo Wenzler." *Develop* 2: 60–4.

Harteveld, C. 2011. *Triadic Game Design. Balancing Reality, Meaning and Play*. Verlag. London: Spinger.

Haynes, L., O. Service, B. Goldacre, and D. Torgerson. 2012. *Test, Learn, Adapt: Developing Public Policy with Randomised Controlled Trials*. London: Cabinet Office Behavioural Insights Team.

Huisman, G., A. Frederiks, B. van Dijk, D. Heylen, and B. Kröse. 2013. "The TaSST: Tactile Sleeve for Social Touch." *Paper presented at the IEEE World Haptics Conference 2013*, Daejeon, South Korea.

Kapp, K. M. 2012. *The Gamification of Learning and Instruction: Game-Based Methods and Strategies for Training and Education*. San Francisco: Pfeiffer.

Katz, D., and M. Bommarito II. 2014. "Measuring the Complexity of the Law: The United States Code." *Journal of Artificial Intelligence & Law* 22 (4): 337–74.

Katz, D., M. Bommarito II, and J. Blackman. 2014. *Predicting the Behavior of the Supreme Court of the United States: A General Approach.* http://arxiv.org/pdf/1407.6333v1.pdf. Accessed August 29, 2016.

Kohavi, R., A. Deng, B. Frasca, T. Walker, Y. Xu, and N. Pohlmann. 2013. "Online Controlled Experiments at Large Scale." *Paper presented at the ACM SIGKDD International Conference on Knowledge Discovery and Data Mining*, Chicago, United States.

Kosters, M., and J. van der Heijden. 2015. "From Mechanism to Virtue: Evaluating Nudge-Theory." *Evaluation* 21 (3): 276–91.

Leeuw, F., and H. Schmeets. 2016. *Empirical Legal Research: A Guidance Book for Lawyers, Legislators and Regulators.* Cheltenham, UK: EE-Publishers.

Leeuw, F. L., and H. B. M. Leeuw. 2012. "Cyber Society and Digital Policies: Challenges to Evaluation?" *Evaluation* 18 (1): 111–127.

McGinnis, J., and R. Pearce. 2014. "The Great Disruption: How Machine Intelligence Will Transform the Role of Lawyers in the Delivery of Legal Services." *Fordham Law Review* 82 (6): 3041–66.

Nielsen, S., R. Turksema, and P. van der Knaap. 2015. *Success in Evaluation: Focusing on the Positives.* Piscataway, NJ: Transaction Publishers.

Olejniczak, K., and P. Śliwowski. 2015. "Towards Behaviorally Informed Public Interventions". *Management and Business Administration. Central Europe* 23 (2): 61–91.

Pawson, R. 2013. *The Science of Evaluation: A Realist Manifesto.* London: Sage.

Shadish, W., T. Cook, and D. Campbell. 2002. *Experimental and Quasi-Experimental Designs for Generalized Causal Inference.* Second edition: Wadsworth Publishing.

Shafir, E., ed. 2012. *The Behavioral Foundations of Public Policy.* Princeton and Oxford: Princeton University Press.

Shaw, I., J. Greene, and M. Mark. 2006. *The SAGE Handbook of Evaluation.* Thousand Oaks, CA: Sage.

Swan, M. 2013. "The Quantified Self: Fundamental Disruption in Big Data Science and Biological Discovery." *Big Data* 1 (2): 85–99.

Tang, D., A. Agrawal, D. O'Brien, and M. Meyer. 2010. "Overlapping Experiment Structure: More, Better, Faster Experimentation." *Proceedings of the 16th ACM SIGKDD International Conference on Knowledge Discovery and Data Mining*, 17–26.

Taylor, L., R. Schroeder, and E. Meyer. 2014. "Emerging Practices and Perspectives on Big Data Analysis in Economics: Bigger and Better or More of the Same?" *Big Data & Society* 1 (2): 1–10.

te Velde, R., J. Steur, and A. Vrankan. 2015. *Gaming en gamification voor justitiële inrichtingen*, edited by WODC. Den Haag: Dialogic.

World Bank. 2015. *World Development Report 2015: Mind, Society, and Behavior.* Washington, DC: World Bank.

Contributors

Maria Barrados retired from the federal public service as president of the Public Service Commission of Canada, having also served as an assistant auditor general at the Office of the Auditor General of Canada. She is currently an executive-in-residence at the Sprott School of Business, Carleton University. She serves on a number of boards and advisory committees. She has a Ph.D. in sociology and continues to pursue her research interests.

Jonathan D. Breul is an adjunct professor in Georgetown University's McCourt School of Public Policy and serves on the United Nations Educational, Scientific and Cultural Organization's Oversight Advisory Committee. Previously, he was an executive director of the IBM Center for the Business of Government, a partner in IBM Global Business Services, and a senior advisor to the Deputy Director for Management in the U.S. Office of Management and Budget.

Nicolaj Ejler is a senior director of Ramboll Management Consulting's Public Policy Practice. He is one of the most experienced evaluators in Northern Europe, having acted as a evaluator of public programs in more than twenty years and advising public sector executives on performance management in more than ten years.

Kim Forss holds a Ph.D. from the Stockholm School of Economics. He is the founder/owner and manager of Andante—tools for thinking AB, a company specialized in research, teaching, and consultancy assignments in evaluation. Over the past twenty-five years, he has evaluated policy and strategy, for example, in the fields of development cooperation, culture, public administration, environment, and research and development in Sweden and abroad. He has worked extensively with organizational analysis for several UN agencies (governance systems in UNEP, reform processes at WHO and UNDP, organizational learning in UNICEF, and a comprehensive evaluation of UNESCO). His research publications include a recent volume on equity-focused evaluation and before that on evaluating complex policy. He is a member of the European Evaluation Society since 1992 and a founding member of the Swedish Evaluation Society, where he has served on the Board for six years, in 2010 and 2011 as the president.

Giovanni Giuffrida is a computer scientist by background who teaches on how to use Big Data to social science students in the new hyperconnected world. Social science research is undergoing a big paradigmatic change as large amount of data is now available in real-time to social and political scientists. He currently teaches in the Department of Social and Political Science of the University of Catania, Italy. He got a Ph.D. in computer science from UCLA.

Caroline Heider has more than twenty-five years' experience in international evaluation. She is currently director general and senior vice president at the Independent Evaluation Group (IEG), a unit that is charged with evaluating the operations and projects of the World Bank Group. Prior to joining IEG, Ms. Heider headed the Office of Evaluation at the World Food Program. She is a member of the International Development Evaluation Association (IDEAS) and the American Evaluation Association. For two years, she served as vice-chair of the UN Evaluation Group.

Steven Højlund holds a Ph.D. from Copenhagen Business School and is the CEO and founder of getQueried. Steven has written several articles on evaluation systems in the European Commission and has more than six years of evaluation experience as a consultant working primarily for the European Union institutions. Currently, Steven works with Big Data as the CEO in getQueried, a company specializing in automated self-service opinion polls.

H.B.M. Leeuw (1985) is a Ph.D. researcher in the Department of Criminal Law and Criminology, Faculty of Law. He holds both a master in criminal law from the Maastricht University (2008) and a master in criminology from the University of Sydney (2009). He has a keen interest in a number of topics concerning criminal law and criminology, many of which are multidisciplinary and international in nature. However, his main interest can be found at the crossroads of the digital environment, behavior, and criminal law/criminology.

Contributors

Frans L. Leeuw (sociologist, 1953) is the director of WODC, the Research, Evaluation and Statistics Center of the Netherlands Ministry of Security and Justice and the professor of Law, Public Policy and Social Science Research at the University of Maastricht. Former positions were the professor of evaluation studies at the Utrecht University, the director of the Netherlands National Audit Office for program evaluation and performance auditing, the dean of the Faculty of Humanities and Social Sciences, The Open University of the Netherlands , the chief inspector of higher education, and an associate professor of social policy research at Leyden University. He was a president of the EES and of the Netherlands Evaluation Society. He has written numerous articles in major social sciences and evaluation journals.

Frédéric Lefebvre-Naré cofounded and comanaged from 1998 to 2005, evalua, a French consultancy dedicated to the evaluation of public policies. He serves presently as CSO of WattGo and Net-conversations, a start-up company and a private research program based on Big Data. He graduated from French Ecole Polytechnique, ENPC, and Ensaé, where he studied econometrics and sampling theory. Since 2014, he is a town councilor in Argenteuil.

Sebastian Lemire holds an M.Sc. in social research methods (with distinction) from the London School of Economics and is currently pursuing a Ph.D. in evaluation at the University of California, Los Angeles. Sebastian brings over ten years of experience managing research and evaluation projects for public and private sector organizations in the fields of education, market development, and social welfare. Before his work as an independent consultant, Sebastian served as a senior evaluation consultant at Ramboll Management, a Danish-based evaluation consulting firm. He has also worked as a research scientist at the University of Washington.

Jonathan I. Mitchell is the manager of policy and research at Accreditation Canada. Jonathan leads Accreditation Canada's national and jurisdictional reports as well as collaborative research projects with academics and health care organizations. He has also led developments to the national and international accreditation programs. Previously, Jonathan was a senior analyst at the Canadian Institute for Health Information. Jonathan is a certified health executive with the Canadian

College of Health Leaders and a fellow of the International Society for Quality in Healthcare.

Tom Negrete has more than twenty-five years of newspaper editing experience, including as a managing editor at the Sacramento Bee and as an editor on the national desk at The New York Times. He currently works at CALmatters.org, a nonpartisan, nonprofit journalism startup covering California public policy issues. Tom led efforts at the Bee to capture and leverage reader data in real time to increase engagement. He is currently working with Northwestern University on leveraging reader data to better understand how journalists might increase civic engagement.

Steffen Bohni Nielsen is a managing director (CEO) of children and educational services at the Municipality of Gribskov in Denmark. He has published widely on issues such as result-based management, evaluation capacity building, and evidence-based policy and practice. He is a former board member of the Danish Evaluation Society and a member of the INTEVAL working group.

Jonas Norén holds a master degree (M.Sc.) in political science and economics. During recent years, he has been engaged as a consultant within the fields of politics, economics, and development assistance. Norén is experienced in evaluation, policy advice, research, statistics, methodological design, and capacity building. From a thematic point of view, he has worked extensively with private sector development.

Karol Olejniczak is an assistant professor at the Centre for European Regional and Local Studies (EUROREG), University of Warsaw, Poland. He has twelve years of experience in evaluation and studies on organizational learning. Since 2008, he is the head of the Academy of Evaluation, an elite postgraduate program for public administration officers in Poland. His main research interests include theory-driven evaluation and behavioral analysis of public policies. He has been a member of INTEVAL working group since 2013.

Gustav Jakob Petersson is a senior analyst at the Swedish Research Council and a director of education at the Swedish National Agency for Education. He holds a Ph.D. in economic history from Umeå University and is currently an associated researcher of the Public Administration

Academy, Södertörn University, Stockholm. He is also an independent lecturer and writer on result-based management and evaluation.

Francesco Mazzeo Rinaldi teaches evaluation research and programming courses in the Department of Social and Political Science of the University of Catania, Italy. He is currently affiliate professor at the KTH, Royal Institute of Technology, School of Architecture and the Built Environment, Stockholm. In the last fifteen years, he carried out training, research, and consulting activities on program and policy evaluation in several regional, national, and international public organizations in the domains of environmental, social, and R&D policy.

Jakub Rok is a research assistant at the Centre for European Regional and Local Studies (EUROREG), University of Warsaw. He received his B.A. degrees in environment protection and geography and the M.A. degree in regional studies. He specializes in theory and measurement of sustainable development at subnational level, as well as in organizational learning in public administration. He has been engaged in a range of national and international research projects. He also carried out applied research and evaluation studies commissioned inter alia by The World Bank, UNDP, the Ministry of Regional Development as well as regional and local authorities.

Maryanne Schretzman is the executive director of the Center for Innovation through Data Intelligence (CIDI). A unit of the Mayor's Office, CIDI, works with New York City's Health and Human Services to conduct interagency analysis and research to identify areas of service need in the City of New York.

Peter Wilkins is an adjunct professor at the John Curtin Institute of Public Policy at Curtin University, Western Australia, conducting research into performance reporting and improvement, evaluation, collaboration, accountability, and governance. He has served as Western Australia's Deputy Ombudsman and prior to this had been the State's Assistant Auditor General Performance Review. He has diverse work experience in Australia, England, Malaysia, and Canada, including roles as an engineer, research fellow, consultant, and thirty years as a public sector manager.

Frank Willemsen is a senior research consultant at the Research and Documentation Center (WODC), part of the Netherland Ministry of Security and Justice. As a methodologist, he advices partners in the field of justice and security (research) on how to relate research designs, data, and types of analysis, including Big Data to policy-related questions. The use of new and innovative (Big) Data collections for policy research and evaluation has his special attention. Next to giving advice, he participates in research projects (including the evaluation of the reorganization of the Dutch Police) and commissions research projects. Previously, He was a researcher at Gfk, an international market research organization. He studied research methodology at the Department of Social Sciences, University of Amsterdam.

Index

Accreditation
  Hospital, 65-69, 72
  Heath care, 61, 67-68, 71
Advanced analytics, 63, 165
American Evaluation Association (AEA), 12, 238, 256
After-action reports, 125-126
Amazon, 25, 244
Analytic Tools 81, 142
Analysis
  Advanced, 63, 165

Big Data, as phenomenon
  Analytics, 2, 6, 20, 62-65, 68, 71-73, 140, 148, 150-151, 153, 165-167, 215-223, 230, 232, 248-250
  Challenges and critiques, 10-12, 22, 79, 166
  Definition, 20-22
  Ethical concerns, 4, 20, 23, 44, 142
  Historical development, 12, 22-27
  Privacy and confidentiality, 4, 7, 43-44, 50, 63, 72, 142-143, 152, 172
Big Data, use of by
  Decision makers, 48, 124-125, 140, 154, 162, 167, 206, 239-240, 250
  Evaluators, 3-15, 19, 27-28, 30, 32, 35-54, 61-65, 72-73, 113-114, 125-126, 137-143, 149-150, 157, 160-167, 172-176, 180-185, 192-194, 206-208, 216-217, 227, 233-234, 238-240, 246-251
  Social media, 7, 80-82
  Social scientists, 36, 52, 92, 217
  Others, 48-49, 126, 138-139, 181-182, 241
Big Data, use in field of
  Transportation, 25, 50, 129-143, 155
  Security, 50, 117-126, 181-182

Health and health care accreditation, 8-9, 46, 49-51, 61-73, 83, 126, 150-155, 161, 171-172, 243, 247
  Private sector, 132, 148, 181
Bing, 245
Black box, 91, 141, 233
  Modeling, 63
  Smart box, 63

California (US), 123, 194, 196, 198-199, 204, 206, 210
Campbell Collaboration, 3, 91
Canada, 61, 65-66, 68-72, 106-112
Center for Innovation through Data Intelligence (CIDI), 147-167
Clustering, 40, 148
Co-production, 14, 251
CompStat (New York Police Department), 150
Computer-assisted data analysis, 63, 131, 149
  Qualitative, 162
  Software tools, 8, 25-26, 28-31, 39, 42, 81, 117, 125, 155, 162, 165, 183, 205
Computer-assisted data collection, 26, 38, 70, 101, 113, 131, 142, 177, 193
Contribution analysis, 106-107, 113, 160, 250
Copyright Alert System (CAS), 97-114
Correlation, 11-13, 23, 25, 67, 71, 79, 81-82, 86-87, 91, 126, 179, 192, 195, 216, 219, 223-229, 234, 241-242, 248-250

Data
  Analysis, 41-42, 44, 49, 73, 114, 143, 149, 162, 194, 199

Databases, 12, 21, 24, 26-28, 36, 40-46, 52, 79, 81, 86, 101, 118, 136, 142, 149, 157, 160, 176-178, 197, 210, 237
Data-driven decision-making, 20-23, 150, 239
Data sources, 4, 6-7, 22, 49, 53, 61-64, 71, 83, 98, 100, 113-114, 162, 176-185, 231, 234, 239-241, 246-248
Emerging data science, 12
Intelligence, 150
Management, 26
Mining, 2, 6, 14, 23, 42, 71, 134, 193, 207, 241
Open source, 26, 64, 79
Scientist, 26-27, 42, 44, 52-53, 64-65, 196, 206, 239, 248
Structured, 24, 177-178
Trust worthiness, 137, 139, 143
Unstructured, 6, 28, 78, 118, 177-178, 249
Data analysis
Active driven, 177-178, 180
Algorithm driven, 178-180, 183
Data processing, 20, 24, 118, 137, 140, 147, 165, 206
Data intelligence, 120-121, 148
Passive driven, 181-183, 185
Qualitative, 32, 62, 162, 205-206
Data sources
Collection, 10, 38, 40, 43, 67-71, 113, 125, 131, 142, 174, 177, 180, 185, 192-193, 239, 247
Design, 8, 24-26, 61-62, 66, 79, 114, 124, 157, 195, 218, 229, 239, 243
Quantitative, 39, 62, 153, 162, 175, 179, 201, 206, 251
Qualitative, 7, 12, 30, 32, 39, 62, 78, 162, 175, 206, 251
Public statistics, 176, 178, 180, 183
Primary sources, 9-10, 12, 14, 62, 64, 175, 178, 246, 248-249
Secondary sources, 12, 15, 21, 62, 64, 114, 175-176, 178, 248
Denmark, 172
Department of Homeland Security (US), 118, 122, 125
Department for International Development (UK), 173, 180
Decker, Paul, 6, 126
Digital piracy, 93, 97-114, 238, 246
Digitalization, 1, 22, 31

Electronic health records, 69-70, 172
European Commission, 148
European Evaluation Society (EES), 12, 238
Evaluation types
Activities, 3, 6, 9, 36
Data, 178
Practice, 46, 48, 183, 185
Process, 9, 176, 181
Results, 54, 240
Evaluators' challenges
Role in the policy process, 240
Learning new designs and tools used by others, 242
Obtain new competencies to manage data, 246
Obtain co-creation, 248
Evaluative information, 130, 137
Evaluative thinking, 166
Evidence-base policymaking, 3-5, 63, 136, 222

Facebook, 2, 7, 9, 12, 38, 77, 80-82, 149, 230, 244
Federal Bureau of Investigation (FBI), 120-123
Forecasting, 87, 91, 93, 104, 135

Gartner, 10-11, 21-22
Global Positioning Systems (GPS), 19, 124-125, 131-135, 141, 171, 247
Google, 7-8, 11, 13, 25-26, 31, 78, 81, 83-87, 93, 98-99, 101, 113, 133, 149, 154-155, 178, 218-219, 221, 241, 244-245, 248

Hadoop, 26, 40
Haystax Technology, 124
Healthcare, 61-73, 97, 155, 243
Hospital accreditation, 65-69, 72

IBM, 27, 63, 139
Information technology (IT), 8, 10, 25, 44, 50, 69, 130
Internet, 1-3, 7-9, 19, 22, 77-79, 83, 97-98, 101, 106, 111, 218, 221, 233, 237, 245, 247, 249
Innovation, 10, 53, 97, 172, 175, 182, 185, 206-207, 244

Japan, 172
Journalism, 14, 194-196, 207

Index

Law enforcement, 119-121, 123, 125-126, 183-184
LinkedIn, 12, 35, 37-38, 81, 238, 244

McKinsey, 63, 69, 129
Machine generated, 1, 28, 77, 178, 231-232
Microsoft, 39, 244-245
Monitoring, 4, 7, 44, 51, 54, 97-98, 124, 130-132, 137-139, 148, 166, 191-212, 237, 240, 242, 250

Netherlands, 80-83, 85, 87, 93, 135, 241

Phoenix (US), 139
Predictive
  Analysis, 4, 13, 87, 191, 193, 206, 221, 241, 248
  Policing, 25, 208, 251
Performance
  Information, 139, 221
  Measurement, 70, 132, 134, 138-139, 141, 148, 166
  Management, 150, 166
  Outcomes, 66-67, 92
Policy
  Policy makers, 6, 9, 54, 92, 97, 140, 162, 165-166, 171, 191, 196, 206, 217, 222, 228, 241
  Policy making, 3-4, 6, 54, 194, 207, 239, 241, 249
  Policy recommendation, 14, 126, 172, 180, 250
Privacy, 4, 7, 43-44, 50, 63, 72, 131, 137, 142-143, 152, 172

Randomized controlled trials (RCT), 240
Real-time
  Evaluation, 3, 191-212, 241, 244, 246
  Monitoring, 31, 83, 131, 133, 191-212
Radio-frequency identification (RFID), 124
Reliability of data, 10, 44, 62, 64, 70, 72, 91, 138-139, 154, 180, 184-186, 246

Representativeness, 36, 79, 140, 231
Rwanda, 180

SCOPUS database, 12, 36, 45-46, 53
Sacramento Bee, 14, 194, 197, 199, 206
Safety, 65-66, 68, 117, 120, 124-126, 130, 135, 243
Security, 13, 50, 91, 117-126, 142, 172, 181-182
Seoul (Korea), 134
Singapore, 84, 135
Smart card, 133
SPSS, 87, 162
Stockholm (Sweden), 25
Super Bowl, 117-126
Sweden, 25, 173, 183-184

Tanzania, 172, 175
Technology
  Technology gap, 20
  Technological shifts, 12
Traffic, 14, 98-99, 120, 125, 129-143, 171, 182, 197, 231, 238
Transit, 119, 122, 129-143
Transport, Public, 13, 25, 50, 129-143
Twitter, 2, 7, 12, 40, 49, 77, 79-82, 125, 149, 178-179, 230-231, 233, 242

United Nations Development Program (UNDP), 173, 175
United Nations Children's Emergency Fund (UNICEF), 173, 181
United Nations (UN) Global Pulse, 78, 172, 177-178, 239, 241-242
United States, 2, 8, 65, 78-79, 98, 101, 106-107, 112-113, 117, 130, 148, 193-195, 198, 211, 242, 247

Validity of data, 7, 10, 62, 64, 72, 83, 91, 107, 149, 180, 184, 186, 226, 229, 246, 250

Western Australia, 132, 138, 142

Yahoo, 25, 244